HOW TO BUY A BUSINESS
WITHOUT BEING HAD

By

Jack (John V. M.) Gibson

SUCCESSFULLY NEGOTIATING THE PURCHASE OF A SMALL BUSINESS

First Edition
June 1996

Second Edition
January 2002

Third Edition
January 2012

Order this book online at www.trafford.com
or email orders@trafford.com

Most Trafford titles are also available at major online book retailers.

© Copyright 2010 Jack (John V. M.) Gibson.
All rights reserved. No part of this publication may be reproduced, stored in a retrieval system, or transmitted, in any form or by any means, electronic, mechanical, photocopying, recording, or otherwise, without the written prior permission of the author.

Printed in the United States of America.

ISBN: 978-1-4269-3618-0 (sc)
ISBN: 978-1-4269-3619-7 (hc)
ISBN: 978-1-4269-8586-7 (e)

Library of Congress Control Number: 2010909187

Trafford rev. 04/20/2013

 www.trafford.com

North America & international
toll-free: 1 888 232 4444 (USA & Canada)
phone: 250 383 6264 ♦ fax: 812 355 4082

Preface

This book has grown over a period of thirty years. During this time I have represented hundreds of business owners who retained my firm to assist them in the sale of their businesses. And in marketing these businesses, I have met and counseled thousands of individuals who contacted me during their search for a business to buy.

After a few years in business, it occurred to us that it would be useful for prospective buyers to have in our reception room a booklet describing the process that a typical buyer might go through during his or her search to find and ultimately buy that "perfect" business. As the years went by, we added a section to help buyers determine how much a typical small business is worth and how much it really earns (or is capable of earning). As our example, we used a cabinet shop with the fictitious name of Doozy Manufacturing Company, which we came to refer to around the office simply as "Doozy."

At first the booklet was only a few pages long, but over the years we added more and more stories about real life experiences: things that a buyer should watch out for and ideas about how to avoid making mistakes during the search and buying process. When Doozy was first published in 1996 it contained no more than thirty pages. Now in my retirement, I have had time to devote to turning Doozy into a real book. It is my hope that the book and our experience will help you in your search.

The examples used in "How To Buy a Business Without Being Had" are intended to be relevant during all phases of the business cycle. Doozy's financial history, however, is from a period unaffected by serious swings in the economy or by the recent recession. The conclusions, advice and recommendations included in the book are wholly those of the author.

Acknowledgements

The author wants to acknowledge the valuable insights of two long-time colleagues at Allied Business Brokers: Sam Cantor and Charles Clark. Also, it is clear to me that this book could not have been written without the tireless editorial assistance of two other members of the Allied team, Cindy Tatum and Sandra Linebaugh. My good friends, Beverly Williams, a published writer, Deborah Mathews and Michael Haviland gave me many helpful suggestions. And, most important, my wife, Lydia, lovingly listened to me moan about my lack of word processing skills while she patiently got me out of more problems than I can remember. Thanks to all.

Table of Contents

Preface — v
Acknowledgements — vii
Introduction — xiii

CHAPTER 1	WHY BUY A BUSINESS?	1
CHAPTER 2	WHAT KIND OF BUSINESS TO BUY?	19
CHAPTER 3	BUSINESS VALUATIONS	31
Part I.	The Elements of Value	32
Part II.	Earnings Multiples and Cap Rates	44
Part III.	Income Averaging	56
CHAPTER 4	ADJUSTMENTS TO FINANCIAL STATEMENTS	65
Part I.	Adjustments to Income	65
Part II.	Adjustments to Net Worth	77
Part III.	Selection of Indicated Earnings Multiple for Doozy	84
Part IV.	Accuracy of Financial Statements	88
CHAPTER 5	EARNINGS CAPACITY AND OTHER VALUATION FACTORS	99
CHAPTER 6	HOW TO STRUCTURE A PURCHASE AGREEMENT	113
Part I.	Terms of Purchase	113
Part II.	The Purchase Agreement	133

CHAPTER 7	**THE CLOSING ON THE SALE**	159
Part I.	The Due diligence Process	159
Part II.	The Closing Process	166
Part III.	When is the Right Time To Buy	177
CHAPTER 8	**CONCLUSION**	183

Glossary of Terms	199
Index	205
Bibliography and Suggested Reading	213
Discussion Questions, Checklists and Study Guides	214
APPENDIX A	A-1
Buyers Agreement (Confidentiality and Non-circumvention Agreement)	A-1
Notes on Value of Goodwill	A-2
Bigger Cabinet Corporation Spreadsheet	A-6
Sample Promissory Notes	A-7
Sample Purchase Contract	A-8
Sample Settlement Sheets	A-12
Confirmation and Bill of Sale	A-14
Sample Profile	A-15

List of Tables

Table 1. Weighted Earnings for Five Years	56
Table 2. Weighted Earnings for Three Years	57
Table 3. Earnings as a Percent of Sales	59
Table 4. Comparison of Income, EBIT and EBITDA	63
Table 5. Summary of Earnings Adjustments	70
Table 6. Calculation of Adjusted and Weighted Earnings	71
Table 7. Doozy Manufacturing Company Statement of Income and Expenses	73
Table 8. Doozy's Simplified Balance Sheet	79
Table 9. Adjusted Earnings (Unweighted) as Percent of Sales	85
Table 10. Cost of Goods Sold Calculation	95
Table 11. Calculation of Present Value of Projected Income and Cash Flow	105
Table 12. Debt Service as Percent of Cash Flow	109
Table 13. Terms of Two Hypothetical Offers	125
Table 14. Allocation of Purchase Price	151
Table 15. Buyer's Non-Cash and Other Tax Deductions	153
Table 16. Purchaser's Twelve-Month Income and Expense Budget (Projection)	190
Table 17. Purchaser's Projected Five-year Income and Cash Flow	193

Case Histories

No. 1	Mismanaging Accounts Receivable	6
No. 2	Landscape Contractor: A Winner	18
No. 3	Photo Processor: An Unfortunate Story	18
No. 4	Managing Working Capital	28
No. 5	Hidden Assets	48
No. 6	Excess Inventory	51
No. 7	Overstated Assets	67
No. 8	Bi-weekly Payroll Issue	76
No. 9	Removing Assets (without informing buyer)	83
No. 10	Overstated Earnings (Cases 1 and 2)	90
No. 11	Understated Earnings (Cases 1, 2 and 3)	91
No. 12	Unrecorded Inventory	94
No. 13	Missing Inventory	100
No. 14	Understanding Cash Flow	109
No. 15	Shareholder Disputes	134
No. 16	Importance of Permits	149
No. 17	Missing Allocation of Purchase Price	152
No. 18	The Need To Confirm Earnings	161
No. 19	Due Diligence Without Financial Records	164
No. 20	Mismatched Inventory	171
No. 21	The Problem of Unbroken Growth	181
No. 22	Bank Account Problem	188
No. 23	Scheduling Management Assistance	189
No. 24	Incorrect Signatures and Shareholder Liability	195

Introduction

This book is for anyone who has ever dreamed of owning a business. During more than thirty years working in the fields of business development and business brokerage, I have seen many people achieve their financial dreams through buying and operating businesses of their own. This has given me great pleasure. The purpose of this book is to assist you in achieving your financial dream through the successful purchase of your business.

Unfortunately, I have also seen a relatively large number of people who became disappointed with the businesses they bought. Many did not achieve their financial dreams. Some prospective buyers never got to the point of submitting an offer to buy a business. I am not sure why. Perhaps they did not have sufficient confidence in their business judgment or never found a business that seemed to match the business of their dreams. Some (thankfully a very small number) who did buy closed their businesses shortly after buying them. And others talked to me about reselling the businesses before they had owned them for very long, often a sign that they were not entirely pleased with their feelings about the long-term prospects of the businesses they had purchased.

It seems that some buyers and some businesses did not make a good fit. This has troubled and perplexed me. I wanted to know what went wrong, so that I could more effectively counsel buyers in the future. Five possible explanations come to mind.

1. **The economy:** Was the economy to blame? Rising prices or rising interest rates, for example.

2. **The business:** Was it the business? Loss of key customers or employees, or weak **cash flow**,[1]
3. **The price:** Did a buyer pay too much for the business and thereby take on too much debt?
4. **Misrepresentation:** Was the business misrepresented in some way by the seller or broker, particularly with respect to financial stability or profitability?
5. **The Buyer:** Or, was the disappointment in some other way the fault of the the buyer? Inadequate management skills, perhaps.

Each of these five factors may have played a role in what went wrong, yet none fully explained why many buyers' expectations were not met. After following up with the buyers of hundreds of businesses, I concluded that some "good" businesses are not good for some people and, conversely, some "not-so-good" businesses are perfect for other people. Two keys to success for the buyer appear to be:

1. Discovering why some businesses and some people make a good fit, and
2. Doing some careful homework before buying in order to learn what makes the business run and what would make it run better.

I was also puzzled by the fact that some qualified buyers passed on purchasing businesses that I felt were unusually good financial opportunities for them. One answer to this puzzle turned out to be that some buyers had been advised (by their bankers or other financial advisors) that the businesses they liked and had considered buying were too expensive. This was, of course, easy advice to give, and often not very helpful, since the advice was usually based largely upon a seller's initial asking price only and not upon any detailed knowledge of the business or of how the business fit into its market or industry.

These buyers often became discouraged and looked no further. They did not have the tools to help them discover what a fair price and terms of purchase might be. Sometimes the gulf between the values that Sellers

---

[1] Certain terms that have precise meanings in the world of small business (or bookkeeping in general) are in boldface type. Some are also defined in the Glossary.

(and their advisors) put on their businesses and the values that Buyers (and their advisors) put on the same businesses seemed too great.

It was not unusual, for example, for an appraiser or financial advisor retained by a Seller to assign a value of, say, $300,000 to a business while an appraiser or financial advisor retained by the Buyer assigned a value as low as $100,000 to the same business. I began to ask myself how, if these were trained and experienced appraisers or advisors, could the differences be so great? How can we make sense of these disparate opinions of value? It is no wonder that some buyers became discouraged and passed up good opportunities. They did not know whom to trust.

While most buyers had the necessary skills to operate a business, they did not have the skills with which to develop with confidence their own **opinions of value**. I have concluded that, generally, the appraisers or advisors were simply attempting to protect their clients' interests and were therefore overly cautious in the opinions they offered.

When buyers did decide to explore an opportunity in depth, often neither the appraisers nor the buyers did adequate homework. They relied much too heavily on a business's federal tax returns and on their year-end financial statements without making adjustments or asking sufficient questions to learn how the statements were prepared. And often they did not tour the business, meet with the owner, or review the business's monthly financial statements. For me, after many years of experience in the field of "small business," I have learned that it is in the monthly (rather then year-end) statements that the answers to many critical questions concerning the value of a business can be found.

Certainly in some cases the **asking price** for the business was too high, particularly the initial asking price. However, as a broker for many years, I can comfortably state that the price at which many (but not all) businesses are sold is considerably less than the initial asking price. It also, sometimes, takes a seller a while to determine when the initial asking price is too steep. Therefore, the initial price sought by the seller is not always a reliable criterion for selecting a business opportunity to explore (or for not considering an otherwise attractive business).

In other cases there was genuine misunderstanding regarding the nature of the business or how the business in question kept (or did not keep) its books. In a few cases there appeared to be a lack of understanding regarding the nature or the quantities of assets that would be included in the sale. For example, the actual value of **inventories-on-hand** can far exceed their **Book Value**, that is, the value at which they are carried on a company's Balance Sheet.

Above all, I learned the importance of writing down clearly and in detail the agreements reached between buyer and seller. Poorly drafted purchase contracts were probably the single greatest source of frustration for buyers of the small businesses that I have worked with. How often have I heard the words: "Don't worry. We can handle that later." Often "later" is too late to avoid costly business interruptions such as the search for a knowledgeable attorney or trying to find the seller and pin him down on loose ends not fully spelled out in the purchase contract.

As important as it is to write things down, it is equally important to understand all the provisions set out in the purchase contract. Too many buyers do not read their contracts in full or fully enough to understand their contents. In their enthusiasm to purchase a business, buyers sometimes sign a contract or sign the closing papers without reading them and discover later that "failing to read" is no defense when it comes to the law.[2] Every buyer should be careful to understand each paper he or she signs, why the paper is important, whom it protects, and what the remedies might be if problems or misunderstandings arise.

Of course, often the parties to a contract have no dispute. They simply want to know what the contract says (what it means), so they can fully and properly satisfy its provisions. And, believe it or not, a year or two after an agreement is signed it may be difficult, even for the attorney who drafted it, to interpret the meaning of some provisions.

It is from these observations that the idea of writing a guide for prospective business purchasers arose. I wanted these purchasers to be able to learn "How To Buy A Business Without Being Had" and without paying too high a price or being disappointed in the financial results of the business after the purchase. It is my hope and belief that if buyers follow the steps set out in this book, they will avoid buying the wrong business and will avoid passing up some great opportunities as well.

When it comes to finances and the future earnings of a business, the cardinal rule for a buyer seems to be summed up in this question: Will

---

[2] There are many good texts on the subject of contracts, including the subject of fraudulent conveyances. One source from which much of the material on these matters is taken is *Business Law* by Louis O. Bergh.

the business, given the skills and other resources that a buyer brings to the acquisition, generate enough "cash flow" to:

- Pay the new owner (the buyer) a reasonable salary,
- Pay the operating costs of the business,
- Provide some reserve cash for future working capital, and
- Pay interest and principal on the debts of the business, including the debts incurred in purchasing the business?

In the world of small business, banks are often eager to provide loans for **acquisition financing**, but later (after the business has been purchased), even if the business is growing, banks are often reluctant to provide additional loans for working capital. Many business owners learn too late that it is best to rely on, and plan around, the working capital provided by the "cash flow" of their business rather than upon "cash" obtained from outside sources.

In learning "How To Buy A Business Without Being Had" we will explore ten distinct steps along the path to success. Each step is important.

TEN STEPS TO SUCCESSFULLY BUYING A BUSINESS

1. Find a business you would like to buy (the *search process*).
2. Study the business, its market, and its industry, visit the place of business, and meet with the owner (*study process*).
3. Review the business's financial statements (*review process*).
4. Adjust or "recast" the financial statements (where needed) (the *recasting process*).
5. Determine a proper **offering price** and **terms of purchase** *(the valuation process)*.
6. Prepare a written offer with price and terms of purchase spelled out in detail (*contract preparation process*).
7. Submit the offer to the seller and respond to any changes he requests (*negotiating process*) and, after the offer is signed by all parties,
8. Conduct a thorough **due diligence** including:

a. inspecting the facilities, inventories, and equipment (and other assets to be included in the sale),
b. confirming the owner's financial representations (about the business's sales history and profitability),
c. obtaining all licenses and other approvals needed to operate the business (the *due diligence process*).
9. Have a qualified attorney conduct the "lien searches" and oversee the formal "closing" on the sale and purchase of the business (the *closing process*).
10. Be sure there is a smooth and successful management transition between you and the former owner after the sale is closed (*management transition process*).

Following each of these steps might at first seem a little daunting. After finding a business to study, however, the total process moves fairly quickly and smoothly. Perhaps it will take a month to complete Steps 1-7, the point at which you have in hand a negotiated and signed purchase agreement. It will usually take another month to complete the due diligence, secure a written commitment from a lender (when necessary) and be ready for the closing. When purchasing a larger business, the due diligence process and obtaining the necessary loan commitments can take longer. Don't rush the process. It's a time to be careful. Most of all, be careful to protect your capital resources.

TIP: More businesses fail because they run out of money than for any other reason. Always learn exactly what it will "cost" to buy a business—the down payment, the closing costs, your first month's rent, any required deposits, and the amount of petty cash or working capital needed to operate the business from the time you buy it until the cash coming in catches up with the cash going out to pay your expenses.

And if the first business you study does not turn out to be the right one to buy, do not worry. You will be better equipped to spot and quickly value and negotiate the next opportunity.

CHAPTER 1
WHY BUY A BUSINESS?

People buy businesses because: (1) they want to be their own boss, (2) they cannot find a job they like or (3) they see business ownership as the best path to building wealth. Self-employed people do in fact seem to be wealthier than other folks. It was recently reported in *Money Magazine* that the median net worth for business owners is $497,000 versus $42,000 for non-business owners.[3]

There are several familiar choices available to help you reach your goal of self-employment and business ownership:

1. Start a new venture by yourself as a home-based business or as an independent contractor. This has become a much more attractive option with the growth of various forms of social media.

2. Start a business by renting an office or other suitable location and leasing or purchasing the necessary equipment and inventory to get started.

3. Go into business with someone else—a partner, your spouse, children or friends, or

4. Buy an existing business.

This book is about this last choice: buying an existing business for yourself.

---

[3] See April 2011 issue of *Money Magazine*, page 68.

Going into business for oneself is becoming an increasingly popular goal for many people from all walks of life. In fact, more new jobs are created each year by the estimated 10 million small businesses in the U.S. than by all the large corporations in the Fortune 500 or by the 10,000 publicly traded companies in the U.S. Small businesses form a dynamic and growing sector of our economy and by some recent estimates provide as many as 70% of all new jobs created each year. Current data about small business and the important and expanding role it plays in the economy, even in times of economic uncertainty, can be found by visiting many web sites, among them: U.S. Bureau of Labor Statistics (bls.gov), CNN.com/small business, Smallbusinesstrends.com or Bricklin.com/smallbusiness.htm.

Finding a location and starting a new business from scratch often takes a long time and often turns out to be considerably more expensive than originally anticipated. Of course, people start new businesses all the time, but start-up businesses do not have a great record of success. Some sources suggest that 50% of all start-ups fail within the first year and 90% do not survive beyond the fifth year. Franchised businesses have lower failure rates than "stand alone" businesses but their income potential seems to be lower as well. CNN.com is also a good source of data to find failure rates for start-ups in various industries. Buying an existing business is less risky and has proven to have other advantages as well.

1. It automatically eliminates a future competitor.
2. It usually saves both time and money.
3. An existing business normally has cash coming in from the first day you take over ownership, so it can pay you a regular salary.
4. If you stay on good terms with the former owner, you may glean valuable tips and leads from him or her that will help you guide the business to its next level.
5. An established business has a credit history.

People who want to go into business for themselves think first of starting their own business from scratch. They often do so because they believe it is less expensive than buying an existing business. In too many cases, the opposite proves to be true. Starting a business usually entails many costs that the owner does not think of. Even when the owner plans carefully and prepares a Start Up Budget and seeks professional assistance from a business counselor, or from one of the government funded organizations such as SBA or SCORE, costs often quickly exceed what has been budgeted. The most overlooked "costs" are the working capital and personal compensation needed during the start-up period. Said differently, many start-up business owners go broke before the new business grows to the point that it can pay an adequate salary.

A realistic minimum budget for a new venture or a new franchise is $30,000. Some business owners will tell you that they developed a successful business with a smaller initial investment than $30,000 but it is wise to plan conservatively. Even with no start-up costs, someone who needs to pay himself a salary of $5,000 per month will have gone through a $30,000 stake after only six months. The real "cost" in this situation would be: (1) the start-up costs, (2) salaries of $30,000 plus (3) the working capital necessary to run the business until that magic breakeven point is reached. Few new businesses are able to breakeven after just six months of operation.

Many profitable small businesses can be purchased with an investment of as little as $30,000, since most small businesses are sold with a down payment of 30% to 40% of the selling price. This means that you can find many businesses with an Asking Price of $80,000 to $120,000 that you could buy for less than the cost of many franchises and less than the cost of starting a new venture on your own. More important is that fact that these businesses are "in operation" and have adequate cash flow to pay their bills, pay your salary and still show a profit. Only a small percentage of businesses are sold for "All Cash." See list below:

Typical Businesses FOR SALE for $120,000 or Less

Advertising agency	Subway sandwich shop	Donut shop
Hair salon	Muffler shop	Tuxedo rental shop
Retail travel agency	Collection agency	Print shop
Coin-op laundry	Ice cream parlor	Needle art shop
Wine & liquor store	Pizza parlor	Flower and gift shop
Bicycle sales & repairs	Vending service	Real estate business
Landscape service	Dry cleaners	Pet shop

and many other types of business

According to the Internal Revenue Service, there are 30,000,000 businesses in the U.S., that is, people or firms that file self-employment

3

tax returns. There are 6,000,000 firms that have employees. Only 8% of these businesses have annual revenues of more than $5,000,000; almost 56% have annual revenues of less than $500,000. So, I suspect that you can find an attractive business for less than you than you thought you would have to pay.

Many people who sell their businesses do so because they are looking forward to retirement, or simply to getting some time off, rather than because the business is failing or has serious problems. In every case the Seller has extensive knowledge of the industry of which the business is a part and should be happy to pass this knowledge along to you.

Former business owners often have well-formulated ideas about how their own businesses could expand and become more profitable. They know their employees, customers and suppliers' habits, quirks and preferences, and can guide you in how to deal with them effectively. And they can advise you about handling the bumps in the road that every business owner has experienced. Their experience is one of the most valuable assets that a business has.

If a business has a good credit history, suppliers will probably ship goods without requiring payment at time of shipment or requiring your personal guarantee. If the business has been established for several years and has a history of generally paying its suppliers on time (or early, to receive purchase discounts) the business will have a favorable credit history. Do not underestimate the value of this hidden asset.

On the other hand, while starting a new business, it may take a long time to find a suitable location and to develop the facilities and contracts needed to establish a profitable business and a positive **cash flow**.[4] It may be difficult to find trained and reliable employees. With a "new" business, it may take months or even years before it grows to the point that it is breaking even and maybe even longer, before it can pay you a salary that matches the salary you earned in your last position. Generally, when buying an existing business, you will not lose salary during your "startup" period and you may avoid some of the typical startup costs associated with a new business. Buying one that has been around for a while provides you with a running start.

---

[4] The term "cash flow" generally is the sum of income + non-cash expenses such as depreciation and amortization less principal payments. See Glossary.

First Generation and Second Generation Business Owners. A business is often called a "first generation" business if it was founded by its present owner. The buyers of first generation businesses become second generation owners and the businesses then become second generation businesses. The differences between the two are instructive.

The first generation owner typically starts his business with little capital and with little formal business training. It is unusual to find a first generation owner who has previously worked in "corporate America." For these reasons the typical first generation owner has limited management skills and little formal knowledge of accounting or bookkeeping. He does not delegate much authority to employees. However, he usually has solid technical skills. As the business grows, this first generation owner goes through a steep learning curve, and over the years, through trial and error, he develops the policies, procedures, business forms, job descriptions and vital contacts that enable his business to survive, operate efficiently and to become (in most cases) profitable. All of these "assets" have value because they would cost money to develop, but their value would rarely appear on the Balance Sheet of the business.

Many times, also, the first generation owner mingles business accounts with his and his family's personal funds. To these owners there is no distinction between "personal" and "business." What the business earns is what they earn. Many first generation owners did not incorporate their businesses; they operate as sole proprietors and file their business tax returns on the Schedule "C" of their individual tax return.

The second generation owner, by contrast, often has less technical knowledge but extensive business training. He tends to keep "business" and "personal" affairs quite separate and, therefore, operates his business as a corporation. The corporation pays him a salary and employee benefits (funds permitting). One consequence of these differences is that first and second generation owners speak, quite literally, different languages when it comes to discussing finance and many other business related matters. A second generation buyer tends to know precise definitions to common business terminology while a first generation/startup owner may not. This is no reflection upon intelligence; it is simply a result of different training and experience.

A second generation buyer may consider buying a particular business because he sees better or more efficient ways of making or marketing a business's products or services. This is what makes commerce work; some people can see a better way of doing things and back their ideas (or hunches) by making investments—an investment in purchasing a business or, after the purchase, an investment in new equipment, facilities, or personnel. There are weaknesses in almost every business, that is, areas that can be improved in ways that will make the business stronger and more profitable. Sometimes the "better way" is to purchase new, state-of-the art equipment; at other times it is simply to operate with fewer assets (fewer trucks or less inventory) and to convert the "excess" assets to cash.

But, it is unwise for buyers, the second generation owners, to discard too many of "the old ways" too quickly. Some were learned through painful and costly experience. Second generation owners should attempt not to repeat the learning curve of the previous owner who is usually quite proud of the business he has created. It is often wise to learn why the owner is interested in selling. There are many predictable reasons but, in my experience, they boil down to one common denominator; the business has grown beyond the skills or "game plan" of the founding owner and needs fresh ideas or energy, or both, to grow to the next level. Be careful not to discard the old game plan too quickly. The following story gives one reason why.

> **Case History: Mismanaging Accounts Receivable**
>
> The buyer of a company with annual sales of $4,000,000 had accounts receivable aged on average to 90 days, longer than had been acceptable in his previous place of employment. He felt he could improve cash flow by implementing some new measures. So, against the seller's advice,
>
> he began to add late fees and interest to the overdue accounts. Before long many older customers canceled their accounts. The buyer did not understand the relationship that the seller had built with them.
>
> What the buyer did not know was that years earlier, the seller, who shipped orders in his company trucks, asked customers if he could ship by the truckload even when they had only ordered a partial load. Many customers agreed provided they could pay as they used the product. The seller readily agreed because truckload shipping was more efficient. However, when product left the plant, the seller booked each truckload as a sale and left the full trailers on his customers' lots. Each truckload was also booked as an account receivable, so it appeared on paper that the accounts were older than they really were.
>
> **Moral: Understanding what has been responsible for success in the past is as important as a buyer's new ideas.**

Unscrupulous Business Owners. Yes, there are some business owners who have done unscrupulous things. In the course of assisting buyers and sellers over thirty years, I have met very few owners and, happily, fewer still that take advantage of an unsuspecting buyer. Far more often, when a buyer senses that something is wrong with a business, the problems are the result of employee misdeeds. If an owner does not seem able to explain satisfactorily, for example, why the reported revenue or margins seem low, or why certain expenses seem unrealistically high, he may not be equivocating or attempting to mislead. He may simply not know. The problems may be the result of employee theft that the owner is not aware of. Be cautious in jumping to conclusions.

Most small business owners are simply trying to feed their families and build up enough equity to retire comfortably. Many spend as little time as possible in record keeping and, as a result, may not have at their fingertips much of the kind of data or answers that you, as a potential buyer, might expect. Moreover, it is natural for an owner to want to cast his business in a good light, that is, to make it appear attractive to a buyer and, so, some owners will embellish their financial results. They might boldly tell a buyer how much money their business has earned (or is capable of earning) even when the financial statements tell a different story.

It is difficult for someone not walking in the seller's shoes to be able to say with certainty that some practice was unscrupulous. There are more often grey areas that make managing a business with absolute fairness to all virtually impossible. Take the issue of calculating employee bonuses or profit sharing as an example. If employees are to receive 10% of pre-tax profit, how is that "profit" to be calculated? The parties to such an agreement may have quite different views of what is considered profit. The problem results from the fact that the "agreement" is not spelled out in writing. One of the things every buyer should learn is that, in the world of small business, many things never get written down.

If an owner has repeatedly engaged in business practices that appear improper or were calculated to take advantage of someone, walking away might be the best response for any buyer. A bad reputation could be expensive to repair. In their enthusiasm to "grow" their businesses, sometimes owners promise more than they can deliver or may exaggerate certain aspects of their business's condition. Perhaps a supplier has told the owner that a "qualified" business must have a $1,000,000 net worth in order to get exclusive rights to some product line. An owner may make some adjustments to his balance sheet in an effort to get his business qualified, knowing full well that the actual net worth is well less than $1,000,000.

The question for the business buyer is to determine if some practice, current or past, has damaged the reputation of the business. If the determination is that, no, neither the business nor its reputation has been damaged, the prudent buyer should continue to find a fair purchase price and resolve to address any issues that have come to light in his purchase contract.

Obviously, some businesses are not worth pursuing. They may have myriad incurable problems. The financial statements may be badly messed up. New technologies may have passed them by. And, yes, some owners may not negotiate with every buyer in good faith or ever agree to accept a price that is a true reflection of a business's worth. For whatever reason, over one-half of the small businesses on the market may never sell: they simply have not grown to the point that they are viable businesses or their problems are terminal.

HOW TO GET STARTED: The majority of small business owners will probably agree with the sentiment that "there's nothing like being your own boss." So, the first step is to be sure that you have that strong desire, that is, the desire to head out on your own into a world where there is no Personnel Department, no Rules and Regulations and no co-workers to chat with when you take a break or need someone else's opinion. Some buyers tell me that another strong motivator in wanting to buy a business is to be free of the restrictions, frustrations, the sometimes endless meetings and other seemingly unfulfilling activities that were part of their present employment. For millions of people, business ownership has been the best investment of their lives and a major step towards achieving their goal of financial independence. If any of these reasons fit you, you are in the company of thousands of Americans who buy or start new businesses each year because they want more control over their lives and their economic future.

Some small business owners tell me that they never doubted that one day they would be in business for themselves. When the opportunity arose, they jumped in with little hesitation. Others tell me that they agonized for months or even years while wondering if they were cut out for self-employment, or to be entrepreneurs, before deciding to buy a business. To help you make this decision, review some of the good sources of information on the web such as the web site of the Small Business Administration of the U.S. Department of Commerce: www.sba.gov/smallbusinessplanner/ index.html. Other helpful web sites are Bizbuysell.com, bizquest.com, and diomo.com.

Let's say that you're convinced that it is more prudent to buy an existing business than to start one from scratch. Now you want to know how to get started. Buyers normally have two big questions. First: Where do I find an attractive business for sale? Second: What is it worth? Regarding the first question, if you haven't found one, there are two main resources:

1. Conversations with people experienced in the field: lawyers, accountants, bankers, business owners and, of course, business brokers and leasing agents, specialists who earn their living representing or assisting business owners

2. Reviewing the "Business for Sale" column in local and national newspapers and trade magazines and, in more recent years, looking through various internet sources. In the papers, some "businesses for sale" are offered through brokers and some are "for sale by owner."

After you have found a business, or perhaps two or three businesses, that appear attractive, it is time to move to Step 2, the Study Process, and learn "how to buy a business without being had." For each business "study" involves learning something about its history, its customers, its industry and about the niche each occupies within its industry. Try also to learn something about the market(s) served by each of the businesses that you have uncovered. It is often helpful at this stage to learn why a seller has put his business "on the market" or, if the business is not formally listed for sale, why an owner is interested in selling.

First, arrange to meet with the owner, or his agent, probably away from the place of business to avoid alarming employees or revealing to others that the business may be for sale.[5] During this initial meeting, try not to sound critical or skeptical. You want the owner to like you and, over time, to take you into his or her confidence. Then, take a tour of the plant or place of business. This

---

5   Confidentiality during this process is very important to the buyer and to the seller. Many things that can be damaging to a business often occur when word gets "out on the street" that a business is for sale.

will probably occur outside of business hours. And jot down all questions that pop into your mind, however inconsequential they may seem.

When meeting the business owner, respect his or her time. Time taken away from running the business may be costly to the owner. Remember also that he or she may have other prospective (and qualified) buyers who are studying the business as well.

The object of your "study" is simply to discover if a business is worth further time and effort on your part. There is no point in getting bogged down in too much study before you have had a chance to complete Steps 3 and 4 (the Review process and the Recasting process). Some buyers may be tempted to discard a business from further consideration after meeting the owner and touring the premises, but in most cases I suggest "hanging in there" until you complete your review of each business's financial records.

TIP: There are many sources of information in addition to the owner and the broker, who want to put the best face possible on the business. And it is natural for you to want to learn more from, hopefully, objective sources. If you are constrained by having agreed to protect the owner's confidentiality, where can you turn? In most communities there are secondary sources available: the Chamber of Commerce, the Better Business Bureau or a trade association. You might check the Yellow Pages Directory and trade publications and you might speak to other business brokers in the area. In some cases you can pose as a potential customer. In other situations you might contact a supplier about becoming a dealer or contact a franchisor about buying a franchise.

A Word About Small Business. Businesses with fewer than 50 employees are considered small. Some economists define "small" as a business with fewer than 100 employees. A small retail establishment might have annual sales (revenue) of $100,000 per employee. A distributorship might have revenue of $1,000,000 per employee. So a business with ten employees might have revenue of $1 million to $10 million. With fifty employees, revenue could range from $5 to $50 million. The majority of small businesses, however, have fewer than ten employees and revenue of less than $1 million.

Small businesses are different from their larger corporate counterparts. The financial press and even some university curricula now recognize them as different. They have less administrative staff. Their owners have little time to study problems; decisions often must be made quickly. This includes being able to spot a good business when it comes on the market and move decisively, if the business seems right for you.

And small businesses are usually thinly capitalized. They have few lines of credit or capital reserves. And, because of these factors, they require a different style of management, a very "hands on" style of management. Owners may have to participate in every facet from handling sales, to greeting customers, meeting their bankers, loading trucks and even sweeping the floors.

A Word About Business Brokers. Brokers generally represent business owners, not the buyers. While learning about a business you found through a broker, most of your contact will be with the broker or agent (or perhaps the seller's lawyer or accountant) who will get answers to your questions. Contact with the owner is usually limited because he is busy running the business and, at first at least, does not know if your interest is serious enough for him to justify taking time away from the business. He is also inclined to protect his business secrets and any information that might assist a potential competitor.

The broker or agent's job is to save clients time and money by presenting their businesses to interested parties and, by screening, to determine if buyers are financially qualified. Business owners do not want to spend much time with buyers who are not financially qualified- they are easy to find. And if word does get out that a business might be for sale, a seemingly endless stream of buyers often appears at every seller's door, interrupting the business and alarming employees.

At first brokers, like owners, may be hesitant to reveal much about a business. Owners and brokers both want to know that you have a genuine interest before dedicating large amounts of time to answering your questions. In fact, the best way to get questions answered is to show interest. This is not a time to act coy. At some point, fairly early in the conversation, most brokers will ask you to sign a **Buyers Agreement** (**Non-disclosure** or **Confidentiality Agreement**) stating that you will keep all information in strict confidence. See Appendix for sample. Only after you sign will the broker or agent reveal the identity of the business. This is perfectly normal and does not obligate you, as a potential buyer, in any way except to keep

Jack (John V. M.) Gibson

all information in confidence, including the fact that a business may be available for purchase.

Profiles, Prospectuses, and Offering Documents. Brokers can and should provide you with a fact sheet or profile of any business you want to look at or study. A good broker will also have for each business, particularly larger businesses (perhaps those with annual sales of $1,000,000 or more), a more detailed write-up called a **prospectus**. That document will contain a description and financial analysis of the business, as well as copies of the seller's financial statements for several years of operations. The analysis will probably include a "spreadsheet" showing operating results from several years on one page, making the year-over-year review and analysis much easier. Spreadsheets sometimes also show adjustments to reported income, but the one below shows revenue and expenses as reported.

DAYCARE BUSINESS—Spreadsheet Without Adjustments

		2009	2008	2007	2006	2005
Total Sales (Revenue)		$185,514	$194,366	$190,488	$175,608	$140,589
Average Sales Per Month		15,459	16,197	15,874	14,634	14,059
Account No. and Name						
515	Daycare supplies	6,093	7,527	8,856	4,921	2,776
525	Daycare food	4,290	1,987	1,643	1,009	1,714
535	Equipment rental	10,662	17,186	437	3,622	307
610	Employee payroll	77,000	80,422	90,157	86,791	56,505
615	Employee advance	0	0	0	0	1,232
620	Contract labor	0	0	0	0	358
630	Payroll taxes	7,444	8,935	10,017	9,643	15,293
700	Rent paid to owner	9,683	41,950	76,500	48,500	41,940
705	Utilities	4,618	5,006	4,010	6,042	3,388
710	Telephone	4,424	4,465	4,113	3,583	4,532
712	Security	4,481	2,635	877	1,131	759
715	Maintenance & repairs	4,181	4,922	6,109	3,810	1,033
720	Office supplies	557	664	98	43	491
760	Transportation	2,162	3,319	1,363	849	847
805	Professional fees	1,700	2,125	2,343	2,194	2,083
815	Bank charges	183	323	304	397	244
820	Bounced checks	1,317	348	0	282	2,514

835	Taxes, licenses & fees	2,940	5,809	6,705	3,248	7,583
840	Insurance	1,327	1,094	1,654	3,517	554
850	Ads, publications, dues	204	215	596	334	523
855	Interest	83	0	671	0	0
860	Student recognition	0	972	0	0	0
865	Postage	58	64	0	32	0
870	Depreciation	10,647	2,638	0	0	0
875	Contributions	0	50	0	0	0
880	Miscellaneous	0	1,430	0	535	225
	Total Expenses	184,414	194,086	207,453	180,483	145,406
	Income (Pre-Tax) Reported	**$ 1,145**	**$ 447**	**-$ 16,717**	**-$ 4,867**	**$ 4,183**

Suggestion. Review the spreadsheet carefully and try to determine what "adjustments" you might make to the reported income. How, for example, could the cost of Daycare Food (account 525) double in one year? Or, how could Taxes, licenses & fees (account 835) decline by 50% in one year? There must be explanations. Look in particular for "lumpy" expenses. These may be for non-operating expenses or, perhaps, for the large expenses that should be spread over several years. Look at account 535 Equipment rental: What kind of equipment does a day care rent? The most important question always is: "How can I make a living from this business?"

The prospectus or profile should also include a description of the assets that are, or will be, included with the business being offered for sale: the furniture, fixtures, and equipment (the FF&E) plus tools and leasehold improvements, with the original cost of each item and its estimated current value. These lists are not always as detailed as the following two abbreviated examples (one for the Daycare profiled above and one for a large industrial equipment sales and rental company) and may not include values, original cost or date purchased, but simply the number and type of items that a seller intends to include in a sale.

Jack (John V. M.) Gibson

1. Schedule of Daycare FF&E—Manager/Owner's Office

Number and Description of Items	Original Cost	Estimated Current Value
1 3' by 6' walnut executive desk	$1,200	$400
1 matching walnut credenza	995	400
2 4-drawer legal file cabinets	120 ea.	160
1 leather high back desk chair	550	250
2 upholstered side chairs w/arms	225 ea.	200
1 fireproof 2-drawer legal file cabinet	500	300
1 HP flat screen 22" monitor (new)	240	180

2. Schedule of FF&E Industrial Sales Co.—Rental Department

	Serial No.	Date Bought	Original Cost	08/31/04 Book Value	Estimated Market Value	Remaining Economic Life
CDI Forklift	4095	11/94	$25,380	$14,530	$16,500	4-6 yrs.
CDI Forklift	4169	11/96	25,380	15,150	16,500	4-6 yrs.
Manlift SM31RT	11062	10/97	18,130	7,645	12,500	6-8 yrs.
A/C Forklift	2310	10/98	24,490	6,910	12,500	6-8 yrs.
Manlift SM42	36146	05/98	19,345	7,555	13,000	6-8 yrs.
Boomlift MZ50	85165	06/02	38,575	12,000	21,000	8-10 yrs.
JCB Backhoe	13230	08/04	26,030	25,230	25,000	9-12 yrs.

Whether you are working with a broker or not, check the offering documents to be sure they include detailed financial statements. If not, ask the seller or his agent to provide them for four full years plus monthly statements for the current year. Later (after you have decided to make an offer to buy a business), ask for federal tax returns as well. It is a big red flag if a seller hesitates to provide any of this information. And it might also be a red flag if the data contained in the tax return differs substantially from the data shown in the financial statements.

Since it is the broker's job to show each business in its best light, these offering documents usually include a "recasting" of each business's financial statements. This recasting includes adding back any non-operating expenses to the reported income and making other adjustments necessary to indicate what the broker (or owner) believes each business has truly earned or is capable of earning. Sometimes it is more and sometimes less than the income that has been reported.

The majority of small businesses are not sold through brokers. They are sold through word of mouth. Whether a business owner is represented or not, it is still important to be careful about not abridging confidentiality and respecting his or her time. Brokers can be useful in helping you, even when you have found a business on your own. But, be aware that the experience and knowledge of business brokers varies greatly. Some states require that brokers be licensed; others do not. All things considered it is wise to use a broker who has some licensure or other professional credentials under his belt.

A sample two-page Profile is included in the Appendix. It includes a short history of the business, the owners' reasons for offering their business for sale and (on page 2) a market (industry) analysis. This detail of information should prepare a buyer to have a productive conversation with the sellers and to undertake his own research into the feasibility of buying the business. For larger businesses the Offering Document will include financial statements for the past four or five years as well as employee rosters (with compensation, title and year hired), a complete listing of assets included in the intended sale (with purchase price and current estimate of value), a summary of monthly sales (often broken down by department) and various spreadsheets. Federal tax returns will probably not be available at this early stage in the buying process.

A Word About Financial Statements[6]. Formats differ considerably. Nomenclature differs as well. Sales can be referred as Revenue and Earnings as Income. Within the Expense Accounts distinct accounts are grouped together as seen on the Daycare spreadsheet on page 12-13. See accounts 715, 835 and 850. At times "grouping" can be misleading. For example, Equipment Rental and Rent may be shown as a single account called Leases. In other cases, non-business related expenses are grouped with business expenses. Account 840 Insurance may include premiums for personal auto insurance as well as employee health insurance premiums. In the Daycare spreadsheet, the accounts are not subdivided. In other businesses expense accounts are divided into several groups (departments) such as:

- Cost of Sales (Production costs) •Research and Development
- General and Administrative expenses •Selling and Marketing

---

6   See Glossary of Terms for definition of a financial statement.

The normal expenses involved in running a business are called Operating Expenses. Certain other expenses, especially Interest, are not considered operating expenses even though they appear to be on some statements of income. So, it is always important when analyzing a business or comparing the results of several businesses to learn how the statements are formatted.

Financial Red Flags. Perhaps, when you reviewed the spreadsheet for **DAYCARE BUSINESS**, you found some puzzling entries. And, perhaps, after discussing them with the broker, they still seemed puzzling. Perhaps the brokers said that there were no financial statements. These are what are termed "red flags." Buyers should always be cautious when red flags appear. Some have been discussed above and some can be resolved through the "recasting" process discussed in detail in Chapter 4. Others might be critical to placing a fair value on a business. The subject of missing documents at the time of the closing is discussed in Chapter 7.

Listed below are some typical red flags to watch for. But, since each business is unique, every buyer should be alert to the possibility of the existence of other red flags that are not listed.

Red Flags Concerning All Financial Statements

1. No statements are available for a business you are looking at, or the statements you have been provided are not up-to-date, or statements for certain reporting periods are missing
2. Incomplete financial statements (perhaps the balance sheet, cash flow statement or accountant's opinion letter is missing)
3. The statements are not prepared (formatted) in a consistent manner from year to year or from month to month
4. The CPA (accountant or bookkeeper) did not attach an Opinion Letter to the Financial Statement or the Opinion Letter stated, in essence, that he could not offer an opinion regarding the accuracy of the Statement.

Red Flags Found on Income Statements (the P&L)

1. Declining year-over-year sales
2. Declining gross profit margins in recent years (or months)

3. Recent increase in cost of labor (measured as a percent of sales)
4. Lumpy expenses in certain accounts (large changes in reported expenses between reporting periods)
5. Unpaid expenses in certain months such as rent or payroll taxes
6. No Depreciation has been taken in the current reporting period

Red Flags Found on Balance Sheets

1. Little or negative Retained Earnings (which may suggest that the business has operated at a loss for many years)
2. Aging Accounts Receivable (as a multiple of monthly sales)
3. Accounts Payable and other Current Liabilities are increasing (as a percent of sales)
4. It appears that certain unpaid expenses (that you have spotted on the Income Statement) have not been added to the Accounts Payable
5. No new Fixed Assets (equipment) has been added for a while
6. Changes in Equity (Net Worth) on the Balance Sheet do not match changes in income shown on the Income Statement

Not all red flags are serious. Some may be, certainly. All are not deal killers either, but all require investigation as well as satisfactory explanations. But proceed with caution: Remember that the seller may not have reviewed his own statements and may be offended if you challenge their accuracy or say things that sound overly critical about the business. Finally, while you are studying a business, be alert to other potential red flags such as anticipated future increases in some "cost of doing business" or things that have nothing to do with financial statements, such as changing markets or changes in technology.

Case Histories. Throughout this book are actual stories of real buyers and the experiences and challenges that they faced. All stories are abridged or edited to reduce the possibility of disclosing the identity of either the businesses or their owners. To begin, let me share two case histories—one a success story and one a story that was not so successful.

> **Landscape Contractor—A Winner.** This company had won many awards for excellence in landscape design but had not made much money despite growing sales. The buyer, a banker, spotted three things that encouraged him to believe the business could be quite profitable: (1) the large cost of (and lost revenue from time spent) preparing for the awards, (2) the interest the seller was paying on several accounts payable and (3) the frequent use of credit cards to pay for routine purchases. The banker bought the company, sold it four years later for a considerable profit and retired at a very young age to a mountaintop in the Smokies. **Moral: Don't overlook good companies with disappointing earnings.**
>
> **Drive-Thru Photo Processor—An Unfortunate Story.** A former store manager, a hard-working and talented guy, was able to buy a shop with a modest down payment. Because of rapidly changing technology he shortly thereafter had to purchase new equipment. Debt service on the equipment was expensive. To help the buyer, the seller reduced the monthly note payments the buyer owed him, but the buyer still couldn't make an adequate living. Chain drug stores began to go into photo processing. Revenue at the photo shop began to decline and the buyer decided to throw in the towel when his lease expired. In view of changes in the industry, the buyer no doubt paid too much for the business, as is often the case when a buyer can only make a small down payment. **Moral: Be sure you can afford the business you want to buy.**

Perhaps a third case history, one about a business that was never sold, would be appropriate also, because many businesses never sell. They seem to have one of three problems: they are overpriced, keep poor financial records, or the seller is just on a fishing expedition and not really interested in selling. With some careful homework, you can determine a fair price and reconstruct reasonably accurate financial statements and overcome the first two problems. I hope this book will give you the tools to do so with confidence.

CHAPTER 2
WHAT KIND OF BUSINESS TO BUY?

Would you have ever thought of buying a cricket farm? A manufacturer of stained glass windows? A school that trains riverboat captains? A company that makes and installs seamless gutters? All are businesses our company has represented and sold in recent years. When thinking about what kind of business to buy, more often we think of traditional businesses such as hardware stores, florists, restaurants or dry cleaners, businesses that have been around for a while and that are part of the fabric of a community.

What would make a business attractive to you? There is an almost infinite variety to choose from. Houses and cars have personalities. We easily fall in love with them. Businesses also have personalities. Therefore, the business that is right for you may be totally wrong for someone else. This is true even when both the "price" and the "financial condition" of a business seem attractive. So, before you buy, consider carefully the non-economic characteristics of any business you are looking at.

As we will learn in Chapters 3, 4 and 5 "numbers" are important and understanding them is even more important. However, all truth is not in the numbers. We can "spread sheet" a business to death doing forecasts and making adjustments to financial statements and still not understand the core business. Many successful buyers focus more on their strategic vision, or game plan, for the business they want to buy. They constantly ask themselves, "How can this "collection of assets" can be deployed both to yield greater returns in the future and to meet my life objectives. This chapter deals with the non-financial aspects of determining if a business is right for you.

There are four broad categories of business found in almost every community: **wholesale**, **retail**, **manufacturing** and **service**.[7] Each type relates to almost every industry. Use the apparel industry as an example. We can wholesale clothing. We can sell clothing retail, we can manufacture clothing, and we can "service" or repair it as in a dry cleaners or tailor shop. There are also some so-called "integrated" businesses, that is, businesses that make, sell, and service their products. A picture frame shop may be a good example. GE may be another example.

Each category has unique characteristics. The "service sector" is the most rapidly growing. It includes **personal services**, **business services**, **repair services**, **professional services,** and many others. In metropolitan Memphis, for example, 62% of the businesses listed in a local directory were in the service sector in 2003, up from 60% in 2000.[8] If every new business has found its way into a directory, I suspect that the service sector today would include over 70% of all businesses. However, since service businesses may have only a few employees, the service sector had a smaller percent of total employment—around 64% of non-farm employment in 2009.[9]

Manufacturing employment has declined fairly rapidly in many parts of the U.S. but still forms the economic base of many cities in the northeast and mid-west. Nationally, manufacturing accounts for only 9% of employment today, down from 12.5% as recently as 2000. Employment in wholesale businesses has declined slightly, primarily as a result of automation, from 4.1% in 2000 to 4.0% in 2009.

In the retail sector, products are sold to the public. Wholesale businesses sell products to the retailers and to other businesses. Manufacturers make the products that we sell or service. Some manufacturers are called "primary" because they process raw materials into such basic products as steel, plastics, and lumber. Other so-called "secondary" manufacturers use the steel, plastics, and wood, for example, to manufacture furniture or cabinets. Some manufacturers simply assemble products from parts that were made by other manufacturers.

---

7   Not included are **extraction** (mining), **food production** (farming) and **real estate** related (motels) businesses.
8   *Who's Who In Memphis Business*, Rodney Baber and Company, www.baberweb.com
9   Employment data, broken down by industry, is compiled by the Bureau of Labor Statistics and may be viewed by visiting www.bls.gov.ces/home.htm.

Service businesses, unlike businesses in the other three sectors, have few tangible products to sell; they generally work on other people's products. They provide services to businesses and to individuals. They repair or clean cars, furniture and clothes. They fix broken bones and windows, test air quality emissions, train and test persons who wish to become licensed, prepare our tax returns, offer financial advice, and provide many other services that we all need.

The service sector has grown most rapidly in recent decades and now constitute the largest sector in the US economy in terms of: **number of total jobs**, **number of new jobs added** each year as well as the **number of businesses**. It is broken down below into five separate categories below. Professional services may seem to overlap business services. The distinction is that they usually require formal training and licensing of some kind. In some states persons without professional degrees or certification are barred from owning or operating certain businesses such as a real estate practice. It is wise to check if any certifications are required in your state.

Changing Industrial Landscape. The landscape is changing more rapidly today than ever before: rapid growth in some industries and decline in others, even the disappearance of traditional businesses in some smaller neighborhoods and cities. Independently owned hardware and drug stores come to mind; many have not been able to compete successfully with the chains. In business, change is a constant. Car dealerships, which were fixtures for years in most small cities, are disappearing because of economies of scale.

Some businesses are declining as a result of changing technology, improvements in labor force productivity, and a more mobile labor force. Other businesses have been able to change the way they make or market their products by adopting more cost effective and less labor-intensive technologies. And some businesses, veterinary practices for example, seem relatively immune to the ups and downs in the economy. People like their pets.

The Information Age. The "old economy" was defined by assets. We could see, feel, touch and even smell the buildings, smokestacks, equipment, trucks and storage yards. A business was defined by (and in many cases valued by) the quantity of physical (tangible) assets that it owned. Today, often the most valuable assets a business owns are its data (information) and other assets such as trademarks, patents or goodwill, assets that cannot be so readily seen, measured or valued.

Many neighborhood businesses and other traditional businesses will always continue to be attractive acquisition targets and will continue to generate attractive returns to buyers. If well managed, the returns can often be very attractive, since they are sometimes overlooked and may sell for very reasonable prices compared to the prices that "information age" companies sell for.

In the "new" economy, businesses that rely upon specialized knowledge, use of computer technology and software (but own quite little in the way of furniture, fixture, equipment or real estate) often offer greater growth and more attractive returns. Tangible assets defined the "old" economy. In today's service oriented and information economy, tangible assets are passé. Knowledge (information) can be your most important asset. Information has other benefits: (1) it is cheap to store (so your cost of rent may be less or virtually non-existent and (2) it is cheap to move, install, maintain and repair, unlike equipment, raw materials and supplies.

A listing of some frequently seen businesses is shown below. A detailed listing of all business types is compiled by the U.S. Securities and Exchange Commission in what is called the SIC (or Standard Industrial Classification) code. The system of SIC codes was replaced in 1997 by a more detailed classification system maintained by the Census bureau called the North American Industry Classification System or NAICS. Both systems may be accessed online.

Traditional Businesses

Retailer	**Manufacturing/Assembly**
Convenience store	Bakery
Liquor store	Cabinetmaker
Fast food restaurant	Awning and blinds manufacturer
Florist	Picture framing manufacturer
Apparel shop	Conveyor system manufacturer
Dealerships (cars, appliances)	Wood pallet manufacturer
Coffee shop	Armored truck bodies
Bike shop	Printing company
Sandwich shop/deli	Funeral caskets and casings

Travel agency
Furniture store
Floor covering
Lumber yard

Wholesale Distributor
Beer distributor
Grocery products
Building supplies
HVAC equipment
Auto parts
Plumbing supplies
Marble and tile products

Repair & Cleaning Services
HVAC repair business
Auto repair shop
Roofing/re-roofing company
Shoe repair business
Muffler shop
Self-help carwash

Security Services
Armored truck service
Guard (armed) service

Stained glass windows
Mattresses and bedding

Personal Services
Personnel agency
Day care center
Hair dresser/beauty parlor
Dry cleaners/coin-op laundry
Landscape services and lawn care

Business Services
Newspaper Publisher
Photography shop
Employment agency
Coupon advertising
Quick print shop
Cleaning Services

Professional Services
Veterinary practice
Insurance agency
Real estate office
School of cosmetology
Accounting practice
Optical dispensary

The specific product or industry (e.g., chemicals, dry goods, building materials, personnel) probably doesn't matter to the typical business buyer, but it seems advisable to find one that your skills and knowledge complement in some way.

Non-Financial Criteria. Try to think of which non-financial criteria would make a business attractive to you (and to your family) and which would make a business seem unattractive to you. Some such criteria to consider in determining if an opportunity is right for you might include the following six:

- **Complementary Skills.** Do you bring any needed or complementary skills to the business, skills that seem to be lacking among the present ownership and employee base? **If you bring something to the business that is lacking, you will "add value"** when you buy it. This is a key to many successful acquisitions.

- **Management Assistance and Non-Competition**. Will the seller of the business stick around after the sale to show you the ropes? How long will he stay and in what capacity? It's always a plus if the former owner will: (1) sign an **agreement not to compete** with you after the sale in any significant way for several years and (2) agree to provide **management transition assistance** for a definite period of time after the sale. Make the seller your friend, since these two factors can be very important to your success. These topics will be discussed in more detail in Chapter 6.

- **Customer Base**. How many long-term customers does the business have? Can you determine how loyal they are to the current owner? Be careful about buying a business that has only a few customers. If one large customer leaves when he learns the business has been sold, you could be in trouble. However, if you feel you could bring new customers to the business, it may be just the right one to purchase.

- **Owner's Management Role**. How would you spend your time if you bought a business? Would you be on an assembly line? Would you spend all day preparing financial forms and reports? Would you spend time calling on customers or solving customer problems? Or in a business like Doozy, (which is profiled in the next chapter) would you be on the drawing board designing new cabinets or, perhaps, new product lines? An important consideration is to be able to fill or delegate essential functions that you are not comfortable with. In any event you will probably perform many different tasks each day.

- **Work Environment.** Do you like the work environment? The work environment is very important because some of us just work better in certain environments. And some work environments are, frankly, dirty, smelly, or hazardous places to be. Work environment includes considerations such as the quality and cleanliness of the facilities, your office environment, and the types of customers, suppliers, and employees you will be dealing with. It also includes thoughts about the way the business does business. Are you comfortable with the way the business markets its products or services? Would you really be comfortable working in the work environment of the business you are looking at?

- **Business Location.** It involves access to markets, customers, and transportation. It also involves distance from home, that is, how long would the commute be. Some people enjoy the drive to work; it is their private time. Others are tired of commuting and want to get home for lunch or be near their church or club.

These are important criteria, but when all is said and done, a business's financial characteristics will probably be the most important. You have to decide if an opportunity, whether it is Doozy or some other, will over time meet your income and other financial objectives. However, if you determine that the business will meet your financial objectives but will not meet your non-financial needs, you should be cautious. Certainly if two businesses appear to offer equal returns, the non-financial considerations should be looked at in some depth.

It is also important to give some consideration to what is called an "exit strategy." Can a business easily be resold? To whom would you sell it? What would make the business more salable in the future? Can you pass it along to other family members? Perhaps the exit strategy may be eventually to sell the business to its employees or to a competitor. Two brief words of advice: (1) don't let the place run down and (2) maintain accurate and current financial records.

Most importantly, do not buy a business only because it seems attractive to someone else, even if that "someone" is your banker or your accountant. You will probably spend more time at the business you buy than you spent working at your last place of employment, so the business must first of all fit your criteria.

When buyers begin looking for a business they generally look for a particular type of business, a custom cabinet shop, let's say, or a motorcycle shop. But when the time comes to decide what to buy, experience suggests that buyers rarely buy what they originally were

for. The search process opens their eyes to exciting businesses
and industries, ones they had never heard or thought of. There is
almost an infinite variety.

Businesses in newer or non-traditional industries often intimidate buyers. Some buyers feel such businesses require unique knowledge or skills and therefore decline to look at these opportunities. But buyers that do look often find that they are easy to manage and utilize skills they already have. Perhaps more importantly, they find these businesses are in rapidly growing fields. Look at the list below. Some of these "industries" did not exist a few years ago. Some have been around for decades. Some are already in danger of disappearing, replaced by newer technologies and changing consumer preferences. Some are sophisticated, some mundane. Few are on the average buyer's radar screen or wish list, yet buyers in each industry are happy with their acquisition.

Non-traditional Businesses

Retailers
Computers and accessories
Reseller of ladies apparel
Pet food store
Health food store
Bonzai products
Aluminum can recycling
RV and mobile home dealer

Business Services
Microfilm record storage
Toner cartridge refiller
Security guard service
Commuter jet booking
Mailbox rental

Professional Services
Business brokerage
Appraisal service
Auctioneer
Dental laboratory

Security Services

Wholesalers/Distributors
Hotel supplies
Material handling equipment
Marble and tile products
Janitorial supplies
Aviation parts supply house
Jewelry supplies
Tour packager

Personal Services
Health and fitness center
Check cashing service
Home cleaning/maid service
Food delivery service
Home health care service
Weight reduction clinic

Repair & Cleaning Services
Computer repairs
Vehicle upholstery repair
Seamless "no drip" gutters
Transmission rebuilder

Home alarm service	Book rebinding
Security software service	Automated carwash
Manufacturers	**Hard to Classify**
Fishing lures	Catfish farm
Software designer	Custom van conversions
Spraywash equipment	Bottler of bottled water
Dry mix food additives	Cricket farm (for medical labs)
Neon signs	Marina

Failure Rates. As mentioned in Chapter 1, knowledgeable sources suggest that over time maybe 50%, or even as many as 95% of start-up businesses fail, while a far greater percent of second generation businesses succeed. However, among different industries the rates of success vary considerably. Some businesses seem almost indestructible. Others seem quite fragile.

It has been observed by many brokers that non-chain restaurants do not survive a change of ownership easily. Many customers are loyal to the former owner who, in many cases, was quite a personality. The rates of survival, ranked by industry, are hard to find, but buying any business strongly identified with the owner could be risky. Mamie's Restaurant or Bob's Auto Repair are often not the same without Mamie or Bob. In fact, some owners are advised to depersonalize their businesses as an exit strategy, perhaps even to the point of changing the business name.

Among franchised businesses, growth and success may depend on how many franchises the franchisor licenses within a trade area. Other businesses, photo shops and video rental shops for example, may be victims of new technologies. Neighborhood drug stores find it hard to compete with large chain operations. Neighborhood businesses are always dependent to a large degree upon what happens in the surrounding neighborhood. Sometimes neighborhoods have room to grow while others are losing population as a result of commercial development or highway construction. Businesses serving a larger market generally reflect trends within the industry of which they are part. Learn if the rate of growth in the industry has been increasing recently or has begun to slow. These factors are as important as either the financial history of a business or the price and terms a seller is willing to accept.

TIP: Many failed businesses (especially those identified with strong owners like Marie or Bob in the paragraph above) spent unwisely or overspent for furniture and fixtures. See Schedule on page 10 for some examples. This overspending is really hidden profit. When you offer to buy such a business, let the owner keep these personal items or reduce the Asking price by the amount of the overspending.

Some things that are beyond the control of a business owner can play a large role in the success or failure of any business in any industry. However, more often the success or failure results directly from actions taken by the purchaser after the business has been acquired. The following Case History gives us a good example.

Case History: Managing Working Capital. A man with many years of industry experience purchased a woodworking shop with annual revenues of around $2 million. He immediately moved the shop to a larger more modern building. It had several loading docks, something that was lacking in the former facility, and was closer to the customer base. The move seemed highly justified. The landlord offered to: (1) build out the office space and make other renovations and to add the cost to the rent or (2) let the purchaser have the building "as is" at the current rent. Purchaser felt he could do the work more economically than the landlord by using company labor, so he took the second option.

During the remodeling the business did not bill out much work, but, since the business had brought in several fairly large contracts, the purchaser was not concerned. After the first year of operations it was obvious that several customers were slow in paying and cash flow dried up. The owner wished he had reserved more cash to cover this kind of situation instead of using so much of his reserves on the remodeling.

Although the business was making money "on paper" it became obvious after several more months that the owner would have to shut down operations and liquidate the assets.

Moral: Be very conservative when you project your working capital requirements.

Now for second big question: How to figure out what a business opportunity is worth.[10] Let's look at a fairly typical small business, a custom cabinet shop. After many years of successful operation, the owner is ready to retire. If you are ready to learn more, let's try to calculate the value of this business in the next chapter.

---

10 Regardless of price, every business should have extensive **financial statements** (see Glossary of Terms) and the owner should make these available to you after you sign a Buyer's, or Confidentiality, Agreement. Be sure to learn if the statements are "originals" or copies and if the owner expects them to be returned.

CHAPTER 3
BUSINESS VALUATIONS

The value of a business is its "fair market" value. That value should be close to the value at which a business can be bought or sold. Since this book deals primarily with "small" businesses, many of which are unincorporated, the valuations are based almost exclusively upon determining the price at which the assets of a business can be bought or sold. In the case of larger incorporated businesses, a valuation might be based upon its net worth, that is, the price at which the stock of the business could be bought or sold. This is an important distinction.

Look at the table below. The market value of the assets of this hypothetical business is $800,000 while the market value of the stock is $500,000. The book values are the values shown on the books or financial records of a business.

	Book Value	Value over Book	Market Value
Assets	$ 500,000	300,000	$800,000
Liabilities	300,000	-0-	300,000
Net Worth	$ 200,000	300,000	$500,000

When someone refers to the value of a business, you must learn whether the value is based upon an asset sale or upon a sale of the stock of a corporation. The discussion that follows concerning the value of Doozy Manufacturing Company is based upon a sale of assets. A discussion of the merits of buying stock in lieu of assets is included in Chapter 6.

Part I. THE ELEMENTS OF VALUE

One of the keys to "not being had" is to understand the "elements of value" and how they are calculated. There are many approaches to determining the worth (or value) of a business; some are appropriate in some situations and some in others. We will look at three commonly accepted approaches (or methods) in this chapter, especially the first two named below. Some other approaches to valuing small businesses are discussed later in Chapter 4 Part III.

- Income or earnings approach
- Asset valuation approach
- Market valuation or "comparables" approach

Because valuing (or appraising) is more an art than a science, the values found are considered "opinions of value" rather than scientific fact. Also, when we start a valuation assignment, we do not know what valuation method is best suited to a given business, but we do know that the use of several different methods is usually advisable. If two methods yield fairly similar results we can usually feel comfortable that the values found are pretty close to a meaningful or reliable valuation. However, if the results differ significantly, it is wise to either (1) employ some other valuation methods or (2) carefully check the data and assumptions used in the methods initially employed.

To help us understand these "elements of value" we will examine in detail a small custom cabinet shop called Doozy Manufacturing Company. It could be located anywhere in the U.S. Doozy is on the market and has retained a broker to help its owner sell the assets of the company for $160,000. The broker has released the following brief profile.[11]

---

11 The profile of a business offered for sale would not normally include the name of the business in order to protect the seller's confidentiality.

> **Company Profile**
> ## CUSTOM CABINET MANUFACTURER
> Doozy Manufacturing Company has been in business for fifteen years. The Company is incorporated as a "C" (or regular) corporation and reports its earnings to the I.R.S. on a calendar year basis. Last year Doozy reported earnings (before taxes) of $12,000 after paying the owner a salary of $48,000 and paying his family's medical insurance premiums. Annual Sales reported in Doozy's latest financial statement were $300,000.
>
> Profits and sales have shown no meaningful growth in recent years and, in fact, have declined slightly. Three years ago Doozy earned $34,000 on Annual Sales of $340,000.
>
> The Company appears clean and well organized. The owner values Doozy's hard assets at $100,000.[12] Doozy currently has four full-time employees plus the owner. The owner's wife works part-time doing bookkeeping. Doozy keeps books on the "cash" method.
>
> **ASKING PRICE: $160,000**

Based on this brief profile, can we determine how much Doozy is worth? Is it worth the asking price? How much would you pay for a "job" that pays you a salary of $48,000 a year, plus pays your family's health insurance premiums and last year's reported earnings of $12,000? The first reaction of many prospective buyers is that earnings of only $12,000 do not seem like very much. Some buyers also wonder why they should pay $160,000 for a business that has only $100,000 in hard assets. These buyers are discouraged and often look no further. Some buyers even feel that they "are being had" because the asking price seems too high.

The prudent buyer chooses to dig a little deeper because he or she senses that the "reported" earnings may not tell the whole story about this company's true profitability. Some buyers like the cabinet manufacturing industry and like the products that Doozy makes. They feel comfortable with the business. For these reasons, they want to learn more.

---

12 The term "hard assets" generally refer to the things you can touch: inventories, real estate, and furniture, fixtures, and equipment (FF&E).

Business Sale Prices. It is difficult to find the prices at which small businesses are sold. The prices are not published in the local newspaper or recorded at the courthouse, as are the sale prices of homes. Most information regarding the sale prices of small businesses is anecdotal. Some pricing information may be learned from attorneys or from brokers. But, because it is difficult to compare one business to another, the conflicting sale prices and **opinions of value** may seem confusing. However, the value of a business and the price at which it will sell is generally closely related to one of two things: (1) its **earnings value** or (2) its **asset value**.

When the actual prices at which small businesses change hands are available, they seem, at first glance, to vary as broadly as the motives and experiences of the potential buyers. The important thing to remember is that what someone pays for a business is usually more closely related to what a buyer feels it can earn, that is to its projected earnings or its earnings value, than to its asset value.[13] When looking at quite similar businesses, the better one may turn out be the one with the fewer assets. Let's review three hypothetical examples of businesses in the same industry: Which business should sell for the higher price?

	Business 1	Business 2	Business 3
Annual Sales	$1,000,000	$1,200,000	$1,400,000
# Employees	4	6	8
Inventory Value	200,000	300,000	400,000
Sales/employee	250,000	200,000	175,000

It might seem at first glance that Business 3 is more valuable. After all, it has greater sales than Business 1 or Business 2 and it has double the inventory of Business 1. But looking more carefully, we see that Business 1 has sales of $250,000 per employee, while Business 3 has sales of only $175,000 per employee. More importantly, every $1.00 in

---

13 The term "earnings" used herein is defined as earnings after paying (or deducting) a salary for the business owner that is consistent with present market salaries for persons in similar positions. The terms earnings, income, and profit are generally interchangeable. "Net profit" or "net income" is the earnings remaining after deducting the cost of any corporate income taxes due. Income value and earnings value are also interchangeable. See Glossary.

Inventory Value in Business 1 seems to generate $5.00 in annual sales. In sharp contrast, each $1.00 in Inventory in Business 3 generates only $3.50 in sales. This means that Business 1 might generate $2,000,000 in annual sales if its inventory were increased to $400,000. (Of course, double inventory does not always mean double sales—these examples are hypothetical.)

Of the three businesses, I suspect Business 1 is the most profitable and therefore more valuable because of three factors important to the success of any business: (1) lower payroll costs (fewer employees), (2) lower rent (it doesn't have to house the additional $200,000 in inventory), and (3) lower interest costs (it doesn't have to pay interest on the additional inventory).

There are several useful shorthand ways to describe the earnings (historic or projected) and the price of a business. For example, they can be expressed as:

1. A percentage of projected or historic annual sales
2. A percentage of the asking price of the business
3. A percentage of the value of the assets in use (Return on Assets or **ROA**)
4. A percentage of the Book Value of business (Return on Equity or **ROE**)
5. A percentage of owner's or buyer's investment (Return on Investment or **ROI**)

Such analytical tools are particularly useful when comparing one business opportunity to another. For example, we can say that one car wash (to use a type of business reasonably easy to compare) shows earnings of 10% of sales while another shows earnings of 15% of sales. Or we can say that a business is on the market at a price equal to five times or six times last year's reported earnings. We can speak the same way about the **Asking Price** of different businesses: one has an asking price of 30% of sales and another has an asking price of 40% or 50% of sales.

Using the five measurements of earnings set out above, let's see what we have learned about Doozy so far. The Broker has made some representations about Doozy's performance from the past year and, optimistically, has given us his opinion of what he feels Doozy might do next year. (Of course, we do not know yet if his opinion is correct.)

Attachment to Doozy Profile	Last Year Actual	Next Year Projected
Earnings (before deducting income taxes)	$12,000	$24,000
Annual Sales	300,000	340,000
Asking Price	160,000	160,000
Estimated Down Payment/Investment	60,000	60,000
Estimated Value of Hard Assets	100,000	100,000
ROA	12%	24%
ROE	Unknown	Unknown
ROI	20%	40%
Earnings as % of Annual Sales	4%	7.06%
Asking Price as % of Annual Sales	53%	47%

Looking at last year's reported financial results it appears that Doozy is earning (before paying income taxes) 4% of Annual Sales and that the Asking Price is 53% of Sales. Also, before additional analysis, it appears that Earnings are 12% of the estimated Value of Hard Assets and that the Asking Price is 60% greater than the estimated Hard Asset value.

Return on Investment. The future or projected earnings are also referred to as a buyer's return on investment or ROI. This is expressed as a percent (%) of the money you invest when you buy a business. Your future profit is the "return" whether your business earns $5,000, $50,000 or $500,000, or more. The "rate of return" can be expressed by dividing the actual or anticipated earnings by the investment (which, in most cases, is the **down payment** paid to the Seller) at the time of purchase of a business. The investment is not the full purchase price unless the full price was paid "in cash."

Example: $12,000 divided by $60,000 = .20 or 20% **ROI**

Down Payment. The larger the down payment, the lower the ROI, and the smaller the down payment, the greater the ROI. All things being equal, the ROI on a $100,000 investment is only 12%. By contrast, the $12,000 return on a $24,000 investment is 50%.

In the illustration above, the $60,000 Down Payment equals the "cash available" which you indicate you can afford to invest. However, the profile is silent on the matter of down payment, so it is not known if the Seller would accept anything other than an "all cash" offer. And it is not known if you or any Buyer could borrow the balance of the $160,000 Asking Price by offering the "hard assets" to a bank as collateral. If either the Seller or a bank will offer partial financing, both will require interest payments. Thus, your future ROI will be the anticipated earnings less the interest charged.

At a price of $160,000 and a down payment of $60,000, the Buyer will have to finance $100,000. If the cost of money (interest) is 8% annual percentage rate (APR), the interest cost will be $8,000 and the **ROI** (based on next year's anticipated earnings of $24,000) will be only $16,000 or 26.7%.[14]

Calculate: $24,000 – 8,000 = $16,000 divided by 60,000 = 26.7% **ROI**

Pre-Tax and After-Tax Profit. A word of caution: Generally, when discussing the profit (or earnings or income) of a small business, brokers, accountants, owners and others are referring to the "before tax" profit. There are several reasons why this is appropriate in valuing a small business or in determining how much to pay for a small business. One reason is that buyers can deduct interest payments (and other expenses) associated with buying a business from the anticipated profit before calculating their taxable income. Many buyers discover that during the first several years after buying a business, there are enough deductions to almost eliminate federal income taxes. In the case of Doozy, it appears that there may be no income tax due from the buyer's first year of ownership. See Table 17 in Chapter 8.

In discussing larger businesses and publicly traded businesses, on the other hand, people usually speak about "after tax" profit when they use the terms profit, earnings, or income. To calculate after-tax profit we deduct estimated federal income taxes from the pre-tax profit. When making comparisons between businesses, always use the same "profit" figure.

The percent "return" that you (or any investor) will find attractive may vary considerably, but it will usually revolve around the questions of "risk"

---

14   The actual first year interest will be less than $8,000 if the Buyer makes monthly principal payments.

and "liquidity."[15] For small businesses, the minimum acceptable ROI is usually thought to be 20% per year or more. Thus, if you made a down payment of $100,000, you might expect your new business to produce pre-tax earnings (after making interest payments and paying you a salary) the first year of $20,000.[16]

Calculate: $20,000 divided by $100,000 = .20 or 20% **ROI**

An ROI somewhat lower than 20% might be acceptable for an established business with very stable and predictable earnings. A higher ROI should be sought for a business with less predictable earnings, fewer assets and fewer years of successful operation. And a much higher ROI would be sought for less stable businesses and those with a high degree of risk.

Risk Factors. This brief paragraph cannot touch on all potential risk factors that might exist with a given business. Each business is different, even when two businesses are in the same industry and located in the same market. Even the safest looking investments involve some type of risk such as one or more of the following. Each could be damaging to the average small business.

- Bank lines of credit are cancelled.
- Interest rates increase significantly.
- Key employee leaves business with little notice.
- Government regulations change or new ones are imposed.
- Important customer decides to do business with a competitor.
- A well-financed new competitor enters market.
- Lease expires and landlord wants a 20% increase in rent.
- A major customer declares bankruptcy, leaving you with an uncollectible account receivable of $100,000.

---

15 For more precise definitions of the terms used, refer to the Glossary.
16 Throughout this book we use "pre-tax" earnings rather than "after-tax" earnings as our benchmark. Most purchasers of small businesses will have enough depreciation, interest, and other acquisition related expenses to reduce taxable income to a minimum for several years.

As a practical matter, the prices at which businesses exchange hands usually range from the value of a business's hard assets (the **asset value**) to ten times the average pre-tax earnings (the **earnings or income value**).[17] It is important to realize that most businesses consist of many different types and quantities of assets. And, of course, a prudent buyer should learn them because much of an established business's value is created through the wise use of the business's assets.

Types of Assets. There are two broad types of assets: **tangible assets** (sometimes referred to as hard assets) and **intangible assets**. The former, which are shown on the Balance Sheet of a business, are those things that we can easily see and touch, such as cash, buildings, equipment, furniture, and inventories. The original cost and current book value of these assets appears on most balance sheets. See Doozy's Simplified Balance Sheet in Table 8 in Chapter 4. There you will see that the tangible assets are divided into two important categories: Current Assets, such as Cash and Accounts Receivable, and Fixed (or Long term) Assets, usually things with a useful life of one year or more.

In contrast, the value or cost of intangible assets rarely appears on the books of small companies. Normally the cost of these intangible assets is expensed, or written off, when they are purchased or created. Sometimes there are no specific intangible assets that can readily be identified. They may be collectively referred to simply as the "goodwill" or "going concern" value of a company. However, these intangible assets are often very important, in fact essential, to the successful and profitable operation of a business. Think of how costly it could be to a business if it lost such assets as its personnel contracts, service agreements, dealership agreements, marketing agreements, business plans, customer lists, and appraisals, or telephone numbers, trade names and logos. In the case of Doozy, what would it cost to replace all the cost sheets and shop drawings for the various cabinets that Doozy manufactures? Intangible assets can and do have substantial value.

---

17 A third useful valuation tool is a review of the sale prices of comparable companies (similar sized companies in comparable industries). Using "comparables" is referred to as the Market Approach to business valuation. Most valuation experts recommend using at least three different valuation methods before concluding what a particular business might be worth.

The **earnings value** of a business usually exceeds its **asset value**. This is certainly true of publicly traded companies that, year in and year out, have **market values** of twice their **book values** or more. See examples below using Price Per Share data from the close of the New York Stock Exchange on September 17, 2008. Each stock shown is considered "blue chip." Only one, QCOM, which had 24% growth in sales the prior year, is considered a "growth" company. The two bank stocks were traded below their **book values,** which is unusual. It is a temporary situation and a reflection of the recent strong decline in housing values across the US.

The average ratio of Market Value to Book Value for the companies shown is 1.93 to 1. Stated differently, the market values exceeded the book values by 93%, a ratio of 1.93:1. By comparison, on the first trading day of the year, January 2, 2008, the ratio for these seven companies was 2.26:1.

COMPARISON OF MARKET AND BOOK VALUES
(*No. shares outstanding* and Market and Book *values* are in *billions of dollars*)

Symbol	Company Name	No. Shares Outstanding	X	Price Per Share	=	Market Value	Book Value	Ratio
JPM	JP Morgan	3.90	X	$36	=	$140	$150	.93
C	Citicorp	8.45	X	19	=	160	190	.84
T	AT&T	5.89	X	28	=	165	110	1.50
FCX	FedEx	.31	X	88	=	27	15	1.80
GE	GE	9.95	X	24	=	239	127	1.90
FPL	Florida Power	.41	X	53	=	22	10.5	2.10
QCOM	Qualcomm	1.64	X	45	=	74	17	4.40
	Average							1.93

Goodwill. The difference between **asset value** and **earnings value** (the price or value in excess of the asset value) is generally known as goodwill. So, when people ask how much are you paying for goodwill, they are really asking: "How much over asset value are you paying?" or "What is the excess value above the book value or asset value of the company being acquired?" A helpful article, "Notes On the Value of Goodwill in Small Businesses," is included in the Appendix.

It is not unusual for the goodwill portion of the purchase price of a manufacturing company like Doozy to range from 25% to 50%.[18] Even though it may not appear that way, no two businesses are identical, so the **goodwill value** may be less than 25% in some and more than 50% in other perfectly normal businesses. The recent sale of a heating and air conditioning business illustrates this point. It is profiled below using year-to-date financial data.

HVAC Service Co.—Summary of Sale Data	
Sales/Revenue (most recent 6 months only)	$250,427
Growth in Sales (over prior 6 month period)	44.2%
No. Employees (including the owner)	2.5
Pre-Tax Income (most recent 6 months only)	$ 62,677
Selling Price	$236,000
Estimated Market Value of Tangible Assets	$ 46,875
Estimated Goodwill Value	$189,125
Goodwill as % of Selling price	**80.1%**
ROA (assume 12 mo. Income of $125,354)	268%
Calculate: $125,354 divided by $46,875 = 2.68	

This HVAC company seems to be able to generate an annualized revenue of around $500,000 ($250,427 x 2) with tangible assets valued at only $46,875. And therefore it seems to have lots of goodwill, probably the result of high customer retention and the very strong ROA. In a good service company, few tangible assets can generate a lot of income. By contrast, a company like Doozy (or a traditional retail business) will require substantially more assets to generate the same sales volume. A good yardstick to use with small businesses is that each $1 in tangible assets (inventory + FF&E) could produce $3 in revenue. For larger, more capital intensive businesses it might require $3 in assets to produce $3 in revenue.

---

18 Many businesses, particularly newer businesses that rely heavily on the skills of the owner, may have no goodwill value. In cases in which the asset value exceeds the earnings value, there is "negative" goodwill. You will also find that there are industry standards relating to the goodwill values in many types of business. While these "standards" may be helpful to you, remember that each business is unique and the standard may not always fit.

Doozy's Goodwill. Let's again look at what Doozy is offering for sale. If Doozy is worth the asking price of $160,000, it appears that the goodwill portion of its value is $60,000 or 37.5%. At a selling price of $150,000, the goodwill value would be only $50,000 or 33.3%.

Book Value of Doozy's Hard Assets	$62,000
Estimated Market Value of Hard Assets	100,000
Asking Price	160,000
Anticipated Selling Price	150,000
Goodwill (price less market value of assets)	$50,000-60,000
Calculate: $60,000 divided by $160,000 = 37.5%	

The amount of goodwill is also related to a company's rate of growth or prospects for future growth. Note that one of the publicly traded companies shown above, QCOM, is felt to have a market value that is 335% greater than (or over three times) its book value.[19]

Calculate: $74 billion − 17 billion = 57 billion ÷17 billion = 335%

Many buyers and their advisors feel it is wrong to pay much for **goodwill.** But good businesses have more goodwill because they make more efficient use of their assets like Business 4 below. It generated $600,000 in revenue on only $150,000 in inventory (Business 1, on page 26, generated revenue of $1,000,000 with only $200,000 in inventory). Goodwill might be summed up as a business's general reputation or degree of name recognition in its market. Goodwill is often what really makes a business run successfully. This is why, when attempting to value two quite comparable businesses, it is often correct to conclude that the one with the fewer assets is the more valuable and, therefore, has more goodwill.

So, as a potential buyer, it is important for you to learn what makes up the goodwill of any business you are interested in. Just because you cannot see these goodwill assets on a company's financial statement does not mean they do not exist and have value. Of course, after some research you may

---

[19] Remember that in talking about a publicly traded company, the market value is the value of its stock (the value of all outstanding shares of stock) and not the value of its assets.

conclude, quite correctly that a given business has no goodwill **value** or even has negative goodwill. Look as these examples:

COMPARISON OF GOODWILL VALUES		
Typical Retail Business	Business 4	Business 5
Annual Sales (Revenue)	$600,000	$800,000
Inventory @ Book Value	150,000	300,000
Fixed Assets @ Market Value	60,000	100,000
Pre-Tax Income	60,000	72,000
Income as % of Sales	10%	9%
Asking Price	$300,000	$400,000
Goodwill Value (at full price)	90,000	0
Goodwill as % of Price	30%	0%
Return on Assets (ROA)	29%	19%

At first glance, the businesses seem comparable: both are offered for sale at a price equal to 50% of sales. However, the Asking Price of #4 includes $90,000 in goodwill. Is this just "blue sky" or does #4 merit this premium over asset value? At a $400,000 asking price, #5 has no goodwill value, perhaps because it has more assets in relation to annual revenue than its competitor. It's assets equal 50% of revenue (($300,000 +100,000)÷$800,000=.5), while Business 4 operates with assets equal in value to only 35% of revenue. Unless some reasonable explanation can be found for this disparity, Business 4 seems to have earned its goodwill.

Notice also that Business 4 has achieved a very respectable ROA of 29%.

Calculate: $60,000 (Pre-tax Income) ÷ $210,000 (asset value) = 29%

However, some businesses for a variety of reasons do not merit any goodwill value. It is important to explore these reasons. If a business has negative goodwill, it is generally felt that its value (and selling price) will be less than the value of its tangible assets. Let's look at the same two businesses again.

Inventory Turnover. Businesses with a good product mix and eager customers are expected to have a better (higher) rate of inventory turnover. This is desirable and is often a component in determining the existence of goodwill, because these businesses will need less inventory to operate profitably. This means that less capital will be needed. Looking at the snapshot below, we can see that Business 4 achieved 3 turns on its inventory while Business 5 achieved only 2 turns. To calculate the turnover rate, simply divide Cost of Goods Sold by Value of Inventory. If we use Purchases instead of COGs to calculate turnover, we are not taking into account changes in Value of Inventory. See Glossary for a further discussion of this point.

Annual Sales (Revenue)	$600,000	$800,000
Purchases (Costs of Goods Sold)	450,000	600,000
Gross Profit	150,000	200,000
Gross Profit Margin	25%	25%
Value of Inventory (see above)	150,000	300,000
Inventory Turns	3 turns	2 turns

Since inventory turnover is one measure of how current the inventories are, we may discover that Business 5 has experienced declining sales and, as a result, has some "dead" inventory. If these factors are true (declining sales and slow inventory turnover), a prudent buyer may conclude that Business 5 has, in fact, some negative goodwill even though the two businesses at first glance appear quite similar. Of course, the "excess" inventory may have recently been purchased.

Part II. EARNINGS MULTIPLES AND CAP RATES

If you invest in long-term U.S. Treasury obligations, you will usually earn about 5% annual interest. Therefore, since 5% interest is the "going rate of return" for the safest and most predictable investment, you would expect business investments to give you a greater return. This "rate of return" is sometimes referred to as the capitalization rate or cap rate.

At a **cap rate** of 5%, the value or price of Doozy would be $240,000 or 20 times its reported earnings of $12,000. Note that this value is more than twice the reported value of the hard assets.

Calculate: If Price (value) x 5% = $12,000 reported earnings

Then: $12,000 (earnings) divided by .05 (cap rate) =

$240,000 Indicated Earnings Value or Price

Is $240,000 a fair price to pay for Doozy? It is certainly not fair if the reported sales and recent earning are the only considerations. Such a high value for Doozy, a multiple of 20 times reported earnings, or 20:1, would assume that U.S. Treasury obligations and Doozy, a fairly typical small business, are both of equal risk and liquidity. Simple logic tells us that this cannot be so. All businesses are much more risky and far less liquid than Treasury bills. Let's look at the effect of higher risk and lower liquidity on the **price to earnings multiple.**

The **earnings multiple** is generally referred to as a **P:E** or price-to-earnings ratio. One of the first questions brokers and others ask about a small business is: "What's the P:E?" You should ask that, too.

Today some fixed income investments and publicly traded stocks and bonds have yields as high as 10% or more per year. These investments yield more than the treasury obligations, or bank certificates of deposit, because they are somewhat riskier. Corporations may fail or they may cut or suspend their dividends, but most of them do not have nearly the same risks as the typical small business.

Publicly traded companies can lose market value quickly in a recession or when problems arise. But, publicly traded stocks and bonds can be sold at virtually any time, so they are quite liquid. And, when the end of a recession is in sight, stocks often rebound in value quickly. It may take many months (or longer) to sell a small, privately held business of any size. The lesson to remember is: **Small businesses are not very liquid.**

U.S. Treasury obligations, on the other hand, are both safe and highly liquid. Their yield (return) is highly predictable; in fact, it is guaranteed. This means two things: (1) that there is little risk that your investment will decline in value (safety) and (2) that your investment can be withdrawn at almost any time (liquidity).

Because of the <u>higher risk</u>, <u>lower liquidity</u> and <u>unpredictable earnings</u>, you (and any other reasonable investor in a small business like Doozy) would seek a return that is higher than the typical return you can find in the stock or bond markets. After all, many small businesses fail each year and very few can be sold quickly enough to raise cash, if a sudden financial need were to arise. Based on these factors **an earnings multiple or P:E of 20:1, or even 10:1, is clearly too high for most small businesses.**

Let's look at some lower earnings multiples and see what effect they would have on the value of Doozy. At a multiple of 8:1, for example, Doozy's earnings value would be only $96,000, much closer to the reported $100,000 value of Doozy's hard assets. At a multiple of 4:1 Doozy would be worth only $48,000.

Calculate: $12,000 x 8 = $96,000 Indicated Earnings Value

$12,000 x 4 = $48,000 Indicated Earnings Value

ASSETS INCLUDED IN A TYPICAL SALE: Unlike many larger businesses, the typical small business leases the space in which it operates. Therefore, when valuing a small business or calculating an earnings multiple (P:E), assume that no real estate (**real property assets**) is included in a sale or in a valuation. Also, most **financial assets** such as Cash and Accounts receivable are normally excluded when a small business is sold. These two classes of assets are customarily retained by the seller. This is so because most small businesses sell to retail customers who pay by cash, check or credit card when an item (or service) is purchased and, therefore, have few or no accounts receivable.[20]

Doozy is somewhat different because it sells custom products, products that may be suitable for only one customer. So, with every custom order, Doozy receives a deposit of about 50% of the contract price and generally receives the full balance upon delivery of the job.

If a business does carry accounts for some of its customers, it may either factor its accounts receivable or have a **line of credit** (secured by its accounts receivable) to borrow against, when additional short-term **working capital** is needed. The amount of "cash" or cash equivalent that a buyer of a small business could expect to find among its assets is usually very little because little cash is needed for normal operations.

---

20 If businesses carry accounts receivable, as is the case in most businesses that sell products or services to another business, it is normal that the "assets" included in the sale include some cash.

In larger businesses, let's say those with annual sales of $5 million or more, that sell most of their products or services on credit, it would be reasonable to expect the seller to include among the assets sold with the business either the accounts receivable or an amount of cash equal to one month's operating expenses. Each industry has different traditions. The important thing is for the buyer to determine what a business's short-term working capital requirements might be.

The following analyses assume that we are discussing a business that has (and will sell) only the following four classes of assets: (Some of these terms are defined in more detail in the Glossary.) In a purchase agreement, each of the assets is assigned a specific value. (Refer to Chapter 6 for details.) The sum of these values equals the purchase price. A related question (which will be dealt with later) is how much of each class of asset to buy, since some businesses have too few assets and other businesses keep far too many assets on hand.

1. **Inventories:** raw materials, parts, work-in-process (or work-in-progress), finished goods, goods held for resale in wholesale and retail businesses, and inventories of rental equipment

2. **Fixed or "tangible" assets:** rolling stock, furniture, fixtures, and shop and office equipment (the FF&E to brokers) and tools of all descriptions. Leasehold improvements are also often included.

3. **Goodwill:** business records, customer lists, orders, forms, logos, drawings, trade names and other "intangible" or "off-balance sheet" assets that are necessary to operate a business. The goodwill portion of the purchase price of a business may often include the Seller's Management Transition Assistance and his or her Agreement Not to Compete with the Buyer.[21]

4. **Supplies:** shop, shipping, cleaning supplies; catalogues, advertising materials; software and office supplies (such as stationery, copier paper and postage stamps)

It is further assumed that the assets that will be sold with the business will be in quantities necessary to operate the business in the "normal fashion" and will be:

---

21 These last two items are discussed more fully in Chapter 6: How to Structure a Purchase Agreement.

1. Free and clear of any debts or liens,
2. In good working order, and
3. Fully insured for their fair market values.

Hidden Assets. We might add a fifth class of assets: hidden assets, that is, assets that do not appear on a company's balance sheet or depreciation schedule. It is not unusual to find hidden inventory. This results from the fact that some small businesses do not bother to count their inventories for many years. For the owners of these businesses it is a nuisance and may result in having to pay more income taxes. Some manufacturing companies estimate the cost of materials that go into their finished products and "write off" these materials when they are purchased. Over a period of years a substantial unrecorded inventory accumulates. Let me give other examples of hidden assets:

> **Case History: Hidden Assets.** In the profile of a ceramic supply company, the broker listed: (1) Catalogues: $15,000, (2) Conveyor System: $40,000 and (3) Goods in Transit: $60,000. But the buyer challenged this because he couldn't find these items on the Balance Sheet. Many companies contract with printers to print their catalogues. In this case, the company had its own print shop and had just run off 5,000 new catalogues ready to ship to customers. There were overhead conveyors attached to the ceiling of the plant. Most of us would assume that they were property of the landlord, but they had been installed by the business owner and were moveable so they were leasehold improvements. The Goods-in-Transit were not counted with the Inventory because these goods were on trucks in transit to customers who had bought them. After some discussion, the buyer agreed that these hidden assets were very real and had value.
> **Moral: There are almost always hidden assets.**

When looking for "assets" it is wise not to rely solely on the list or description of assets provided by the business owner or his broker. While I was working as a broker, my preference was to walk through each room in a facility, with the owner if possible, and jot down a brief description of every piece of equipment that I found and my estimate of its current value. When stumped I would ask the owner: "What is this? What's it for? Where did it come from? Is it still used in the business and what did you pay for it?" I found that owners usually remembered quite distinctly how their assets were acquired and what they cost.

Then I would do the same thing outside, walking through the yard and parking areas examining the signage and any other (movable) items of potential value. This practice also helped me spot areas of concern such as environmental hazards. I normally found several useful (and sometimes quite valuable) assets during my tour of a business that did not appear on the company balance sheet or on the Schedule of FF&E. For example, the signage alone (i.e. neon lighting, pole lighting) could easily have cost $20,000, even in a relatively small business.

One reason to pay particular attention to the type and quantity of assets on hand is to learn how a business is organized. Another involves collateral. If a buyer intends to borrow money to assist with the purchase, lenders always want to see a lot of collateral, that is, assets against which they can file liens to help secure their loans. Finally, every buyer should want to learn at some point during the process of buying a business what assets he is taking title to.

The Question of Excess Assets or Inventory. Businesses that have more assets (than would be necessary to operate "in the normal manner") may sell for higher prices than the following analyses suggest. The presence of "excess" assets or "excess" inventory may also help explain the difference between a seller's opinion of value and the value calculated by a buyer. The two most frequently encountered classes of "excess" are vehicles and inventory. The buyer may not have to purchase the excess but, first, the buyer must know how much is normal.

Since no two businesses are exactly alike, it is best to think in terms of adjusting information regarding any given business to what is the norm in its market area or industry. If, for example, the value of inventories "on hand" is $100,000 and the norm for such a business to "operate in the normal fashion" is only $50,000, the estimated $50,000 surplus might either be (1) excluded from the sale or (2) be included in the sale and added to the purchase price (and to the estimated "fair market value") of the business. If possible, find out from the owner, a trade association or from a broker what the "norm" is.

If the excess inventory is in good and marketable condition, it really does not cost the buyer anything to buy it, because in the course of a few months the buyer would need to replenish this inventory. Said differently, excess inventory in good and marketable condition does not always increase the price you would pay for a business, because it is often consumed after the sale in the normal course of business. If, however, there is more than several months' excess, you, as Buyer, may want to include a provision in the Purchase Agreement that states that one of three things will occur:

1. The Seller will reduce the inventory on hand to "normal" levels by the closing date on the sale of the business,
2. Excess inventory will be purchased by the buyer at closing but will be valued at less than its **replacement or original cost**, say at 75% of original cost, or
3. Excess inventory will be purchased in the future from seller without discount on an "as needed" basis, but not later than six months after the closing

How Much Inventory is Normal? Businesses turn over their inventories at different rates. The ideal turnover rate depends upon the product mix, lead time needed to reorder, reorder quantities necessary to receive price discounts and other factors. Three to four "turns" a year is pretty normal. So, if a business had purchases of $400,000 a year, it would maintain an inventory of about $100,000 with four turns. This would be a three-month supply. If a business like Doozy can replenish its inventory with a week of lead time, a one-month supply (one-twelfth of annual purchases) or less may be normal. If a business has only two turns a year, it probably has (1) too much inventory or (2) some inventory is obsolete. In either event an explanation is needed. See section titled How Much Inventory To Buy in Chapter 6.

The answer to what constitutes a "normal" inventory is more than simply calculating the proper amount of total inventory. A business can have different types of inventory. It may have raw materials, parts and finished goods. Each of these inventories will have sub-sets. In other words, there may be too many parts of one kind and far too few of several other kinds, but the total value may seem about right. It is therefore important to have the right balance of inventories as well as the right amount. You do not want to buy a business and discover shortly thereafter that you have to shut down operations because you have run out of essential part.

TIP: Normal inventory levels can vary throughout the year. Some businesses have seasonal fluctuations, which makes normal levels trickier to calculate. In advance of the busy season, inventories may seem too high. However, at the end of the season inventories may seem too low, but businesses do not want to end the "season" with merchandise they cannot sell during the next season. And they would have to discount it to clear the shelves for incoming merchandise. If inventory should turn over four times, "normal" equals about two month's sales. But, instead of using average sales to calculate "normal," use projected sales for the coming two months.

Not all changes in inventory levels result from seasonal fluctuations in sales and not all changes are bad. Let me share a story.

Case History: Excess Inventory. A distributor of heating and air conditioning equipment ended the year with far too much inventory for "normal" conditions. Worse, much of it was cold weather equipment. Several well-qualified buyers passed up the business because of this overhang of winter inventory. What the buyers did not take into account was that the manufacturers wanted to clear out their inventories and offered their distributors a discount if they reordered before the end of the year. Three months later one manufacturer had a 6% price increase. So, even if the distributor had to borrow money to buy the "excess" inventory, it saved money in the long run. The excess inventory, if the buyers had agreed to buy it at the seller's original cost, was a bargain. **Moral: Learn why inventories are higher than normal.**

Buildings and Other Real Property Assets. Is a building an "excess" asset? If Doozy owns the building it occupies and therefore does not pay rent, how can we value the business? Or compare Doozy to similar businesses that do not own real estate and do pay rent? To do this, the following three steps are generally recommended:

1. Exclude the value of the building (or other real property asset) from the asking price of the business,
2. Deduct an appropriate cost of "rent" from the reported earnings and, then

3. Add back to the reported earnings any building related expenses, such as real estate taxes, for which the landlords would normally be responsible.

These steps facilitate the calculation of the **fair market value** of the business alone. Of course, whether you would prefer to buy Doozy's building or rent it from the Seller is a normal subject for negotiation. You may even wish to neither rent nor buy Doozy's building but to move the company to a new facility.

Suggestion: Learn which assets are carried on the Balance Sheet of a company and which ones were "written off" or expensed when they were purchased. Many companies expense or write off several classes of short-lived assets when they are purchased, so the value of assets on the Balance Sheet may seem discouragingly low. Hand tools, for example, are almost always expensed. Some companies, such as dental labs, may expense all of their precious metal purchases because they are not resold and are consumed fairly rapidly. Others expense the cost of assets with a longer life, such as a three-year supply of catalogues, rather than put them on the Balance Sheet. As we learn later, Doozy wrote off the entire cost of a new truck rather than depreciating it over several years

---

SELECTING THE RIGHT EARNINGS MULTIPLE: Most small businesses change hands at prices that range between two and six times their "pre-tax" earnings. The HVAC company profiled earlier sold for almost exactly two times (twice) its annualized pre-tax earnings. The multiple for established manufacturers is more likely to range between four and eight times pre-tax earnings. This higher "price to earnings multiple" or ratio is a reflection of the fact that manufacturers require more assets to operate than do typical retail or service companies.

Larger, publicly traded businesses are valued on the basis of their "after-tax" earnings and, in normal economic times, will trade on the stock market (or sell) at much higher earnings multiples. Look at the price to earnings multiples (P:Es) listed in the Money and Investing section of the Wall Street Journal or in other financial publications. In normal times the average earnings multiple or P:E ratio may be 12:1. For some "high tech" companies the P:E may be 50:1 or more, but these companies are growing (or anticipated to grow) very rapidly.

The U.S. Small Business Administration (SBA) in its publication "Checklist for Purchasing a Business" recommends that no small business be valued at more than 4 to 5 times its annual earnings, or a P:E of 4:1 or 5:1. While this advice may be a little conservative, the SBA guidelines cited below can be very instructive. Review them carefully. Remember that, unlike the publicly traded stocks sold on Wall Street, when speaking of small businesses, the earnings are "pre-tax" not "after-tax" earnings.[22] There can be quite a difference.

SBA VALUATION GUIDELINES

1. **10 Times Earnings**—Old established businesses with large capital assets, excellent "goodwill" and excellent future earnings prospects. Only very few small, privately held companies fall into this category.

2. **8 Times Earnings**—Old established businesses that are successful and have predictable sales and earnings growth but require considerable managerial care.

3. **7 Times Earnings**—Strong, well-established businesses that are sensitive to the general economy, and are vulnerable to recessions. They require considerable managerial ability, but little specialized knowledge on the part of the owners.

4. **5 Times Earnings**—Medium size businesses that require comparatively small capital investment and only average managerial ability. These businesses are highly competitive but the established "good-will" is of distinct importance. Market value of assets should be fairly close to the purchase price.

5. **4 Times Earnings**—Medium size businesses that require comparatively small capital investment and only average managerial ability. These businesses are highly competitive but have less goodwill value than a more established company with

---

22 The federal income tax rate for larger companies is around 35% of the pre-tax income. If a company has pre-tax income of, say, $500,000, the after-tax income is $325,000. Calculate: $500,000 – ($500,000 x .35) = $325,000. If this company is worth $4,000,000, the P:E for the pre-tax earnings is 8:1. In after-tax earnings, the P:E is 12.3:1. **Calculate**: $4,000,000÷325,000 =12.3.

more stable sales and earnings. Market value of assets should be close to purchase price.

6. **2 Times Earnings**—Businesses, large or small, which depend upon the special, often unusual skills of one or a small group of managers. They involve only a small amount of capital, and have few tangible assets, such as inventory or equipment, and are highly competitive with high "mortality" rates.

7. **1 Times Earnings**—Personal service businesses. They require little or no capital. The manager must have special skills and thorough knowledge of his subject. The earnings of this type of business depend upon the manager's skill rather than his "organization" or staff. The owner can sell the business including its reputation and "plan of business" but not his skills. The earnings of these businesses are normally the Seller's "take home" pay.

While the SBA checklist can be helpful, it did not mention one factor that can have a large bearing on the proper multiple to select. That is interest rates or the "cost" of money. If money can be borrowed at 5%, a higher P:E might be used than when the cost of money is 12% because the ROI will be greater. Let's refer to Doozy again and calculate the effect of different interest rates on ROI. Let's assume Doozy will earn $24,000, the company sells for $160,000 of which $100,000 is borrowed, and money costs 8%. After deducting interest on a $100,000 loan, the ROI on a $60,000 down payment is 26.7%. See calculations below. Interest rates affect earnings considerably and so the value of businesses could fluctuate with changes in interest rates.

Calculate:

1. @ 5% interest: $24,000−5,000=19,000÷60,000=31.7% **ROI**
2. @ 8% interest $24,000−8,000=16,000÷60,000=26.7% **ROI**
3. @ 10% interest $24,000−10,000=14,000÷60,000=23.4% **ROI**
4. @ 12% interest $24,000−12,000=12,000÷60,000=20.0% **ROI**

DOOZY'S EARNINGS MULTIPLE: There are two separate analyses that are useful in selecting the appropriate earnings multiple: (1) reviewing the **earnings history** (what a business has earned over the

How to Buy a Business without Being Had

past several years) and (2) calculating the **earnings capacity** (what a business could earn in the future) which will be discussed in Chapter 5. Assuming for the moment that the information provided by the Seller is accurate, what P:E ratio do we use to value Doozy? To discover this, try to match the SBA categories and the **earnings history** set out in Table 1 below.

Doozy manufactures kitchen cabinets. This is a business that does not usually require a great amount of managerial talent or technical skill. Therefore, goodwill may not be of much importance in this business. On the other hand, goodwill may be a more important element than is first apparent.

As shown on Table 1 below and on Table 3 on page 50, three years ago Doozy made $34,000 on sales of $340,000, but last year reported pre-tax earnings of $12,000 (on sales of $300,000). Why this apparent decline? The industry appears stable. Business acquaintances suggest that Doozy's owner may not be spending much time at his business in recent years. If this is so, it probably isn't necessary to discount Doozy's **purchase price** for any anticipated future drop in earnings. The business may simply need the full-time attention of an owner who can bring new energy and enthusiasm. While the acquaintances may be correct, let's look further and see if we can find a fuller explanation for this apparent decline.

With the information at hand so far, Doozy looks like a "four times earnings" business with an earnings value of only $48,000 (4 x $12,000), significantly less than its estimated hard asset value of $100,000. More importantly, at a value of $48,000 there is no goodwill.[23] The **goodwill value** would, in fact, be negative. Before we conclude that a P:E of 4 times earnings is appropriate for Doozy, more analysis is needed.

---

23   This discussion of earnings multiples is too brief to cover all relevant factors. To select the appropriate multiple, there are services that many brokers subscribe to which provide comparable market data on businesses that have been sold. Typical multiples can be calculated from it.

Jack (John V. M.) Gibson

Part III. INCOME AVERAGING

It's hardly fair to judge a business's earnings capacity or the value of a business on only one year's performance. Doozy has ups and downs like most businesses. The average of several years' earnings would probably be more indicative of Doozy's true earnings and market value. A period of three to five calendar or fiscal years is usually considered a good base period for the purpose of income averaging; but sometimes the business cycle is longer, stable and relatively predictable.[24] This also should be taken into account.

Doozy's reported earnings for five years are shown in Table 1 below. The $18,000 average earnings over the past five years are considerably more than last year's $12,000 reported earnings. While the difference of $6,000 between the five-year average earnings and last year's may not seem significant, it represents an apparent 50% increase, which is very significant.

Because earnings over the last few years appear to be trending downward, rather than relying on an earnings average, it may be fairer and more accurate to "weight" Doozy's earnings according to their closeness to the present. One method for doing this is to multiply the earnings by a "weight" and then average the "weighted" earnings. The selection of weights varies and is quite subjective, but normally the last year (or most recent period) is given the highest weight.

Table 1. Weighted Earnings for Five Years

Year	Reported Earnings	Weight	Weighted Earnings
Last Year	$12,000	x 5 =	$60,000
2 Years Ago	20,000	x 4 =	80,000
3 Years Ago	34,000	x 3 =	102,000
4 Years Ago	10,000	x 2 =	20,000
5 Years Ago	14,000	x 1 =	14,000
	$90,000	15	$276,000
	÷ 5 yrs.		÷ 15
Average:	**$18,000**	**Weighted Average:**	**$ 18,400**

---

24 It is important to look at the earnings since the end of the last calendar or fiscal year and to look at monthly financial statements as well as the annual statements. If timely monthly statements are not available, every business should have some form of monthly sales record available that the owner or broker can share with you.

This weighted average of $18,400 is higher than the five-year simple average of $18,000. In the example shown the weighted average is only 2.2% higher than the simple average. But it is comforting to learn that both averages are higher than last year's unimpressive earnings. For other businesses, we find that the weighted average is far different from the simple average.

If we use the **weighted average** of $18,400, it appears that the value of Doozy is around $75,000 (4 x $18,400 = $73,600). The weighted average is usually a better indication of value than a value derived by using only last year's reported earnings because it takes into account: (1) the business cycle and (2) the growth trend of a company or industry. If, for example, Last Year had earned $40,000, the weighted average would jump to $27,740.

Some buyers feel that only the most recent earnings should be considered in putting a value on a business. However, generally a weighted average is more accurate for cyclical businesses. Remember, though, that the reason we study the past is to help us anticipate the future more accurately, so the more thoughtful buyer will base his opinion of Doozy's value on what that company might be expected to earn in the future. (You can believe the owner has ideas about what future earnings will be, so ask him when it seems appropriate.)

We still have two significantly different values: the indicated **weighted earnings value** of $75,000 and the **hard asset value** of $100,000. Which value should we trust or should we trust either one? Let's first look at a different weighting and a different analysis period. Table 2 shows the results of using only a three-year "look back" period.

Table 2. Weighted Earnings for Three Years

Year	Reported Earnings	Weight	Weighted Earnings
Last Year	$12,000	x 5 =	$60,000
2 Years Ago	20,000	x 3 =	60,000
3 Years Ago	34,000	x 1 =	34,000
	$66,000	9	$154,000
	÷ 3 yrs.		÷ 9
Average:	**$22,000**	**Weighted Average:**	**$17,111**

Note that "average" earnings have gone up and the "weighted average" has gone down with the different weighting and "look back" period. Both averages in Table 2 are still quite close to the averages obtained in the analysis set out in Table 1. This would normally suggest that we are on the right track, since we should expect values found by using different methods of analysis to be relatively close. If they are not close, it may be because an inappropriate measure of value is used.

The average of the four averages is $18,877, slightly higher than the weighted average found in Table 1 and 57% higher than last year's reported earnings of $12,000. Which average should we use? In fact, we should not rely too heavily on any of these averages, because the weightings only tell us about the past. It is usually more important to learn what a business is capable of earning. To learn what Doozy is capable of earning we might analyze the reported $34,000 earnings from three years ago more closely. These earnings may be more indicative.

RELATIONSHIP BETWEEN SALES AND EARNINGS: How does Doozy's earnings history relate to its sales history? Annual sales have been fairly stable, while earnings appear to have fluctuated widely. Because Doozy is a custom shop (and reports sales when payment is received), this fluctuation in earnings may simply result from the timing of receipt of payments. For example, Doozy may have received a check for a large job in the first week of January, even though all the "costs" were paid the preceding year. In the following analyses we will look for explanations for these apparent fluctuations on both the "cost" side and the "sales" side.

There normally is no good reason why earnings are not a relatively consistent percent of sales. We expect rising sales to be associated with higher earnings margins, that is, earnings will be a somewhat higher percent of sales in good years and somewhat lower percent in slow years.

In Table 3 (below) we see that earnings have apparently declined sharply from 10% of sales three years ago to only 4% of sales last year. If there has been no economic recession or rise in interest rates, or other external causes of decreasing profit margins, we would expect to find some fairly obvious internal explanation. We do see in Table 3, as expected, that reported sales for the best years have the highest margins (percent of reported sales). Note: Doozy's five-year sales history is from a period: (1)

How to Buy a Business without Being Had

unaffected by serious swings in the overall economy and (2) during which inflation averaged about 3% per year.

It is reasonable to assume that, if earnings equaled 10% of sales three years ago, earnings could do so again.[25] If this proves so, Doozy may be worth much more than $75,000. Assuming sales of $300,000 and pre-tax earnings of 10%, we find the following suggested earnings and business value:

Calculate: 1. $300,000 x 10% = $30,000 suggested earnings

2. $30,000 x 4 = $120,000 suggested value (price)

If we assume that: (1) sales should be in the $340,000 range, with an enthusiastic new owner devoting full time to the business, and (2) earnings should be in the 10% range, the fair market value of Doozy may be higher than $120,000. It's good to keep an open mind about this possibility.

Table 3. Earnings as a Percent of Sales

Year	Sales	Earnings	Profit Margin
Last Year	$ 300,000	$12,000	4.0%
Two Years Ago	320,000	20,000	6.25%
Three Years Ago	340,000	34,000	10.0%
Four Years Ago	300,000	10,000	3.3%
Five Years Ago	264,000	14,000	5.3%
Total:	$1,524,000	$90,000	5.9%
Average:	**$ 304,000**	**$18,000**	**5.9%**

Note that the profit margin goes up as annual sales go up and declines as sales go down, but this relationship is not perfect. Four years ago sales did rise from the prior year, but the percentage (margin) declined

---

25 Keep in mind also that the reverse could also be true; but without further analysis it is not possible to know whether pre-tax earnings of 3.3% (four years ago) or 10% (three years ago) of sales is more accurate.

from 5.3% of sales to only 3.3% of sales. It appears that more analysis is indicated.

Adjusting Reported Sales. Explore whether some of Doozy's sales three years ago were actually completed in the prior year. This often occurs in businesses that report sales on the "cash basis" as Doozy does. Doozy may have received a check in the last week of the year and not deposited it until January. A look at the general ledger and bank deposits for the last several Januarys can shed light on this. Also, we should check the date on which Doozy's bank posted the year-end deposits.[26]

Of course, if actual sales three years ago (based on dates of delivery or on dates of receipt of payment) turned out to be less than $340,000, the reported earnings of $34,000 would exceed 10% of sales (and may exceed the 11.76% of sales shown later in Table 9 at the end of Chapter 4). In custom shops, one check could be $10,000, or greater, so the date a check was deposited will alter the sales reported for a month (or year) and therefore alter corresponding "averages."

In a typical retail business it is more likely that a deposit would not exceed average daily sales, but some smaller retail businesses deposit their sales receipts only once a week or have no set routine for making deposits. More often, fluctuations in daily, weekly, or monthly sales are the result of the number of days that a store is open for business. Average daily sales can actually be up when the reported monthly sales are down as a result of Sunday closings and the like.

Finally, many owners are conscious of the income tax consequences of recording year-end sales because the more sales reported, the more taxes owed. Some owners consciously hold up making deposits for a few days. Many times, reported December sales are lower than expected while January sales are higher. Adjusting monthly sales is often necessary to calculate correct profit margins. For this reason, it is helpful to obtain (from the owner or broker) a Summary of Monthly Sales. Large businesses

---

26 Sometimes it is not feasible to undertake this level of analysis at the early stages of buying a business. However, after submitting an offer, it is fair to ask the owner for more detailed information. As will be discussed later, an offer should give the buyer the right to verify all financial representations made by the seller. Or an offer might simply say: "This offer is contingent upon Buyer's approval of Seller's financial records." After receiving an offer a seller should make all financial records, including copies of bank statements, available for review by a buyer.

How to Buy a Business without Being Had

often break down sales by department (i.e. Rental Department, Sales Department, etc.) but for most businesses the Summary might look like the following. Does anything appear out of line to you?

Summary of Monthly Sales (attachment to Business Profile)

Month	2002	2003	2004	2005	2006
January	12,304	14,586	15,201	14,121	18,526
February	9,643	9,898	12,665	12,974	14,566
March	13,334	13,998	15,531	17,765	19,334
April	15,987	17,804	19,324	20,563	24,332
May	17,545	19,987	21,348	23,334	24,977
June	18,322	19,345	22,576	27,776	32,544
July	17,654	20,337	26,688	30,768	34,494
August	18,002	18,002	24,451	33,553	39,402
September	17,655	17,655	24,998	30,566	34,429
October	15,332	15,332	19,987	19,998	26,433
November	16,302	16,117	19,030	18,112	23,302
December	18,664	19,906	22,444	21,368	21,287
Total:	$190,744	$214,310	$244,243	$270,898	$313,626
Percent Increase		13%	14%	11%	16%

Remember that sometimes sales are not recorded in "cash basis" businesses (like the business profiled above) until the sales receipts are deposited into the bank account. This appears to be the case for the sales reported for December 2006. Note that in each of the prior years shown the December sales exceeded the January sales by about 50%. However, in 2006 the December sales exceeded the January sales by only 15%. In fact the reported December sales of $21,287 in 2006 were less the November sales, a very unusual situation for this type of business. December sales in the prior years exceeded November sales by about 20%.

If we assume that actual December 2006 sales were 50% above the January sales of $18,526, they would be around $27,000. If this turns out to be true, then the actual annual sales would be around $320,000, or 18% greater than the prior year's sales. A check of the dates of the January 2007 deposits will enable you to confirm or to disprove our assumption. Holding

61

back deposits may simply result from a busy holiday schedule, but it often seems to occur when a business is growing.

Understanding the seasonal nature of a business is always important. It is particularly important to keep in mind when making projections of the future Cash Flow of a business. When monthly sales are seasonally low, it may be impossible to cover all the fixed expenses from Income or from Cash Flow: the Rent, Payroll, Taxes and debt obligations will have to be paid somehow. Look, for example, at the reported February sales in the **Summary of Monthly Sales** above. How much Income would you have with sales of under $10,000 in February 2002 or 2003?

Suggestion: If a business has highly seasonal sales, and the seller is offering some "seller financing," ask the Seller if he will accept a lower monthly Note payment during a predictably slow month. If monthly principal and interest is $3,000, offer the Seller $1,000 or $1,500 in February. Or, even better: offer the Seller a Note with a "skipped" month, that is, one month with no Note payment or one payment each year of "interest only," that is, a payment without any principal.

Cash vs. Accrual Accounting. What we see on the written page is very persuasive. However, in the case of first generation businesses in particular, we have to look beyond the written page, that is, beyond the financial statements we are handed. Sometime both sales and expenses are underreported. In other cases, the sales may be reported accurately and the expenses are understated. The answer to this puzzle is the timing of posting the information.[27] A business may record (post) its sales when they are made, which is "accrual" accounting. More often, sales are recorded only when payment is received, which is "cash" accounting. Learn which accounting system each business uses.

---

27 There is another answer also. Operators of many small businesses are absorbed with business operations and have little time for bookkeeping and may have little knowledge of accounting. Many do not prepare monthly financial statements or review them for accuracy. It seems irrelevant (to operating the business) until it comes time to sell. When financial statements are not available, other records may be used to confirm sales: checkbooks, bank statements, cash register receipts and sales tax report forms that are required by many states to be filed monthly.

How to Buy a Business without Being Had

Doozy reports on the cash basis. It records sales when payment is received and records expenses (liabilities) when payment is made. Unpaid bills are therefore not recorded as expenses. Understanding the financial reporting practices is indispensable in preparing an accurate analysis and opinion of value.

STANDARDIZING FINANCIAL STATEMENTS: Often we observe that one business does not earn as much as another quite similar business. We instinctively assume that something is wrong with the business that earns less. If the reasons are not immediately obvious from looking at two sets of financial statements, it is helpful to "standardize" the statements. One tool for doing this is **EBIT** (earnings before interest and taxes). In calculating EBIT we add income taxes and interest expenses to the reported after-tax income. Be careful not to add back any "business" taxes, but only the "income" taxes.

If we add back depreciation and amortization expenses as well, the result is called **EBITDA** or earnings before interest, taxes, depreciation and amortization. A business, often a recently acquired business like Business 3, as profiled in Table 4 below, can have a lot of interest, depreciation and amortization expenses, and therefore appear not to be profitable. But such a business may have a higher EBITDA than businesses to which it is compared and in reality be more valuable. Review the illustration below. Which business is worth more? EBIT and EBITDA should be done for each year in the "look back" period.

Table 4. Comparison of Income, EBIT and EBITDA

	Business 1	Business 2	Business 3
Annual Sales	$300,000	$400,000	$500,000
Cost of Goods Sold	200,000	250,000	320,000
Gross Profit	100,000	150,000	180,000
% Gross Profit	33.3%	37.5%	36%
Depreciation	5,000	20,000	25,000
Amortization	0	10,000	20,000
Other Operating Expenses	65,000	100,000	125,000
Total Expenses	70,000	130,000	170,000
Income from Operations	$30,000	$20,000	$10,000

Jack (John V. M.) Gibson

Interest	0	10,000	15,000
Pre-Tax Income	$ 30,000	$ 10,000	$ (5,000)
% of Sales	10%	2.5%	(1%)
Income Taxes @ 15%	4,500	1,500	0
Net Income	**$25,500**	**$8,500**	**$(5,000)**
% of Sales	8.5%	2.125%	(1%)
EBIT	**$30,000**	**$20,000**	**$10,000**
% of Sales	10%	5%	2%
EBITDA	**$35,000**	**$50,000**	**$55,000**
% of Sales	11.6%	12.5%	11%

Look first at Net Income (the "bottom line"). Most of us would say Business 1 is worth more since it has a profit margin of 8.5% of sales and it seems to have earned three times what Business 2 earned. Business 3 had a loss, but if we look at Sales (the "top line") most of us would say Business 3 must be more valuable. If we look at the **Gross Profit** margin, an important element of value, it appears Business 2 may be worth more. But, when the statements are standardized through the use of EBIT and, in this case, EBITDA, all three businesses look much more comparable. EBITDA as a percent of Sales varies only from 11% to 12.5% while Net Income as a percent of Sales varies from (1%) to 8.5%.

Now back to Doozy. What is she really worth? After finding and making some indicated adjustments to her financial statements, she may be worth more than it originally appeared.

CHAPTER 4
ADJUSTMENTS TO FINANCIAL STATEMENTS

Part I. ADJUSTMENTS TO INCOME

Is $75,000 a fair price to pay for a business with $18,877 in average annual earnings and a $48,000 a year salary? Or is the $120,000 suggested value a closer indication of Doozy's fair market value? These questions lead to the observation that reported earnings (the earnings shown on the financial statements and tax returns of a business) often differ significantly from actual earnings. Earnings may be more or less than reported, but the earnings of small businesses are generally more, primarily because of strategies to reduce or defer income taxes. Other logical reasons are as follows.

Understated Earnings. Reported earnings could be less than actual earnings if companies:

1. Use faster depreciation write-offs for tax purposes than real economic depreciation.[28]

2. Have paid for certain non-operating expenses such as wages paid to family members who did little actual work for the company.

---

28 Let's say Doozy bought a new truck for $17,500. Doozy could write off the entire cost as a Section 179 expense and have a depreciation expense of $17,500. Alternatively, Doozy could elect to write the cost of the truck off over five years and only take a depreciation expense of $3,500. In the later case, Doozy's earnings would appear to be $14,000 higher, or more than double the $12,000 earnings reported. However, this accounting change would not double the value of the company.

3. Have pre-paid other expenses such as insurance premiums.
4. Have paid for non-recurring costs such as expensive additions to their physical plants.
5. Have (correctly or not) failed to report or record all sales.
6. Have accumulated inventories worth more than the value shown on their Balance Sheets (see Table 10 for a fuller discussion).

Non-operating expenses may include country club dues, meals for family members, unnecessary pieces of equipment, expensive furniture for the executive office, and gas and insurance for personal vehicles. The list is long. These are expenses that have nothing to do with responsibly operating a business. The **non-recurring expenses** are lumpy (and often "big ticket") expenses that pop up only from time to time: an expensive repair, a new roof, printing a catalogue, a training seminar out of town, one-time legal or medical expenses or an auditing fee. These expenses are best spread out over several years or over their "useful life."

The matter of excess inventory is important not only because most small businesses have more than is carried on their Balance Sheets but also because it represents hidden value. If a store has over ten years accumulated a "cushion" of $100,000 worth of unrecorded inventory, we can assume that, on average, the Income has been understated by $10,000 a year. With a 4:1 P:E ratio, this "inventory cushion" could increase the value of the business by $40,000.

Calculate: $100,000÷10$ years=$10,000 x 4=$40,000

Overstated Earnings. Reported earnings could also exceed actual earnings for several reasons. Bills for rent or insurance premiums may not have been paid on time. There may be, for example, unusual "one-shot" items included in the reported sales, such as damage awards from a lawsuit, or proceeds received by the company from a life insurance policy. It is not unusual to find from time to time that customer deposits (made for future delivery) are included among the reported "sales." From the business owner's standpoint such "receipts" appear to be the same as any other type of receipt.

There may be substantial, unrecognized bad debts among the accounts receivable or there may be severe distortions in income caused by inaccurate accounting for inventories. Some inventory items may be old or damaged

How to Buy a Business without Being Had

and, therefore, not be saleable at their stated book values. The point is that **you should never accept financial statements of a small business as gospel.**[29] We must usually look behind the statements to discover the reality of the financial condition of a company.

> **Case History: Overstated Assets.** A company tendered a contract to purchase a large equipment dealership for a price of over $2 million. This price was contingent upon Purchaser's ability to confirm the representations (values) shown on seller's Balance Sheet. Upon inspection the buyer found that many pieces of new equipment (that were still carried on the Balance Sheet at their original cost) had been leased to some of the company's customers and were damaged in some fashion. Since the seller, in the Purchase Contract, guaranteed the inventory values on his Balance Sheet, the buyer obtained an appraisal of the damaged items. When the Book Values of the equipment were written down to values indicated in the appraisal, the price was adjusted downward and the seller received almost nothing at closing. **Moral: A buyer should always require a seller to warrant the accuracy of company's financial statements.**

RECASTING FINANCIAL STATEMENTS: If the initial price that you are considering paying for a business is based only on a "multiple" of reported or averaged earnings, you must "recast" both the income statement and the balance sheet into a standard format to help you determine if the reported earnings are "under" or "over" stated. This is done in various ways, including utilizing these two broad types of adjustments: (1) add to the reported earnings all pre-payments, overpayments, non-operating expenses, and excessive benefits that a company paid to the owner or to family members, and, then, (2) deduct any unrecorded liabilities, such as past due trade accounts payable and accrued

---

29 A "financial statement" always includes two parts: an Income Statement and a Balance Sheet and often also includes a Cash Flow Statement. The Income Statement is also referred to as a Profit & Loss Statement or P&L.

employee bonuses or profit sharing.[30] Costs that are deducted from Expenses and added to Earnings are called "add backs."

First Review: Review of Annual Statements. For every business you are seriously considering, look at the results for three or four years "spread out" side by side. Review the spreadsheet in the Appendix. And review the spreadsheet on page 12-13 that shows very lumpy expenses from year to year. Why, for example, is Equipment Rental so high in fiscal 2008? Why is Rent so high in 2007? Why is Insurance so high in 2006? Finding out why expenses are lumpy is often very instructive.

Putting the statements into a spreadsheet format is an easy way to spot errors in bookkeeping and potential hidden income. And when you get monthly statements, put them into a spreadsheet as well. It can reveal a lot about how a business is managed.

Both the reported income and the reported expenses on a financial statement can be misleading. There are many reasons for this. Some financial statements are quite accurate. Nevertheless, it is wise to check out their accuracy when considering buying a business and wise to consider what adjustments you could make to normalize the statements. Keep in mind that the adjustments can be **positive** or **negative**, that is, they can add to or subtract from the reported income. The goal of a buyer is to discover what the expenses and earnings would be if you were running the business.

The timing of payment of insurance premiums is one frequently observed example of a positive adjustment. If a $12,000 annual premium is paid in December and the business owner wrote off the entire premium, how should the statement be adjusted? We could recast the statement by only recognizing one month's expense ($1,000) in that year. The balance ($11,000) becomes an asset called Pre-paid Insurance, which should be added to the business's Balance Sheet and $11,000 should be added to the reported earnings. Conversely, if it were observed that the rent or insurance

---

30 Unrecorded expenses are important enough to be the subject of a separate book. Some business owners are unaware of this potential problem. Owners let bills and invoices stack up and do not record them until they are paid. But these expenses are real and must be considered when calculating income. The key is to review the accounts payable and the Balance Sheet to see if there is a change in Total Liabilities (including accrued expenses) from period to period. If, for example, accounts payable totaled $20,000 on 12/31 and are $30,000 on 6/30, a negative adjustment to earnings of $10,000 for the first six months of the year could be indicated.

How to Buy a Business without Being Had

premiums (or other invoices) were not paid by their due dates, we may have to make negative adjustments to earnings.

Our look at Doozy's recorded annual expenses indicates there are at least five expense categories that warrant review and may result in adjustments to the Income Statements for the five-year "look back" period. Upon completing the review it appears that three categories require positive adjustments, one requires a negative adjustment, and one did not require an adjustment. How will this affect Doozy's earnings and its market value? Let's look at these five potential adjustments:

1. **Purchase of delivery vehicle:** Doozy bought a low mileage delivery vehicle last year for $15,000 and wrote it off as a Section 179 deduction in one year. Normally, it would be written off (depreciated) over three to five years, at $3,000 to $5,000 per year. Thus, we have a positive adjustment of $10,000–12,000. See column 1 in Table 5 below. The lower adjustment of $10,000 is used.

2. **Family health insurance:** Doozy last year paid over $4,000 for family health and life insurance. Should the portion that covers non-employee family members be included in your adjustments? Probably not, since many companies still offer family health insurance coverage, but it is reassuring to know that Doozy can afford the cost.

3. **Bad accounts receivable:** Doozy still carries two "bad" accounts receivable on its books, one from a $2,000 sale four years ago and another from a $4,000 sale five years ago. Neither debtor can be located, but the debts should be written off, thereby reducing income in the year in which the "bad" debts were incurred and reducing the net worth in each year, including the current year. Since there appear to be no bad debts on the books from the last three years of operation, apparently Doozy has learned not to extend unwarranted credit to its customers. This is also reassuring.

4. **Payments to owner's wife:** Doozy's owner is paying his wife $200/week to do some bookkeeping and office work at home. This appears to be $10,400 in hidden annual earnings.

5. **Payments to remodel home office:** Two years ago, Doozy paid $6,000 for new cabinets, furnishings and remodeling a home office, where the owner's wife does her part-time bookkeeping.

Regarding item 4 above, payment for bookkeeping, it seems fair to add back only the difference between salary paid to Doozy's owner's wife ($10,400) and the cost that a local bookkeeping service would charge for the same work. A few telephone calls suggests that, based upon the number of checks that Doozy writes each year, several local firms would charge about $1,500. The difference of $8,900 is pretty significant. After deliberation, it is decided to be a conservative and only "add back" 2/3 of the potential savings (roughly $6,000) to the reported earnings each year.[31]

After the appropriate adjustments are added in Table 6 below, the weighted average earnings conservatively appear to be $28,800 or 60% more than the $18,000 average reported earnings for the last five years ($90,000÷5) and over twice the reported earnings for last year. To determine the weighted average earnings, observe the calculations in Tables 4 and 5. Using the same 4:1 P:E, Doozy now appears to be worth slightly over $115,000!

Calculate: $28,800 x 4 = $115,200 Suggested Valuation

Notice that the largest adjustments were found in the last two years. If we add $16,000 for last year's adjustments to the $12,000 reported earnings, Doozy may have actually earned $28,000 or 9.3% of last year's sales of $300,000. Actual earnings from two years ago would have been $32,000 (10% of reported sales) if all the adjustments are added. (To review reported sales and % of sales refer to Table 3.) It now looks as if the notion that actual earnings are a relatively fixed percent of sales is borne out by our review.

Table 5. Summary of Earnings Adjustments

	Vehicle Depreciation	Bad Debts	Wife's Salary	Home Office	Earnings Adjustments
Last Year	+$10,000		+ $6,000		$16,000
2 Years Ago			+ 6,000	+$6,000	12,000
3 Years Ago			+ 6,000		6,000
4 Years Ago		-$2,000	+ 6,000		4,000
5 Years Ago		- 4,000	+ 6,000		2,000
Total	**$10,000**	**-$6,000**	**$30,000**	**$6,000**	**$40,000**

---

31 A detailed recasting would also include adding back payroll taxes of 9.85% ($591).

How to Buy a Business without Being Had

TIP: Check whether a business has credit cards. Check the balances. Use of credit card for routine purchases is a dangerous and costly practice. One "add back" I look for is interest charges included on various invoices. Often interest is charged on late accounts payable, which inflates the cost of goods. And interest is sometimes charged on credit card purchases, as in the landscape contracting company mentioned in the second Case History. If you feel you can arrange to pay your bills on time, all the interest charges are hidden earnings.

Of course the "weightings" and "look back periods" would change, if change seems indicated. For example, you may feel that a look back period of only three years is more realistic. As seen on Table 6, Weighted Average Earnings are $28,800 for the full five-year look back. Doozy's Weighted Earnings for the past three years average are $33,000, which is 14.6% higher. But +14.6% is still significant.[32] Actual Earnings (unweighted) for the most recent three years are even higher: $33,333 per year. Which "earnings" figures to use is a matter of judgment.

Table 6. Calculation of Adjusted and Weighted Earnings

	Reported Earnings	Adjustments	Actual Earnings	Weight	Weighted Earnings
Last Year	$12,000	+$16,000	$ 28,000	× 5 =	$140,000
2 Years Ago	20,000	+ 12,000	32,000	× 4 =	128,000
3 Years Ago	34,000	+ 6,000	40,000	× 3 =	120,000
4 Years Ago	10,000	+ 4,000	14,000	× 2 =	28,000
5 Years Ago	14,000	+ 2,000	16,000	× 1 =	16,000
	$90,000	+$40,000	$130,000	15	$432,000
					÷ 15

Weighted Average Earnings After Adjustments: $28,800

---

32 To calculate $33,000, use a 3-2-1 weighting, add: ($28,000x3) or $84,000 + (32,000x2) or $64,000 + 40,000x1 or 40,000=198,000. Then: $198,000÷6=$33,000. Other weighting may also be useful.

71

> **Suggestion.** Try using different weightings and "lookback" periods to see the effect on weighted average earnings. Try it for Doozy and for any other business you are looking at. If the three-year look back period seems more appropriate, we could use a weighting of 5-3-1 as used in Table 2. The 5-3-1 weighting indicates Weighted Average Earnings of $30,667, just 6.5% above the $28,800 shown in Table 6.

Can you feel secure in offering to buy Doozy for $115,200, the value we get after making adjustments to income? Would the seller accept $115,200? Maybe we should use the three-year Weighted Average Earnings of $30,667, which at 4:1 indicates a value of $122,668, or the unweighted three-year average of $33,333. Not quite yet! There is a little more work to do before we can answer that question.

First, it is wise to review the company's expenses again, particularly expenses for the past year, since it is quite important to be able to conclude with conviction what percentage of sales the actual pre-tax earnings are (and could be in future years). To do this, it is very helpful to review the monthly financial statements, especially for the past year. Second, as we discuss in the next section of this Chapter, we must not rely solely upon the income approach to value; we must take a good look at the asset value of the business, as well.

Second Review: Review of Monthly Statements. Our second review focuses on Doozy's **monthly** expenses, whereas the initial review looked only at **annual** expenses. We reviewed employee compensation expenditures first, since that is the largest single expense account. As we looked we tried to note any large deviations from the average monthly compensation expense. We discovered that "payroll" as a percent of reported sales in December, the last month of the fiscal year, seems to have jumped. We asked the broker why payroll had jumped. He explained that Doozy paid a $3,000 bonus to the owner's wife on the 30th of December last year.[33]

As seen below on Doozy's Statement of Income and Expenses, employee payroll expenses for the year are $78,000, an average of $6,500 per month,

---

33 Looking at the financial statement for the 12th month of the fiscal year can be very helpful since expenses that month tend to reflect the owner's desire to pay bonuses when possible and to reduce taxable income.

or 25% of Sales. However, in December payroll expenses are, in round numbers, $9,500, or 46% above the monthly average. This deviation was the result of the $3,000 bonus, not of employee profit sharing, as originally thought. Note also the $15,000 depreciation expense shown at the bottom of Table 7. Since the "excess" depreciation of $10,000 is included in the earnings adjustments in Table 5, the depreciation expense shown on a restated Income Statement would be only $5,000.

To help with the monthly review, see if the broker has a spreadsheet of monthly expenses. If not, ask for copies of the monthly "financials" and create your own spreadsheet. It can help you spot other one-time charges or, perhaps, unpaid bills.

Table 7. Doozy Manufacturing Company
Statement of Income and Expenses

Sales (checks received and deposited)	**$300,000**
Less: Cost of Materials and Shop supplies @24%	72,000
Gross Profit	**$228,000**
Expenses:	
Owner's Salary	$48,000
Employee wages, including bonuses	78,000
Payroll Taxes (9.85% of wages and salaries)	12,800
Rent (4,000 sq. feet @ $4.50/sq. foot)	18,000
Insurance (medical, general liability and auto)	10,000
Utilities	14,400
Telephones	4,200
Office Supplies	2,400
Miscellaneous taxes, including personal property and gross receipts taxes, and licenses	2,600
Gasoline (two vehicles)	3,000
Advertising, including Yellow Page Directory	2,600
Part-Time (vacation) employees (see Note 1)	4,000
All Other Expenses (see Note 2)	1,000
Sub-Total:	$201,000
Depreciation (Section 179 expense of van)	15,000
Total Expenses:	**$216,000**
Income (Pre-Tax):	**$12,000**

Note 1. Calculate vacation for 4 employees x 2 weeks = 8 weeks x 40 hours=320 hours @ $12.50/hour = $4,000

Note 2. Includes interest on used van purchased in June for $15,000: Calculate: $15,000 @ 6% = $900 /2 = $450

It seems clear that this $3,000 "bonus" should be added to the $28,800 earnings previously calculated for last year (see Table 6) so the adjustments are now $19,000 and adjusted earnings appear to be $31,800.[34] A deeper look at other expense accounts may reveal additional "non-operating expenses" that would increase actual earnings more, but none appear significant except, perhaps, the $450 paid in interest on the new van. This is a non-recurring expense that a buyer will not have. See Note 2 above at the bottom of Table 7.

With this last adjustment, the adjusted pre-tax income for the last year is $31,800 or 10.6% of Sales, well above the 4% calculated using the $12,000 shown on the Statement of Income and Expenses. See Tables 3 and 7 for reference. Using the 4:1 P:E again and the estimated $31,800 earnings, we now have an indicated value for Doozy of $127,200. Keep in mind that the $31,800 is after deducting $5,000 in depreciation expenses.

Calculate: $31,800 x 4 = $127,200 estimated valuation

Perhaps with more digging you may find additional positive adjustments! Aren't you glad you took a deeper look at Doozy? Ten other buyers had looked at Doozy and quickly lost interest because reported earnings looked too low. These buyers had failed to restate Doozy's earnings or her net worth.

Suggestion. After making adjustments to Doozy's Income Statement, examine again the spreadsheet in the Appendix for Bigger Manufacturing Co., a cabinet manufacturer with annual sales over $4,000,000. Bigger has a large showroom and sells to the retail public as well as to contractors. What "add backs" are indicated and what would the indicated pre-tax income be after making adjustments? Examine each line item carefully. Bigger appears to have had a negative

---

34 To be conservative in putting a final value on Doozy, it may be wise not to use the highest of the indicated estimates of pre-tax earnings found so far: $28,000, $28,800, $30,667, $31,800, $33,000 and $33,333.

operating income in five of the past seven years. In three of those seven years it wasn't even able to pay the owner a salary, yet it was appraised at over $1,000,000 and paid its owner and the owner's children combined salaries of $356,423 in the most recent year.

Owner's Compensation. No adjustment was included (in Table 5) for owner's salary because it ($48,000) seemed in line with compensation paid at similar businesses in that year. However, if Doozy had paid its owner a base salary of $78,000 instead of $48,000 and no adjustment were made, the company would have shown a profit in only two of the last five years and would appear to be worth much less than $124,000. It is advisable to begin your recasting process by selecting a reasonable owner's salary (and benefit package) for the market in which the business is located and to adjust reported earnings upwards or downwards accordingly.[35]

With Bigger, for example, we might have begun the recasting process by inserting salaries of $40,000, $45,000, $50,000, $55,000, $60,000, $65,000, and $70,000 for the seven years shown on the spreadsheet. Since it is a much larger company, the manager/owner at Bigger should be expected to earn a salary considerably higher than the manager/owner at Doozy. Making these (or similar) adjustments would give a much more realistic picture of Bigger's actual earnings.

> **TIP:** You can find comparable salaries by visiting useful websites like: salaries.com. and cbsalary.com. The latter, for example, says that a lathe operator/woodworking earns (in March 2009) on average $24,093 nationally and $22,951 ($11.25/hour) in Memphis. A shop manager nationally earns $51,277 and $44,455 in Macon, Georgia. In Los Angeles, shop manager salaries ranged from $42,207 to $77,750 with an average of $56,091.

Other compensation issues involve employee wages, accrued wages, vacation pay and the timing of making payroll. Study the following Case History.

---

[35] A caution for buyers is that sellers understandably resist buyers who pay themselves more compensation than the down payment that the sellers receive.

> **Case History: Bi-Weekly Payroll Issue.** After submitting an offer on behalf of a buyer, the seller gave me a copy of his latest monthly Income Statement that I, in turn, shared with the buyer. Earnings were almost $7,000 less than in the prior month. The buyer became anxious and asked that I withdraw his offer and return his earnest money check. I urged him to give me a chance to discover why earnings appeared to drop so sharply. He agreed. It turned out that: (1) the business paid its employees every two weeks and (2) there were three pay periods in the past month. After adjustments were made, the past month's recast income actually was $20,000 and exceeded the prior month's recast income by $9,000. The buyer was pleased and the sale went through as planned. The prior month had payroll expenses of $48,000 (rounded). The recent month had payroll expenses of $72,000 (rounded). Adjusting for the 26 bi-weekly payrolls in a year of $24,000, normalized payroll would be about $52,000 month. **Calculate as follows: ($24,000 x 26 weeks= $624,000) ÷12 months = $52,000 Moral: Always ask. When in doubt, check it out.**

Missing Financial Statements. Some smaller businesses do not have published financial statements. Sometimes the most recent financial statements are several years old and have not been reviewed, even by the owner, for accuracy. While this can be unsettling, particularly to a first time buyer, other useful financial documents can be found for almost any business. These might include:

1. State Sales Tax Report forms (almost every business must file them)
2. Copies of the business's bank statements and cancelled checks (look at the **general ledger** if checks are computerized)
3. Copies of local property tax and federal income tax forms
4. Copies of invoices from suppliers, phone and utility companies
5. Copies of lease agreements with landlords and insurance policies
6. Quarterly or monthly payroll reports showing wages, payroll taxes and withholding, and the annual W-2, W-3, and W-4 forms sent to the Internal Revenue Service

From these documents a fairly accurate picture of most small businesses will emerge. These documents, however, cannot be assumed to be 100% accurate. Instead they give a picture of what is happening over time. If, for example, monthly purchases from suppliers are higher (in excess of price increases or general inflation) in the current year than in prior years, it can be assumed that sales are growing and, conversely, if purchases are lower, that sales are declining.

If the financial statements are missing, they cannot be recast. Instead they are constructed from scratch, check by check, a process that may produce a more accurate picture of the financial condition of a company than the recasting process. This process is not as time consuming as it may seem; the typical small business may only write 20 to 25 checks per month. Often these businesses employ a payroll service, so there is only one payroll check per pay period.

TIP: Learn how the financial statements are prepared and who posts the checks to the various accounts. Some charges may not be posted to the proper account, but more importantly to you, when you review individual checks you may discover that some accounts include some unusual entries. I have seen country club dues posted under Office Supplies and children's dental bills posted under Medical Expenses. A check-by-check review can be very instructive.

Part II. ADJUSTMENTS TO NET WORTH[36]

These adjustments involve company Balance Sheets. The previous adjustments involved company Income Statements. Doozy is reported by its broker to have tangible assets worth $100,000. How could it be possible to buy a business for only $48,000 or $75,000, the preliminary estimates

---

36 The term "net worth" refers to the net book value of a business: its assets less its liabilities. It is shown on the Balance Sheet. After making adjustments, we can calculate a business's "adjusted net worth." Remember not to confuse a business's fair market value with its net worth. They may be quite different. See Glossary.

of value, when a business has assets worth $100,000? The answer is that you can't, because a prudent owner, acting in his own self-interest, could liquidate the business for the value of the assets. There is normally little incentive to sell for a price less than asset value or the value that an orderly liquidation would bring.

To reconcile a disparity between **earnings value** of a business and its **asset value** we must adjust (or recast) the values shown on its Balance Sheet.[37] There are many things to analyze in Doozy's case. If Doozy's accountant had elected to take rapid depreciation, some assets (such as the delivery van) may be worth more than their present Book Value. On the other hand, some items of inventory may be old or obsolete and have a market or liquidation values well below their Book Value, the value shown on the Balance Sheet, or below their original cost.

A business's **adjusted asset value** would be its minimum transfer price, if that value were higher than the earnings value. Any business should be worth its adjusted asset value because you or the owner should be able to liquidate the assets at close to this price. In my experience, most businesses have assets that are not fully reflected on their Balance Sheets and those businesses may, therefore, be worth considerably more than their Net Worth or, if the seller retains the liabilities, more than the book value of the assets. When speaking of a possible stock sale, the minimum transfer price would be the **adjusted net worth** (or net asset value).

Let's take a look below at Doozy's Simplified Balance Sheet to see if we can determine what its **adjusted asset value** might be. It appears that some values are understated and that some important assets are not shown on its Balance Sheet at all. We also find that several classes of liabilities are unreported, but the net balance sheet adjustments (the difference between the reported Book Value and the Market Value) found are close to the $40,000 in positive income adjustments found in Part I of this chapter and shown on Table 5. This confirms our feeling that Doozy has "hidden" income.

---

37 The Seller should consider that there are costs involved in liquidating, such as legal and sales fees and generally some on-going operating expenses. Sellers sometimes say that they could liquidate their business for more than a buyer is offering, but often they do not consider the expenses associated with liquidation.

Table 8. Doozy's Simplified Balance Sheet

Type of Asset	Book Value	Market Value	Adjustment (+ or -)
Accounts Receivable	$15,000	$9,000	-$6,000
Raw Materials and Finished Goods	40,000	50,000	+ 10,000
Pre-Paid Insurance	1,000	0	- 1,000
Vehicles—Depreciated	6,000	16,000	+ 10,000
Equipment Less Depreciation	0	17,000	+ 7,000
Miscellaneous Dies	0	4,000	+ 4,000
Miscellaneous Tools	0	4,000	+ 4,000
Customer Contracts	0	?	?
Sub-Total	**$62,000**	**$100,000**	**$38,000**

Type of Liability[38]			
Accounts Payable	$12,000	$15,000	+ $3,000
Accrued Salaries	0	3,500	+ 3,500
Accrued Taxes	0	1,400	+ 1,400
Accrued Interest		100	+ 100
Note to Bank	15,000	15,000	0
Sub-Total	**27,000**	**35,000**	**8,000**
Net Worth/Value	**$35,000**	**$65,000**	**$30,000**

TIP: When attempting to value the FF&E (which may have $0 value on the company Balance Sheet), check the insurance coverage. It is rare for a company to over insure and rarer for an insurance company to issue a policy based on inflated asset values. Many policies include a detailed list of the specific assets that are covered in a policy.

---

38 If Doozy is holding customer deposits, they must be shown as Liabilities because they will have to be repaid if the work is not performed. Also, accrued payables, such as accrued salaries and earned vacation, must be considered. It would be awkward (as well as unfair) if several employees opt to take vacation immediately after a business is sold and the seller expects the buyer to assume this expense. The normal rule is: Expenses incurred before the closing on a sale are normally paid by the seller (unless a contract states otherwise).

Jack (John V. M.) Gibson

The assets shown on the Balance Sheet seem to have a fair market value of $100,000, the value indicated in the brief profile that the broker prepared for prospective purchasers. A physical inspection of the plant quickly leads to the conclusion that several classes of quite valuable/hidden assets are not carried on the Balance Sheet at all. They were not valued by the broker or mentioned in the profile. They include the first three assets shown below and possibly the fourth:

1. Unbilled work-in-process (or work-in-progress)
2. Shop and office tools and supplies
3. Customer contracts for future delivery of goods
4. Pre-paid insurance premiums

The first category, unbilled work-in-process, is perhaps the easiest to value because this "work" is already sold. From a "walk through" inspection it is obvious that the shop is full of partially completed cabinets, part of several rather large jobs for which Doozy has firm, written contracts. Some cabinets are complete except for the doors; others are complete except for painting or other finish. Still others are in an initial stage of fabrication. Work-in-process is easy to value for Doozy. It may be more difficult to value in a non-contract manufacturing business.

After reviewing the jobs in shop the owner discloses that they have a combined contract price/value of $30,000 and are 75% complete, a value of $22,500. We cannot assign the entire $22,500 to this asset because Doozy, like all companies, must earn a profit. After some thought it is concluded that a fair market value would be 70% of the contract (or completion value), or $15,750.[39]

The shop and office supplies take somewhat longer to value, since there are many different categories to count or inspect. The broker, based upon his experience with other companies of a similar size, feels that a value of $10,000 will be quite conservative. The broker adds, helpfully,

---

39 Normally these calculations cannot be made very accurately at this stage in conversations with a seller. Sellers are reluctant to reveal this much detail or to take the time to make these calculations with every potential buyer. Instead, when a purchase contract is prepared, the contract will include language such as the following: "This Contract is contingent upon there being on hand at time of closing unbilled work-in-process of $15,750, valued at 70% of Seller's contract price." The seller may feel that 80% is fairer, so this becomes a point of negotiation.

How to Buy a Business without Being Had

that the buyer can always reserve the right in a formal purchase offer to count and value each class of "on-balance sheet" and "off-balance sheet" assets.[40] In this manner the final sale price of the business will be adjusted if any of the assets have been sold or removed from the business prior to the completion of a sale.

The third "missing" class of assets is customer contracts. Many businesses, especially retail businesses, do not have customer contracts. In contrast, service companies may do all their business by contract. Since Doozy is a custom manufacturer, it does all of its business by contract. Contracts describe the job to be done, set out a price and terms of payment, a date for completion or delivery of the finished products and perhaps a penalty for late delivery.

Doozy has $80,000 worth of cabinet written work orders on the books (a 90-day backlog based on annual sales of $320,000) in addition to the work-in-process. In some businesses, contracts (such as contracts for janitorial services or cell phone service) are billed monthly and may be cancelled at almost any time. Their value depends largely upon the terms of cancellation. By contrast, Doozy's contracts (work orders) are one-time contracts and are non-cancelable. So, if they were negotiated at a price that includes a reasonable profit, they have value.

Since Doozy's **profit margin** (pre-tax) is around 10%, we can assume that the orders "on the books" will also produce a 10% profit or about $8,000. If this future profit is valued at a P:E of 4:1, it could be worth $32,000.[41] The method for valuing contracts differs by industry. In the security alarm industry, the rule of thumb is to use a percent of annual or monthly billing. The key is to verify that the contracts were not accepted at too low a price to produce a profit for the buyer.

---

40 Many brokers, particularly in the case of somewhat larger businesses, include in their profile or other offering document a detailed listing of all assets in a business with market values or replacement costs.
41 $32,000 may seem like a high price to pay for contracts. Yet in many industries contacts are sold to other firms (that may need to fill in some work). Also, these contracts have been negotiated and sales commissions paid, saving a buyer these costs. In the case of Doozy, the $32,000 is part of the goodwill that the buyer of the company will receive.

Jack (John V. M.) Gibson

TIP: Sometimes, but rarely, business owners are anxious to demonstrate that their businesses are healthy and take on new contracts at very low prices, prices that have no profit. If the backlog of orders appears to have spiked recently, some form of additional analysis may be in order before setting a value on contracts for new work. If at the same time the balance of Accounts Receivable outstanding in the 60 day or 90 day column has increased more rapidly than Sales, it is possible that these "new" sales have been made to less than creditworthy customers. This could certainly be a red flag.

The value of Doozy' assets (including accounts receivable) may now be roughly summarized as follows:

Fair Market Value of Assets on Books	$100,00
Value of Assets Not on Books	
1. Value of Work-in-process	15,750
2. Value of Supplies-Estimate	10,000
3. Value of Unperformed Contracts-Estimate	32,000
Estimated Total Asset Value	**$157,750**

Suggestion. After reviewing the balance sheet of any business and compiling a rough list of assets that may be included in a sale, ask the seller (or ask your broker to ask the seller) two important questions:

1. Are there any assets used in the business that you (the seller) intend to keep?
2. Are there any assets used in the business that you own outside of the business, that is, assets that were never put on the company Balance Sheet? A truck, for example.

The answers are often very revealing. Many owners want to exclude a company vehicle (if they do not own a personal car), computer, desk, clock, or memorabilia. It is difficult to know the right time to ask these questions, but they should be asked long before the closing. Let me share another story.

> **Case History: Removing Assets.** After a contract had been signed and a closing date set, the buyer walked through the plant with a list of FF&E that seller had provided. The buyer wanted to learn if the assets were still "in use" and he proceeded to check off on the list each asset that he found. When he got to the seller's office, he checked off the executive desk. The seller said that the desk was not included in the sale; it had been his father's. The buyer said, "Okay" and proceeded down the list. He asked if the clock on the wall was included. Again the seller said, "No." And then he asked about the computer. The seller said, "No" a third time. At this point the buyer thanked the seller for his time and went home. The next day he called me and said he no longer wanted to buy the business because the seller had misrepresented several things. He added that if there are these many "misrepresentations" there are probably others as well. **Lesson: It is difficult for some sellers to part with family and "personal" items, but this doesn't greatly diminish the value of a business. Ask for a replacement allowance.**

The preceding three Balance Sheet adjustments for unrecorded assets are not intended to constitute a complete valuation or appraisal. They are simply intended to assist buyers in making a preliminary estimate of the kinds and quantities of assets that would be conveyed in a sale of a business. This information is rarely obvious from looking at the Balance Sheet or other business records. Of course, the kinds, quantities, and mix of assets vary from business to business and industry to industry, but the quantities and values discussed for Doozy are realistic.

In the Balance Sheet review, no adjustments were made for unrecorded liabilities because only the assets are being offered for purchase. In other situations a detailed review of the liability side of the Balance Sheet would be in order, especially when a buyer is considering a stock purchase. Also, no adjustment was made for pre-paid insurance because the total premiums of $10,000 paid in the past year (refer back to Table 7) seem in line with costs. Often, however, some portion of the premiums are pre-paid and should appear on the asset side of the recast Balance Sheet. If Doozy's insurance expenses had been, say, $20,000, further review would be indicated.

TIP: There may be attachments to the financial statements that no one has mentioned. At some tpoint during your review ask whether there are any schedules, accountant's notes or opinion letter accompanying (and therefore an integral part of) the statements. These can be very instructive. Sometimes, the person preparing copies is simply in a hurry and only copies the income statement.

Part III. SELECTION OF INDICATED EARNINGS MULTIPLE FOR DOOZY

Using the SBA guideline of 4 times restated earnings, Doozy is probably worth $115,000 to $125,000, depending upon the "look back" period selected and other factors discussed in Part I or Part II above. It now appears, however, that we could use a valuation guideline (earnings multiple) of 5 times earnings, because the restated earnings are much more stable and predictable than the reported earnings originally appeared. The asset value we have uncovered so far seems to support a higher valuation for the business as well.

It appears that Doozy's earnings are in actuality growing (as a percent of sales). This is a key indicator of value, since it may indicate that the company is operating more efficiently or that its products are of such a quality that they command a higher price in the marketplace. Growing businesses, whether the growth is in profit margins or in "top line" sales, quite logically should sell at a higher multiple of earnings, or P:E, than businesses that show no growth. Why? Because future earnings will probably exceed the historic earnings.

Doozy's adjusted earnings of $31,000 ($28,000 + bonus) for last year are almost double the adjusted earnings ($16,000) from five years ago. And earnings for the last three years now appear to average almost 11% of sales, even though reported annual sales have declined from their peak three years ago. This is quite an improvement from the **margins** shown on Table 3 and from the 4-6% margins shown below for the two oldest years. With this promising picture of Doozy's recent performance, a P:E ratio greater than 4:1 may be in order.

Table 9. Adjusted Earnings (Unweighted) as Percent of Sales

	Adjusted Earnings	Reported Sales	Percent of Sales
Last Year	$ 31,000	$ 300,000	10.33%
Two Years Ago	32,000	320,000	10.00%
Three Years Ago	40,000	340,000	11.76%
Four Years Ago	14,000	300,000	4.67%
Five Years Ago	16,000	264,000	6.00%
	$133,000	**$1,524,000**	**8.72%**

Adjusted earnings in recent years look quite stable as a percent of sales. Perhaps the owner has learned some important lessons. We can therefore assume with a relatively high degree of comfort that future earnings will be 10% of sales or more. It is also comforting to learn that Doozy can achieve 10% of sales even when the owner has apparently spent some time away from the business. Perhaps, if the new owner were to spend more time at the business (than the present owner), sales would begin to increase again.[42]

The average margin of earnings (see Percent of Sales) is considerably higher for the three-year "look back" period (10.73%) than it is for the five-year look back period (8.72%). While the difference between 10.73% and 8.72% seems to be only 2%, remember that 10.73% is actually 23% greater than 8.72. And the 10.33% achieved last year is 76% higher than 6.0% achieved five years ago. These are highly significant differences. The following calculations use data from Table 9.

Calculate: Restated Earnings ÷ Total Sales for Five Years:

$133,000 ÷ $1,524,000 = 8.72% of sales.

---

[42] A word of caution about time spent on the job. A current owner can make the operation of a business seem almost effortless, because the products, markets served and operating procedures are so familiar. Even the simplest task may take a new owner much longer. Every buyer seems to start with the assumption that he or she can "do a better job" than the previous owner. It is easy to see what the owner has done wrong. It is sometimes difficult to see what he has done right.

Calculate: Restated Earnings ÷ Total Sales for Three Years:

$103,000 ÷ $960,000 = 10.73% of sales.

If a 5:1 P:E ratio now seems warranted, the income value of Doozy is in the range of $150,000 to $170,000, much more than the $100,000 estimated market value of the tangible assets and close to the estimated $157,750 asset value.[43] Both estimates of value are in the range of the Asking Price of $160,000. We can calculate these values in several ways: (1) multiplying last year's restated earnings of $31,000 by 5 to suggest a value of $153,000, or (2) multiplying the $34,333 average actual earnings for the last three years ($103,000÷3) by 5 to suggest a value of $171,666.

Here we have two Income Values: (1) $153,000 and (2) $171,666. Should we rely on the one derived from last year's earnings alone, or the one representing an average of several years? Should these values be given different weights? Arguments could be made both ways, so in this case a simple average of the two seems indicated.

Average Weighted Income for Three and Five Year Periods

Calculate: $153,000 + 171,666 = $324,666 ÷ 2 = $162,333

With the higher valuation now indicated, there is a **goodwill value** of $50-60,000, which is about one-third of Doozy's indicated **fair market value**. This seems in line with the spread between the present market value of the tangible assets (equipment, inventory, supplies and financial assets) and the intangible assets (goodwill) found in other small but well-established cabinet manufacturers.

Since the values indicated seem to support each other, it is probably not necessary to do other value analyses. However, an experienced broker or industry group can usually provide information regarding the third basic valuation method: the market approach to value or **comparable sales method**: i.e. prices at which similar companies have recently sold. Such

---

43 A word of caution about which earnings multiple to use: When interest rates go down, the multiple tends higher and when rates go up, the multiple tends lower. Example: At a price of $150,000, assuming all the money was borrowed, 10% interest would be $15,000, almost half of Doozy's restated earnings. At 5%, interest would be only $7,500.

information is always helpful, if available. But remember: because each business is unique, the user of such "comparable" sales data must be alert to the need to adjust the data of a comparable business to the subject business (in this case, Doozy) before drawing any conclusion about value.

The market approach is used extensively in valuing real estate but is used less in valuing businesses. In most real estate markets we have at hand information that lets us test the validity of market data. We can determine the location and the square footage of a house. So, we know that two houses on the same street should sell for about the same price if they are about the same size (square footage) and in comparable physical condition. If one house is offered for a substantially higher price, it probably has more square footage. But if, for example, two coin-op laundries are for sale, one for $100,000 and another for $200,000, we do not know how to explain the difference in values so easily.

Suggestion. If you like a business and the owner insists that it has been profitable but you cannot confirm a positive earnings history, ask the seller for his personal net worth statement. If the seller has owned his company for a long time and says that he has made a lot of money, these "earnings" should show up in a robust personal net worth. Simply observing the size of house the seller lives in and the cars his family drives will not indicate net worth because it will not indicate the level of debt the seller has. This suggestion should be undertaken cautiously and at the right time, probably after your original offer to purchase has been declined.

The **process of adjusting earnings** and net worth can seem almost endless to first time buyers. For other buyers the process is quite quick; they may already have certain yardsticks in mind. They want a small manufacturing business with at least a ten-year track record, and with excess capacity, that they can buy for no more than 35% of annual sales. And they want an annual return on their investment (ROI) of at least 30% after all expenses, including taxes. What yardsticks would define an attractive business for you?

If different values have been found through the use of different methods, it is always useful to find some way to rank or weight the different values. Should some values be discarded? Should some be weighted more highly than others? The process of reconciling values can be very useful, particularly if the values differ substantially.

Part IV. ACCURACY OF FINANCIAL STATEMENTS

The prime objective of analyzing financial statements is to determine their accuracy and, ultimately, their reliability. Let's face it: the financial statements of many small businesses are not very accurate. Little time and attention goes into their preparation except for purposes of reporting income to the federal government. However, the statements may be very reliable, that is to say, we can figure them out with a little effort. A lot of people beside yourself will need to rely upon them: your bank or other lender and your suppliers, that is, the people that you want to extend credit to you. One key to reliability is to see if statements are prepared in a "consistent" manner year-over-year and month-over-month.

Another important objective of the review process is to get a feeling for what a business is really doing and to see if it can meet your goals. Are costs under control? Have costs risen more rapidly than revenue? Is revenue growing? Is the business making money? And does it have a positive Cash Flow? Are there changes that could be made that would increase earnings or Cash Flow in the future? These are all important questions but have little to do with accuracy.

What is meant by "consistent"? This term is often heard but rarely explained. I look for several things, such as the following nine. Apply them to any business you are looking at. How many "yeses" and how many "noes" would you count? A lot of "noes" would make it difficult to determine profitability.

1. Are the statements for different years prepared in the same manner? Are the monthly statements prepared in the same manner as the annual statements?

2. Did the same person prepare the statements for each of the periods reviewed? Did the person who prepared the internal statements also prepare the year-end federal tax returns?

3. If statements (or tax returns) were prepared by a CPA, ask if company has used the same CPA for several years. Has the company frequently changed CPAs?

4. Do figures on the annual federal tax return match figures on the company's Income Statement and Balance Sheet? Are there obvious reasons for any discrepancies?

5. Do the financial statements match the company's bank statements? If not, are the reasons obvious?

6. Do the "retained earnings" shown on the most recent Balance Sheet equal the sum of: the Equity on the prior Balance Sheet plus the pre-tax earnings on the current Income Statement?

7. Does the Cost of Goods on the Income Statement reflect changes in the value (amount) of Inventory? Sometimes Inventory is only valued at the end of the year for tax reporting purposes, but the new Inventory value is not put on the internal statements.

8. Is the Depreciation account posted in a consistent manner from period to period? Sometimes depreciation is only taken at the end of the year, making it difficult to compare financial results from different periods.

9. If a certain expense item is accrued on one Income Statement, is it also accrued on other statements?

All of these are good questions to keep in mind, but be wary of getting bogged down in too much detail. Too much analysis can lead to paralysis, as has been said many times. All truth is not in the numbers. Try to stay focused on what you are trying to learn, that is, will the business, in your opinion, in the future earn enough to meet your financial objectives?

In Doozy's case the net effect of the review process was positive: **adjusted earnings** exceeded **reported earnings**. It was relatively easy to make the adjustments necessary to "recast" the year-over-year earnings into a consistent format because the financial statements are essentially accurate. But, in many businesses this is not so. Review the Case Histories below. Adjusted earnings may be much less than reported earnings. Looking, for example, at Case No. 1: If the equipment used in the rental fleet is written down (depreciated) as it should be, adjusted earnings would be much less than the reported earnings.

Case No. 1: Overstated Earnings. A heavy equipment sales and rental company reported over $500,000 in pre-tax income on its most recent year-to-date financial statement and over $700,000 for the last full year. This seemed a most attractive trend to a group of potential buyers. It turned out, however, that the reported numbers were misleading because the owner had not written down (or depreciated) the book values of some of the new equipment that he had been using in his rental fleet. After deducting appropriate depreciation charges, it was determined that the income, at best, was a breakeven situation. **Moral: Check (1) whether depreciation has been taken in the current year and (2) whether book values of rental equipment and other equipment have been written down.**

Case No. 2: Overstated Earnings. The owner of a small retail business proudly handed me his latest year-to-date financial statement. It showed a significant increase in profit. After scanning the statement it became clear that Rent for the last month had not been paid and Payroll for the last week had not been posted. Instead of the $10,000 profit shown, true monthly profit was closer to average monthly earnings of $5,000. **Moral: Check obvious expenses on monthly statements: Often they have not been posted** (through no intent by the owner to misrepresent company earnings).

TIP: A buyer's adjustment process is for his edification, not for the seller's. While it is intended to confirm the representations that a seller has made concerning his business, it is not intended to educate the seller, that is, to show the seller that his business has in reality earned more than he thought it had earned or may be worth more to you than he is willing to sell it for.

The next three case histories involving embezzlement illustrate this point. Of course, embezzlement is the product of lack of adequate financial controls or oversight by the owner. It bears repeating that keeping accurate books and records is not instinctive to most first generation owners; they are focused on running and growing their businesses. Only later do they find that their lack of oversight became obvious to employees, some of whom found ways to take advantage of the situations.

Case No. 1: Understated Earnings-Liquor Store. While the owner was attempting to sell his store, we asked several times why the reported gross profit margins seemed low. If he used industry standard "mark ups" the gross profit margins should have been higher. The owner was at a loss to explain this. We thought that some money was being spent for non-operating expenses or, perhaps, bottles given as promotional items. With the low "margins" shown on the store's financial reports, we were unable to sell the store. Some months later the owner called to tell me that my questions had spurred him to look more closely at the daily sales reports. There he found the obvious answer: a long-time employee was not ringing up all the sales. Instead of putting all sales proceeds into the cash register, he was putting the proceeds of the unrecorded sales in his pocket. **Moral for buyers: A business showing little profit on paper may, in fact, be quite profitable.**

Case No. 2: Understated Earnings-Restaurant and Bar. This bar was located near a university and was constantly packed, but showed no profit. The Cost of Goods seemed much too high. In fact, one month COGs reached almost 90%. (COGs should have ranged between 25-35%.) The owner seemed at a loss to explain this so I invited a restaurant man to join me for drinks at the bar one evening. This is what we found: The place was crowded as usual. Everyone was having trouble getting service. Students kept coming in to "work" the evening shift and, we soon discovered, kept leaving shortly thereafter. They simply had gone back to the kitchen, eaten a free meal, and soon left for their evening classes. No wonder service was slow and the Cost of Goods so high. **Moral: Financial statements do not have the last word when determining if a business is viable or attractive.**

Case No. 3: Understated Earnings-Forklift Distributor. The owner of this well-established, growing business wanted to retire. The financial statements, month after month, showed reasonable earnings, but the cash balances in various accounts were declining. The owner was convinced that the statements were being properly prepared. Operating expenses seemed in line. Purchases seemed in line also. Finally, I asked the bookkeeper to run a Cash Flow statement, but for many months she declined to do so. It turned out that she was reversing the depreciation

> charges on older trucks in the rental fleet, thereby creating fictional profits. It appeared to me that she had taken the cash. **Moral: Financial statements should have three components: the P&L, the Balance Sheet and the Cash Flow statement. Ask to see all three. And review them. They should be in agreement.**

Business owners are usually unaware of misstated earnings. For many owners it made little difference what the statements showed until time to prepare the annual tax returns or to offer the business for sale. Some misstatements are from recent reporting periods, but many have "been on the books" for a long time. Doozy, for example, carried several bad (uncollectible) accounts receivable on its books for several years. Some companies carry hundreds of thousands of dollars of uncollectible accounts on their Balance Sheets. Some carry inventories that are widely under or overstated.

Sometimes, if the financial statements seem to contain many inconsistencies, the best way for business buyers to proceed is to ignore prior years and concentrate instead on the current year. Simply reconstruct the books for the current year check-by-check and account-by-account. This is not as onerous as it might seem. Many businesses write surprisingly few checks. Expenses for many accounts can be "reconstructed" from source data like leases, utility and phone bills, and insurance policies. Accountants call this process of reconstructing "forensic accounting."[44] They don't seem to like to do it, preferring, in my experience, to rely largely on "published" reports.

The more obvious reasons for misstated earnings are listed below. Some produce negative adjustments and others positive adjustments to earnings.

1. **Pilferage** of cash, supplies, or inventory (by owners, employees, or customers): *positive*.
2. **Embezzlement** of cash or equivalent: *positive*.
3. **Inventory issues:** Inventories may not have been fully or accurately counted in years: *positive or negative*.

---

44 Forensic accounting is a little like archeology; the archeologist has to guess the shape of a pot from the pieces he can find. Accountants have to "reconstruct" financial statements from what they can find or surmise.

4. **Unpaid bills:** Lags in posting accounts payable or checks. Sometimes checks have been written but not mailed and bank balances appear favorable: *negative*.

5. **Employee benefits**: Mandatory bonuses, vacation pay and retirement plan contributions are not booked as expenses. Few small businesses audit these accounts consistently: *negative*.

6. **Pre-payment of expenses:** Many businesses do this at the end of the year to reduce taxable income: *positive*.

7. **Payment of personal and family expenses:** This is the matter of non-operating expenses. Always ask the owner (or broker) to list them-they can add up: *positive*.

8. **Lags in booking sales or purchases** of new items of inventory: This makes the reported inventory appear lower than it really is.: *positive*.

9. **Extravagant or unnecessary purchases** by owners: One owner of a modest business spent $6,000 for the "executive" desk in his office: *positive*.

10. **Bookkeeping errors:** Expenses for similar items are posted to different (incorrect) accounts over many months: *neutral*.

11. **Inventory accounting practices:** Use of LIFO accounting (during periods of increasing prices) could understate the value of Inventory greatly and therefore understate earnings: *positive* See following discussion.

INVENTORY: ISSUES AND OPPORTUNITY. Since the Inventory is the most expensive asset included in most acquisitions, it warrants additional mention. Correctly or incorrectly, some companies write off (expense) the cost of their inventories when they are purchased, so their value is never shown on the Balance Sheet. When inventories are shown on the Balance Sheet, it is not clear how they were valued unless the financial statement contains footnotes telling us how. Even then, there may be some discrepancy between the explanation in the footnotes and reality, unless statements have been audited. In that case the counting and valuing has been monitored and the values shown can be relied upon.

Jack (John V. M.) Gibson

> **Case History: Unrecorded Inventory.** A dental lab that made crowns and implants had a lot of precious metals (gold, silver, and platinum) in its inventory none of which showed on its Balance Sheet. During the year preceding the proprietor's divorce, purchases of these precious metals seemed to rise substantially while gross profit (and the bottom line) appeared to decline. On paper, earnings were dismal. When the inventory was counted, it turned out that the opposite was true: inventory had increased substantially and the lab had in fact been quite profitable. **Moral: When purchases increase, see if book value of inventory has changed. If it hasn't, it may be concealing profits.**

Many companies carry their inventory on the books at "original cost." This "cost" may be well below current "replacement cost." When an item of inventory is sold, it may be difficult to determine if the Book Value of the Inventory is reduced by the original cost or by the current replacement cost, unless inventories are computerized. Even then, the values shown on the books are often not accurate because of shrinkage, breakage or obsolescence.[45]

Sometimes this "exchange" of old and new items of inventory produces an artificial profit and sometimes a loss. So, over a period of years the Book Value of the Inventory can become much less than or can exceed its current or fair Market Value.

If the inventory is not computerized, owners have a choice of what values to use when they "take inventory" at the end of the year. Let's say that a store counts the 1.75 liter bottles of Makers Mark Kentucky bourbon and then "extends" the count at some cost per bottle. The oldest bottle in inventory cost $21.00 and the most recent cost $22.00. Which "cost" should be used? Using the lower cost will appear to reduce profit, while using the higher cost increases profit, if the store properly records its Cost of Goods on its Income Statement. To avoid this quandary, some businesses use a blended or average cost.

If a store makes no effort to adjust the Cost of Goods to reflect changes in inventory, the resulting Gross Profit and Gross Profit Margin cannot be relied upon. See Table 10 below. It can appear "on paper" that a store is

---

45   It is useful to learn the difference between LIFO (last in, first out) and FIFO (first in, first out) inventory valuation methods. LIFO tends to understate earnings, particularly if replacement costs have been rising.

making money and that purchases have not increased, while the Inventory and the Gross Profit Margin are actually declining. Let's say that a "good" liquor store or other retail store should have at least a 25% Gross Profit (or a Cost of Goods Sold no greater than 75%) and Store 1 appears to meet this criterion. But, as illustrated below, if the Inventory had in fact declined, the actual Gross Profit may be much less. If Purchases are pretty level as shown below, when Inventory increases, margins (and profits) go up and when Inventory declines margins go down.

Table 10. Cost of Goods Sold Calculation

	Store 1	Store 2	Store 3
Reported Sales	$400,000	$400,000	$400,000
Beginning Inventory	?	120,000	150,000
+ Purchases	300,000	300,000	300,000
- Ending Inventory	?	150,000	120,000
=Cost of Goods Sold	300,000	270,000	330,000
Gross Profit	$100,000	$130,000	$70,00
Gross Profit Margin	25%	32.5%	17.5%

TIP: Determining the Gross Profit (as a % of sales) is always important to analyzing a business correctly. Has it gone up or down recently? Has the gross profit margin (percent) fluctuated significantly? If Purchases have gone up, it always appears that the Gross Profit margin has gone down. But, without knowing if the value of Inventory has changed, it is not possible to tell. The key is to understand how to calculate the Cost of Goods Sold (see Table 10) and to use that calculation instead of relying simply on the amount of purchases (or the cost of items purchased).

It is tempting to rely upon financial statements exactly as they have been prepared, but, as we have seen, they often do not tell enough about a business to give a buyer confidence. Many wonderful businesses can be found and purchased at fair prices if we look a little deeper and learn through some basic analysis what a business has really been doing.

SUMMARY: For every business a buyer seriously examines or considers purchasing, he should perform these steps or calculations before attempting to select an earnings multiple or conclude what a business is worth.

1. Confirm the top line results, i.e the sales, making necessary adjustments
2. Prepare five-year spreadsheet of sales and expenses
3. When appropriate, split expense accounts like Taxes and Insurance into smaller and more meaningful groupings
4. Adjust or recalculate the Gross Profit (and Gross Profit margin) to take into consideration changes in inventory levels, if Purchases (instead of Cost of Goods Sold) is used on the Income Statement
5. Make year-over-year adjustments (both negative and positive adjustments) where lumpy expenses are out of line or where any expenses appear not to have been paid when due
6. Delete any non-operating expenses where appropriate
7. Make adjustments for large one-time or non-recurring expenses
8. If all expenses (such as employee vacations and bonuses) are not fully accrued, add them to the adjusted Income Statement
9. Find or calculate appropriate owner compensation, adding back to Income any excess compensation or benefits (adjust to market)
10. Make adjustments to Balance Sheet to reflect necessary changes, such as in the case of overstated or understated assets or liabilities
11. Select indicated P:E or earnings multiple

TIP: Look at the Balance Sheet again. Has the original cost of the Fixed Assets changed from year to year? Has the amount of the Depreciation expense changed from year to year? If Depreciation expenses are declining, the owner may not have invested in new equipment. This could suggest that Income in recent years has been overstated a little.

An excellent source for learning more about analyzing financial statements is "Fire Your Stock Analyst" by Harry Domash. Mr. Domash discusses in much greater detail some of the topics discussed above: valuation ratios, cash flow, historical sales, earnings growth and much more. His perspective is analyzing publicly traded stocks but most of the analysis is equally applicable to smaller, privately held companies.

CHAPTER 5
EARNINGS CAPACITY AND OTHER VALUATION FACTORS

EARNINGS CAPACITY: In the last chapter we analyzed what Doozy's earnings history has been. The question now is, "What could Doozy earn in the future?" Does Doozy have the "capacity" to grow and, if so, can we determine how what will that growth cost? And do you have the skills to support and manage that growth? There are many items to think about when trying to determine the **earnings capacity** of a business. Let's look at some:

- **Market Characteristics:** Is the market or trade area strong enough to absorb additional sales of the products or services a company is sells? Can it absorb more custom cabinets each year? What kind? Perhaps a competitor has recently gone out of business or a new well-financed competitor has recently entered the market with high efficiency equipment. If a retail business, are there changes planned to the street system, such as new stoplights or new Interstate Highway exit ramps?

- **Plant Capacity:** Is the physical plant adequate to produce more cabinets (handle more sales) without leasing additional space or purchasing new equipment? This seems to be the case with Doozy, but not all businesses have excess physical or plant capacity. Check to be sure the present equipment is in good repair and working properly. Or, better yet, have someone with specific industry knowledge check the equipment for you.[46]

- **Capital Requirements:** Does the business need immediate capital for operations or for its plant and equipment? Does the business have a delivery truck? Does it have a reasonably new computer system? Are some assets missing? Do the assets in place at the business seem to match the assets listed in the profile or on the Balance Sheet? I have seen businesses where aging owners reduced inventories and deferred maintenance during the years or months preceding a sale. If this has occurred, you may have to assume the cost of replacing some inventory or upgrading some equipment (a hidden cost) immediately after buying the business. See Case History below.

> **Case History: Missing Inventory.** A buyer offered to purchase a business for $240,000. The listing price included inventory of $100,000. The terms of purchase were: $100,000 down payment and a note for the balance, said note to be adjusted for any change in inventory between the time the offer was accepted and the day of closing on the sale. The owner, realizing that change in inventory values would not change the down payment, reduced the inventory by $50,000 during the month before the closing. By so doing he put an extra $50,000 in his pocket, but the buyer did not have sufficient inventory to operate. The $100,000 down payment was all he could squeeze together, so he had to borrow money from family to replace this missing (and badly needed) inventory. **Moral: Always state a minimum inventory value in your contract.**

- **Employee Productivity:** Can the present employees at Doozy be expected to handle more work without reducing the quality of that work? Ask the owner or check with industry sources to discover what "output per man hour" should be. Output pertains to office and sales employees as well as to warehouse and shop workers.

---

46 Checking the equipment can sometimes be a delicate matter to business owners, since they quite properly regard buyers as future competitors that may open a similar business somewhere in their market area. Again, this matter can be handled as a contingency in the eventual purchase contract.

- **Employee Retention:** Will key employees stay with the business after it is sold and can employees easily be replaced at or near their current level of compensation? It would seriously impact future earnings if the new owner could not quickly replace key employees at or near their current salaries.
- **Efficiency:** Are there more efficient ways by which Doozy can operate or by which Doozy can manufacture or market its products? What will it cost, if anything, to increase production or sales efficiency? Often older businesses have not invested in the newer, more efficient equipment that is readily available, while newer competitors have. Can the shop or business be laid out so that materials can be handled more efficiently, or so there is less waste?

Answering these questions will help you to forecast your sales and expenses and to prepare a budget. Both of these steps should be completed before submitting an offer to buy a business. Your broker, as well as friends in the industry, can assist you.[47]

Forecasting. It is important to forecast both sales and expenses. To do this requires making a few assumptions. Let us first assume for the moment that you are comfortable forecasting 12% growth a year for the next five years. At this rate, after five years Doozy's annual sales will have grown to $528,700, a 76% increase over last year's sales of $300,000. To accommodate this growth, will Doozy need more space? Need to hire more employees? Purchase additional equipment? If the answer is yes, any additional costs must be included in your projected expenses and in your monthly budget.

In smaller manufacturing plants, there is often excess capacity. The buildings are large enough and the equipment adequate to handle more sales than they currently produce. This seems to be so with Doozy, since it reported sales three years ago of $340,000.

---

[47] Remember, while talking to friends, that all information about a business opportunity must be treated confidentially, including the fact that a business may be available for purchase.

Let's now assume that there has been 5% inflation in each of the last two years.[48] If that is so, $340,000 three years ago would represent sales of $374,850 last year, an increase of 11% over the $340,000 and 25% over the $300,000 in recorded sales last year. So, if inflation has in fact risen by 5% a year, we know that Doozy has at least 25% **excess capacity**, that is, the capacity to increase sales by 25% without having to increase its physical plant or equipment. This is reassuring to know.

Calculate: $340,000 x 1.05 = 357,000 x 1.05 = $374,850

Doozy's owner suggests that the plant could easily have handled sales well in excess of $340,000 three years ago. To back that up, he provided a breakdown of monthly sales showing three different months when the plant sold over $35,000 worth of goods that year. With monthly sales of $35,000, what would the plant "capacity" be next year?

Potential Annual Sales: $35,000 x 12 months = $420,000 two years ago

Potential Inflation Adjusted Sales:

$420,000 x 1.05% x 1.05 x 1.05 = $486,000 next year

These historic monthly sales numbers suggest that the plant may have the capacity to produce 50% more than last year's reported sales of $300,000. For the actual buyer's complete first year forecast of income and expenses, see Table 16 in Chapter 8. This **excess capacity** is another hidden asset because it appears that Doozy could produce sales of almost $500,000 without requiring more equipment or renting additional space. But be careful. Because Doozy achieved monthly sales of over $35,000 in three different months does not mean that Doozy could achieve sales of $35,000 for twelve consecutive months. Remember also that Doozy's reported sales are based on "date of receipt of payment" and not on when the work was actually performed.

---

46 While 5% inflation is used below, current (2010) inflation is unusually low—about 1%. Be careful when calculating inflation. Actual rates for many regions and cities are compiled by the Department of Labor, Bureau of Labor Statistics. In recent years inflation has been well under 5%.

How to Buy a Business without Being Had

RECONCILIATION OF VALUES FOUND: The question now is how to reconcile the different values indicated. Remember that in Chapter 4 we discussed three methods of valuation and concluded:

- Income method suggests: $150,000-$172,000 value range
- Asset method suggests: $157,750 value
- Comparative method suggests: value unknown

To reconcile our values, we might first see if there are any other applicable valuation methods. Then we must look for external factors that impact Doozy or may impact Doozy in the future. Some of these may indicate a discount in value while some may indicate a premium. Remember that the consistency of earnings found after making adjustments indicated replacing the initial 4:1 earnings multiple with a 5:1 multiple.

Other Valuation Methods. There are a few other valuation methods, or approaches, that knowledgeable buyers and analysts use, including: (1) **replacement value,** (2) **discounted cash flow value, and** (3) **percent of sales.** In the first method, we must determine the cost of replacing or "duplicating" the business in its present form. Surely we would not pay more for a business than it would cost to build it from scratch.[49]

To determine **replacement value,** we must determine the cost to (1) duplicate the physical facilities and tangible assets in their present (not new) condition, and (2) duplicate the income stream. Thus, we would estimate how much it would cost, in addition to replacing the hard assets, to build up sales to the $300,000 range (in Doozy's case) and, thereby, replace the income stream of a business.

---

49 One interesting method not mentioned is the Excess Earnings Method. It has been used by the U.S. Treasury Department since the days of prohibition. Essentially the appraiser uses this method to calculate the value of the intangible assets. To do so he calculates a return on the tangible assets (which are known) and subtracts that return from the total return (earnings). The "balance" of the earnings is then assigned to the intangible assets, using a rate of return that reflects the estimated risk involved-generally 20-25%. The goodwill portion of a company's value is thus estimated to be 4 to 5 times the "balance" of the earnings. In the view of the IRS, this method proves the existence of goodwill value, even when owners argue there is no goodwill. See Pratt, page 285.

Jack (John V. M.) Gibson

The **discounted cash flow** method requires: (1) forecasting Doozy's future earnings and cash flow and then (2) discounting the future cash flow to its **present value**. For example, if next year's cash flow is projected to be $100,000, we discount this amount by the current cost of money (or more if the business appears unstable). Assuming a cost of money of 10%, the present value of the $100,000 projected cash flow is $90,000.

Now, turning to Doozy, assume for purposes of this calculation that the $31,000 pre-tax income will grow at 10% per year for the next five years. The present value of Doozy's future cash flow stream may be calculated as shown below in Table 11. To get First Year Cash Flow, we add the projected ten percent increase in income ($3,100) and any non-cash expenses such as the $5,000 depreciation (the restated depreciation for last year) to the Base Income. We deduct no debt service payments that a buyer may have in the future. We look only at Doozy as it is today.

In most cases a buyer will have less taxable income and more depreciation than the seller had, since the buyer, when calculating future depreciation, will use the higher market value (or purchase price) of the depreciable assets instead of the lower Book Value of the assets carried on the seller's Balance Sheet.[50] Of course, the amount of annual depreciation expenses will increase if new equipment is purchased during the five-year "look forward" period.

Next, multiply the cash flow by the indicated discount of 10%: the first year, multiply $39,100 by .90. The second year multiply $42,510 by .81 (.90 times .90), and so on, and then add the sums derived, giving an estimated **present value** for Doozy of $168,854 using the **discounted cash flow method** of valuation (if our assumptions are valid).

Look again at the **Present Value of Future Cash Flow** in Table 11. Would you pay $32,406 (the present value) for a **projected cash flow** five years from now of $54,926? If not, maybe a discount rate greater than 10% is appropriate (maybe 12% or even 15%). There are no guarantees when it comes to projecting earnings or cash flows, so caution is always advised.

---

50 All of Doozy's equipment has been fully depreciated, including the truck. In making adjustments we elected to "add back" $10,000, leaving $5,000 in depreciation. This assumes the cost of the truck will be depreciated over 3 years. ($15,000 ÷ 3 = $5,000). The buyer of Doozy valued fixed assets at $45,000 and took $9,000 annual depreciation. See Tables 14 and 15.

Table 11. Calculation of Present Value of Projected Income and Cash Flow[51]

	Base Income	Add 10%	Depreciation	Cash Flow	Discount
First Year	$31,000+	$3,100+	$5,000	$ 39,100	90%
Second Year	34,100+	3,410+	5,000	42,510	90X90
Third Year	37,510+	3,751+	5,000	46,261	90X90X90
Fourth Year	41,261+	4,126+	5,000	50,387	90X90X90X90
Fifth Year	45,387+	4,539+	5,000	54,926	

Present Value of Future Cash Flow

First Year	$39,100	X	.90	=	$ 35,190
Second Year	42,510	X	.81	=	34,433
Third Year	46,261	X	.73	=	33,771
Fourth Year	50,387	X	.656	=	33,054
Fifth Year	54,926	X	.59	=	32,406
		Estimated Present Value:			$168,854

The third method, **percent of sales method**, is the simplest. Many similar businesses in many different markets sell at or near the same percentage of annual sales—30%, 40%, 50% of annual sales, or more in some industries. Percentages may not vary much from one community to another because similar types of business in many industries must purchase and maintain approximately the same complements of equipment and inventory. This is particularly true of franchised businesses such as a UPS Store, Jiffy Lube or Subway Shop.

For example, in some markets, laundromats are priced close to 90% of annual sales. Thus if sales are $100,000, a laundromat might sell for $90,000, all things being equal. A typical retail shop may sell for 35-40% of the past

---

51 The actual discount is 100%-90% or 10%, roughly the cost of borrowing. If the cost of borrowing is less, a lower discount rate might be used. This discount can change year over year as economic and business conditions change. The Future Cash Flow is then multiplied by the discount to bring it back to a Present Value. Thus, next year's projected cash flow will be $35,190 in present dollars. Calculate: $39,100 x .90 = $35,190.

year's sales. Subway sandwich shop prices average around 45% of annual sales in markets I know. Check with local sources, including your broker, to see what percent (or range) should apply to the type of business you are considering. After learning the usual percentage in your area, be sure to make any upward or downward adjustments that seem appropriate. For example, laundromats with new equipment should be worth more than ones with ten-year old equipment, because future maintenance and utility costs may be less.

These percents are certainly not guaranteed and should be used cautiously. They are only "rules of thumb." Each business is different but, within certain industries, sales data on comparable businesses indicate that the sales prices tend to cluster around a certain percent of annual sales.

For better or worse, excluding certain popular franchises, similar businesses within the same market area cannot always be found, so industry standards, such as the **percent of sales** method, are only useful starting places on valuing a business. However, if "comparables" can be found, it is important to make all appropriate adjustments, and use EBIT and EBITDA before drawing conclusions.

After various suggested values for a business have been found, we should "reconcile" them. Some values may be of dubious validity because of limited backup data. Other values may not appear applicable to the subject. You must rely more on the values that appear appropriate. In other words, the process of reconciling disparate values is as much an art as it is an exact science. It is in attempting to reconcile values derived by different methods, and in determining which ones to rely upon, that questions arise about valuation factors that have not previously come up.

OTHER VALUATION FACTORS: There are many factors not found in financial statements that can impact the value of a business. Try to develop your own list of factors and consider them carefully. My short list includes the following ten. Experience has shown that in virtually every valuation these ten factors play a role. Although there may be some change in the importance or weight assigned to each factor, they (and the foregoing discussion about methods of analysis) are as applicable to the success of small neighborhood businesses as to businesses with annual sales of $10,000,000 or more. Analysis is not limited to financial analyses. Let's look briefly at these "other" factors.

1. **Competition.** How much competition is there? Who are Doozy's competitors? What effect if any do they have on how Doozy conducts its business and prices its products?

2. **State of the Economy.** Where is the economy within the business cycle? Is the overall economy still expanding? Is a slowdown in the economy anticipated? How would it affect business? What's the state of the economy in general?

3. **Trade Area.** What is the business's market or trade area? Can it be expanded? Is it contracting? What will it cost to expand into other trade areas?

4. **Stability of Market.** Is the market (for custom cabinets like those in Doozy's product line) stable? Growing? How fast? Are Doozy's sales growing at the same rate as the market? Should Doozy's growth rate match the rate of growth in its market area? If it has not kept up with the market, have you found reasons why it hasn't?

5. **Key Employees.** Are there management or technically skilled people who will stay with the business after it is sold? Can you readily find people with the necessary skills to operate the business if some of them leave?

6. **Position/Reputation of Company.** How well established is the company in its market? When was it started? What is its reputation within the community and within its particular market? Is it getting referrals from satisfied customers? Ask the owner how he gets new business.

7. **Financial Condition.** What is the company's financial condition? Does it need more working capital to fund present or anticipated growth? Can it qualify for a line of credit? Are the assets in the business managed well? If there are accounts receivable, are many of them old? Are the inventories overstocked or understocked?

8. **Stability of Profit Margins.** How stable has the Gross Profit margin been over the last few years? What should it be? Are there any obvious explanations for deviations in the reported **gross profit margins**?

9. **Reason(s) For Selling Business.** What are the seller's motives for selling and what are his future plans? Does he, perhaps, intend to open a competing business?

10. **Location of Business.** Will the location be desirable in five years? If not, can you get out of the lease by then? Location is related to the size of the trade area. Thus, location may be a much more important factor for smaller neighborhood businesses.

Remember, what will happen in the future under your direction is far more important than what occurred in the past under the previous ownership. Can the business be improved in any critical areas under you leadership? If your answer is a resounding YES, try to identify the specific areas in which improvement seems attainable.

Ask yourself questions like: Can the **inventory turnover** be improved? Can output per man-hour be increased? If the inventory levels were decreased, how much would the **ROA** and **cash flow** increase? Would a new compensation plan encourage the employees to take a stronger interest in the business? What can you realistically do to make the business more competitive and profitable? You cannot find the answers to these questions by relying solely upon reviewing financial statements. You must try to understand the business.

In the final analysis, you must weigh the values indicated by the different valuation methods. **Replacement value** may be indicated for a given laundromat. The **percent of sales value** may be a more appropriate yardstick for a drycleaners, since its value is influenced by the sale prices of comparable businesses in neighboring areas. Where few comparable businesses exist, **earnings value** may be the most reliable measure of all.

How Much Is A Fair Price? Whatever value you assign to a business and whatever price you are able to buy it for, keep in mind that whatever the business earns, cash flow must be adequate to accomplish things: (1) pay your salary, (2) pay your debt service and (3) provide for any working capital requirements.[52] Let me share a short story.

---

52 See Glossary of Terms for definition of Working Capital.

How to Buy a Business without Being Had

> **Case History: Understanding Cash Flow.** A buyer called me six months after buying his business and said: "You told me that the business was earning about $10,000 a month and I relied on that. I have paid myself $10,000 each month and now I can't pay my bills." What he didn't tell me was that Sales had increased substantially and he therefore had to increase his inventory, which soaked up much of the cash flow. He learned that growth is often hard to manage and that growth is expensive. **Moral: Learn the difference between income (earnings) and cash flow. Even though a business is making money, growth can soak up all the cash flow and leave you struggling.**

Experience suggests that no more than two-thirds of projected cash flow should go towards debt service. So, in the case of Doozy, with Cash Flow of around $39,000 (see Table 16 for a detailed pro forma income and expense statement) over the twelve months after a sale, debt service (the sum of principal and interest payments referred to as the P&I) should not exceed $26,020. **Calculate:** $39,000 x .667=$26,020. Using this guideline, let's calculate how much a buyer can afford to pay for Doozy by looking at different offers: <u>prices</u>, <u>terms</u>, and <u>interest rates</u>.

Table 12. Debt Service as Percent of Cash Flow

	Offer 1	Offer 2	Offer 3	Offer 4	Offer 5
Purchase Price	$150,000	$150,000	$160,000	$170,000	$170,000
Down Payment	50,000	60,000	60,000	60,000	60,000
Balance Due	100,000	90,000	100,000	110,000	110,000
Interest Rate (APR)	7%	8%	9%	9%	7%
Term of Note	4 years	4 years	5 years	5 years	5 years
Monthly P&I	2,395	2,441	2,076	2,283	2,178
Annual Payments	$ 28,735	$ 29,295	$ 24,910	$ 27,401	$ 26,137
Percent of Cash Flow	73.7%	75.1%	63.9%	70.3%	67.0%

The conclusion appears to be that a buyer can comfortably buy Doozy at the Asking Price of $160,000 with a down payment of $60,000, or even $50,000, if the seller will accept a note for $100,000 to $110,000 with a term of at least five years and interest of around 7% APR. The key variable seems to be the five-year payout.

With rapidly growing businesses, buyers can sometimes safely pay a price that might require debt service of almost 100% of forecast cash flow (more than 100% of forecast pre-tax income!). With traditional "bread and butter" businesses, however, businesses that are affected by the ups and downs of the economy, two-thirds of cash flow is a good yardstick to keep in mind.

Misrepresentations and Their Effect on Business Value. Sometimes sellers do misrepresent things about their businesses both verbally and in their financial statements. And their agents often repeat the misrepresentations to buyers. Most of the "misrepresentations" are unintentional and not intended to take advantage of an unsuspecting buyer. Some misrepresentations are, in fact favorable to the buyer. But since it may not be possible to spot every misrepresentation, a well thought out and carefully drafted purchase contract (which is discussed in detail in the next chapter) is always the best defense.

The most common misrepresentations involve Inventory, which is usually the most expensive "asset" included in a business sale. Whether Inventory values are overstated or understated, this fact will come to light during the due diligence process (see Chapter 7) and, with a well-drafted contract, the purchase price will be adjusted accordingly at the closing on the sale. Actually, understated inventory values may in fact be a positive sign for a buyer instead of a red flag. Normal business practices differ but some Inventory may have been written off at time of purchase or written down in value at the end of the fiscal year. Frequently understated inventory can result in understated profit. This difference between actual and reported inventory values is often referred to as the "inventory cushion."

When a seller says something as an inducement to a buyer such as "I know the Balance Sheet only shows an Inventory of $100,000, but I am sure that there must be $200,000 worth out in the warehouse," take the seller up on that representation. The seller's statement is not intended to defraud, even if $200,000 turns out to be somewhat exaggerated. Put in your purchase contract some wording like:

> "This Price includes current Inventory items with a value (or original cost) of $200,000."

Try to determine when the cushion was created. In some cases owners have not changed the inventory values on the books for five years. If, as in the example above, a business actually has a $100,000 cushion consisting of salable merchandise in good condition, the business's earnings have been underreported by $100,000 or $20,000 per year. Of course, if inventory values (or other asset values) are overstated, the reported earnings likely are overstated.

What is more common than a pattern of repeated unscrupulous practices is some one-time event in the past (perhaps the result of an owner's effort to reduce taxable income) that might in fact be a misrepresentation. Some owners have intentionally misrepresented something to the detriment of a customer, an employee, a supplier, a bank or to some taxing authority. Again in my experience, the occurrence of such events is limited. Nevertheless, many buyers tend, understandably, to shy away from a business after a red flag regarding misrepresentation comes to light.

Misrepresentations can involve every aspect of a business: the sales, the value of certain assets, the condition of the assets, the stability of the workforce, and, of course, the business's growth and income potential. What is the prudent buyer to do in the face of obvious misrepresentations? Almost always, the best advice to a buyer to avoid paying too much "blue sky" or purchasing non-existent assets is: "**Let your contract do the talking.**" Be sure to obtain a properly drafted purchase contract before committing to buy a business. Of course, even with a proper contract it can be dangerous to buy when the misrepresentations cannot be resolved or when it seems clear after careful review and analysis that a business will not meet your expectations. As stated in Chapter 1, some businesses are bad businesses and are not saleable.

CHAPTER 6
HOW TO STRUCTURE A PURCHASE AGREEMENT

Part I. TERMS OF PURCHASE

When you have decided to prepare an **offer to purchase** a business and have decided what you feel is a fair price, there are some other important decisions (choices) to make before submitting an offer to the seller. These include:

1. Choosing whether to structure the purchase (and sale) as an "asset sale" or as a "stock sale"

2. Determining which assets to include in your "offer to purchase" (see Which Assets to Purchase section below) Or to buy the assets as offered?

3. Deciding how much of each class of assets to offer to buy: How much raw material? How much inventory of resale merchandise? How many vehicles?

4. Deciding whether to pay "cash" for the business or ask the Seller to accept payment over some time period, that is, to accept "terms" (see To Pay Cash or Terms section below)

5. Choosing which "contingencies" to include in your "offer to purchase" (see Contingent Nature of Contracts in Part II)

6. Determining how to allocate the purchase price among the assets to be purchased (see Allocation of Purchase Price in Part II)

7. Determining how (in what form) to "take title" to the business (see Taking Title in Part II)

ASSET SALE OR STOCK SALE: There are two methods to purchase a business: Buy the stock of the corporation from the shareholders or buy the specific assets (including, of course, the goodwill) from the corporation or directly from the owner if the business is not incorporated. This decision is easy if the business is not incorporated because no stock has been issued.[53] Sometimes, the form of sale is a combination of the two methods. In such a case, the buyer will purchase the corporate stock and also purchase some assets, such as non-compete agreements, from individual shareholders directly. Normally a non-compete agreement is between the buyer and the majority shareholder. However, sometimes, if several shareholders have been active in the management of the business, it is prudent to have agreements with more than one shareholder.

If a stock purchase is contemplated, a buyer may also choose not to purchase all the outstanding stock. He may want only to buy a controlling interest, which may be 51% of the issued and outstanding stock or, in some cases even less that 51%. This alternative, however, is seldom used in buying a small business for several reasons: (1) there may be state laws that protect minority stockholders in closely held corporations and (2) the stockholders may have entered into buy/sell agreements with each other that prevent any sale of shares of stock unless all stockholders consent to the sale and all the outstanding shares of stock are sold.

Even if the business is incorporated, it's usually best to buy the "assets and goodwill" rather than the "stock." This is so because, when you buy stock, you buy the whole corporate structure and, thereby, inherit whatever undisclosed liabilities or skeletons there may be lurking in the corporate closet—like latent tax deficiencies, unfavorable leases, lawsuits, or other old claims that haven't settled. Even if the Seller agrees to "hold you harmless" from any undisclosed liabilities, there could be many unforeseen problems (or financial liability) arising from obligations that were incurred by the

---

53 There are several types of corporations: "C" corps, "S" corps and LLCs. It is advisable to become familiar with the characteristics of each. Usually the best place to begin is with your accountant.

corporation prior to the date of your purchase. If you buy stock, these obligations could become your obligations.

Let me give two examples of the kind of things that could happen. In the first example a former employee brings a lawsuit against the corporation after you buy it. He alleges that he was wrongfully dismissed (by the former owner) and sues the corporation for back wages and damages of $100,000. While neither you nor the former owner believes the suit has merit, you end up spending $25,000 in legal fees, take a lot of time away from the business and incur many sleepless nights.

In the next example let's assume that, at the time you bought the corporation, it owed $20,000 to a supplier of one of its main lines of goods. The **payment terms** that the supplier has extended to the corporation for many years are "net thirty days with 2% discount" for payments made within 10 days. The $20,000 invoice was not paid within these terms, perhaps because both you and the seller were preoccupied with matters relating to the closing on the sale of the business, and as a result the supplier cancels the line and gives it to a competitor. It may have been a very important line, a line that you liked, and one of the reasons you bought the company.

If you had purchased the assets instead of stock, you would have requested from this supplier before the closing a letter giving you the right (perhaps exclusive rights) to handle this line of merchandise in your market area. You probably would have also requested in your purchase contract that the balance due all suppliers be paid by the seller before the closing or paid from closing funds. These are prudent safeguards.

In some cases buying "stock" is perfectly OK, particularly if:

1. The selling corporation has carried appropriate insurance coverages,
2. The financial records will pass an independent audit,
3. The shareholders personally will "indemnify" you from possible future losses resulting from events that occurred during their period of ownership, and
4. The shareholders will permit you to defer (or hold back) a substantial amount of the purchase price until all their contractual commitments (the commitments set out in the Purchase Contract) have been satisfied.
5. Corporation has sufficient cash to meet its obligations.

The chief advantage to buying the outstanding stock (instead of the assets and goodwill) is that everything is "in place." You normally won't need new licenses, bank accounts, leases, employment agreements and the like before taking over. And you might be able to assume existing dealership or supplier agreements without having to qualify for them in your own name (and credit situation), a sometime lengthy process.

If the decision is made to purchase corporate stock, it may still be prudent to buy other assets "outside of the corporation" as well. This is appropriate when some assets are owned individually by the majority stockholder (or by other persons involved in the sale) rather than by the corporation itself. An example is a "non-compete" agreement with the owner or majority stockholder. Most buyers expect a former owner not to compete with him (her) after the sale and, therefore, purchase a non-compete agreement. This "asset" is not owned by the business and the business (whether it is a sole proprietorship, partnership or corporation), therefore, is not responsible for the fulfillment of the agreement; the individual owners or stockholders are.

Lease Purchase or Option Purchase. A third way to buy a business is to lease it from the owner with an option to purchase it later at an agreed upon price. This mechanism is not often used but should be part of a Buyer's tool kit. A seller is very unlikely to agree to simply lease his business (as in leasing a building) because a seller wants or needs some cash at the closing. Often the seller has bills to pay off as well as certain closing costs and a brokerage fee. The way to resolve the lack of down payment in a lease/purchase is to lease with an option to purchase. Instead of selling the business outright at closing, the seller sells an option. The option price becomes the down payment. From the buyer's point of view, he gains time to decide if a certain business will help him reach his goals.

Buyer and Seller still negotiate a price for the business. Parties enter into an option agreement to buy the business within the option period (typically a year or two) at the negotiated price. The price for the option might be as little as $2-3,000. Or it might be $20-30,000. The price represent the money the seller will lose or forego by not getting paid for a year or two, including interest he would not earn from a larger down payment. If he received All Cash and the agreed upon price for the business were $300,000, and interest rates were 6%, the seller would "lose" $18,000 a year or $36,000. The option price is paid to Seller at closing. Sometimes part of the option price is credited towards the price of the business, but what the option really does is hold or guarantee the price of the business for a certain time period. For that a seller is entitled to compensation.

The Parties also must agree to a lease payment (usually a monthly payment). Let's assume the lease payment on a $300,000 acquisition is $4,000. Usually a portion of this payment is credited against the purchase price. In other words, the lease payment is treated as a partial payment of principal and interest. If, for example, 50% of the monthly lease payment of $4,000 is credited toward the purchase price, the price will be reduced by $2,000 each month. If the buyer exercises his "option to buy" at the end of two years, then the price is effectively reduced by $48,000.

In a Lease Purchase Agreement there would normally be additional covenants between the parties to cover the operation of the business while it is under option (see discussion of buyer and seller warranties in Part II of this Chapter). In other words, the seller would have to protect himself against the possibility that a buyer could harm or destroy his business if it were not properly managed. Three typical covenants would be:

1. limit the compensation a buyer could pay himself
2. require buyer to pay company bills on time
3. require buyer to give seller timely financial reports

At the end of the option period the buyer would have the "option" whether to proceed with the actual purchase or not. If the buyer does not exercise his option the seller would then be free to sell his business to someone else.

WHICH ASSETS TO PURCHASE: The concept of which assets to purchase does not occur to all buyers, but making the right decisions about assets can impact your future success. Most businesses have some non-operating assets, that is, assets that are not used in the business and are, therefore, not essential to its present or future operations. Sellers feel that a business cannot be broken up and, at the beginning of the negotiating process, expect the buyer to buy "everything on the books" or "everything you see here." If you determine that a business has too many (or some unnecessarily expensive) assets, it may be wise to exclude some in your initial offer.

If, for example, the owner or other family members are driving large, new pick-up trucks with all the bells and whistles while more modest vehicles would be adequate, do not hesitate to suggest that these assets be excluded. Often there is unused equipment in storage or sitting idle. Sometimes the furnishings in the executive office are far more extravagant than necessary.

In most business transactions, inventory is the most expensive asset, so it merits your most careful attention. Let's look at a retail furniture store. How much inventory should the business have? A sixty-day supply? A ninety-day supply? Or more? Normally thirty or more days elapse between acceptance of an offer and the closing, so sellers usually have time to sell any excess or unwanted inventory as well as any other assets you may elect not to buy. In regard to inventory, it is wise to include in your purchase contract a clause that limits the amount of inventory you agree to buy. See discussion below on How Much Inventory To Buy.

Other sellers will instinctively want to exclude from a sale all financial assets such as cash and accounts receivable. However, it may be appropriate for the seller to leave in the business enough cash to provide you, the buyer, with a level of working capital necessary to operate the business. This is particularly true with businesses that sell their products on credit as opposed to the typical retail business in which customers pay for their purchases at the time of each sale. **If the needed working capital is not included among the assets purchased, the buyer will have to provide it from other sources.**

How to Treat Customer Deposits. In the case of Doozy, the seller will give you (not sell) all or part of the deposits the customers made when their orders were placed. Legally, deposits are not an asset of a business, even though they may be recorded (incorrectly) as Cash under Assets on the Seller's Balance Sheet. If a customer's deposit is shown under Assets, the same amount should be included under Liabilities, because deposits must be returned, if an order is not filled. Often deposits are prorated between buyer and seller based on some formula, generally a formula relating to the percentage of completion of each order at the time of the sale. If an order has not been started, the full deposit would be given to the buyer. In some cases it might be fair for the seller to give the buyer the full deposit less the cost of marketing and other costs that the seller has already absorbed.

When a business (or its owner individually) owns its business premises, buyers face the "asset" decision of whether to purchase the real estate or simply to lease it from the seller. It generally seems wise not to be burdened by the additional debt associated with buying the real estate, unless the buyer is convinced that the location is desirable and the price is attractive. Sometimes it may be prudent to move the business to another location, in which case the buyer will neither buy nor lease the real estate. In other cases, a seller may make a buyer an attractive deal if the buyer does agree to buy his business and associated real estate.

How Much Inventory To Buy. Another decision is to decide how much of each asset, or class of assets, to purchase. This decision most often impacts inventory. If the inventory on hand appears too low to permit the business to operate efficiently, the buyer might require the seller to increase his inventories. The buyer may also stipulate that as of the date of closing there are on hand inventories of raw materials valued, say, at not less than $100,000. Likewise, inventory might be too high, so the buyer may decide to cap the value of raw material inventories that he will purchase at, say, $50,000 and cap total inventories at $125,000.

The seller will probably resist excluding or discounting any part of the inventory but a prudent buyer should be careful. If the amount of inventory on hand appears to be far above necessary levels, a buyer might put one or more clauses in the purchase contract such as:

> *"Excess inventory will be valued at its Book Value or replacement cost, whichever is the lesser, less a 10% discount."* Or *"Any inventory in excess of $100,000, valued at Seller's original cost, will be discounted by 20%. If inventory value exceeds $200,000, the excess will be excluded from the sale."*

Of course, the proper discount could be greater than 20% depending upon the age and condition of the inventory in question. The buyer could also offer to purchase the excess inventory from seller on an "as needed" basis. There are many ways to handle excess inventory. If a seller has not conducted a complete count of the inventory for many years, he may be quite surprised by how much is on hand. Since any "excess" inventory will increase the sale price of the business, a seller should be willing to give the buyer favorable terms as an inducement to take all the inventory on hand at the time of closing.

Jack (John V. M.) Gibson

TO PAY CASH OR TERMS: There are essentially two ways to pay for a business: (1) pay "cash" or (2) pay "on terms." Most small businesses are sold on terms, that is, the buyer makes a cash down payment at time of closing, and the seller accepts a **promissory note** (see sample Note in Appendix) for the balance of the purchase price. There is a third payment option called **assumption of debt**. Often the final terms of sale are a combination of Cash, Note, and Assumption of Debt. Let me illustrate with summaries of three possible terms of sale.

Hypothetical Terms of Sale	Offer 1	Offer 2	Offer 3
Cash Paid at Closing	$150,000	$60,000	$25,000
Cash Paid 90 Days from Closing[53]	125,000	0	25,000
Assumption of note on truck	0	15,000	15,000
Assumption of Accounts Payable	0	70,000	40,000
Note to Seller—1-Year Maturity	0	30,000	0
Note to Seller—5-Year Maturity	0	115,000	200,000
Purchase/Selling Price	**$275,000**	**$290,000**	**$305,000**

Terms can differ considerably. However, a down payment of at least thirty percent (30%) or one-third of the selling price is generally expected. Assumption of some of a seller's debt is essentially the same as a larger down payment. Notice above that with a larger down payment, the Selling Price is less.

Terms of Promissory Notes. Usually note payments (principal and interest or **P&I**) due seller are: (1) level, that is, the payments of P&I do not change during the term of the note, (2) they are paid monthly, and (3) the first payment is due 30 or 40 days from closing. There are several common variations to the standard terms of promissory notes taken back by sellers. These (and other) variations could be useful during the negotiating process. It is highly unlikely that a bank would accept such variations, though.

---

54 The 90-day deferred payment might: (1) pay for management assistance (2) protect buyer from undisclosed liabilities (3) assure buyer of collectability of accounts receivable or (4) cover a variety of other short-term situations. It is always wise to hold back some money.

1. Parties may agree to start with lower monthly note payments and increase them over the term of the note. For example, note payments may be set at $1,200 per month for the first year and increase to $2,000 per month during succeeding years.
2. Parties may agree to an adjustable interest rate, with the interest rate on the note changing yearly to reflect changes in the prime rate (the rate that banks give their best customers) or some other customary rate.
3. First payment of P&I may be deferred until 45, 60, or even 90 days after the closing to give the buyer a little breathing room.
4. Buyers may reserve the right to skip one or more monthly payments (of principal-not interest) during a year because of the seasonal nature of some businesses.
5. Buyers may pay interest only for the first several months.
6. There may be separate notes to pay for different parts of a business such as a note for the value assigned to Management Assistance and another note for the rolling stock. One note might be paid directly to the seller and another note paid to the corporation that owns and is selling the physical assets.
7. Notes for management assistance and non-competition may not require interest, since at time of closing seller has not "performed" these services.

The typical maturity for promissory notes is 3-5 years. When buying smaller, less well-established businesses, a shorter maturity is not unreasonable. For larger businesses a longer term is common. Some buyers may also want a **balloon note**. In such cases the seller might accept a note amortized, perhaps, over 5-6 years but require a balloon payment (the balance of the principal) at the end of three years. This has the advantage that: (1) buyers get smaller monthly note payments during the early years of ownership and (2) sellers get paid off more quickly. See sample Notes in Appendix.

If the owner is really committed to selling, you are much more likely to buy at a favorable price and on favorable terms. Whatever the agreed upon price and terms, most sellers will expect a personal guarantee from you (and your spouse) as well as specific collateral to back up the Note. The collateral for the Note is usually the assets of the business (the assets being sold) rather than "outside" assets, that is, assets such as your personal residence. Sometimes it is reasonable to expect the seller to release some of the collateral as the buyer pays down a note.

All notes call for penalties (late fees) if note payments are not received on time. Late fees are added to a note and accrue interest if they are not paid on time. Typically a payment is late if received 10-20 days after the due date. The late payments are generally not onerous but are stiff enough to encourage compliance on the part of the buyer. If there is a string of late payments, virtually every note permits seller to foreclose on or to repossess the assets assigned to seller as collateral or even to take back the entire business. In most situations, neither buyer nor seller wants foreclosure to occur.

A note may contain a **default clause** that specifies that full payment is due upon default (non-payment of one or more monthly payments) by buyer. In such cases there is no "cure" and there are no late fees, simply a demand for full payment. Such a provision is not in a buyer's interest.

A seller can take back (hold) several notes as shown in Offer 2 above. The one-year note, for example, could be for payment of a non-compete agreement. This note may carry no interest, since the Seller will not have "performed" until after the year is complete. It is useful to think of paying for different assets over different terms, while contemplating your offers.

For a seller, the key to accepting an offer "on terms" is to feel protected, that is, to believe that the collateral is adequate to cover the deferred obligations of the buyer in case he is forced to repossess the business or has to liquidate the assets. Rightly or wrongly, the seller worries that the buyer may not be able to "keep the business together" and pay him off under the terms of the purchase agreement.

Security Agreement. When notes are secured by specific items of collateral, a Security Agreement is attached to the Note. This agreement spells out in detail the buyer's obligations to the seller and the specific procedures the seller must follow in order to regain possession of the collateral. There is another use for security agreements that a buyer should not overlook: if properly drafted, they make the sellers feel secure accepting offers to sell "on terms" rather than requiring "all cash" offers.

In a typical security agreement, a buyer may be required to:

1. Keep all collateral at all times in good repair, adequately insured, and housed on business premises,
2. Allow secured party to inspect premises and collateral after reasonable notice,
3. Not sell or transfer secured property without express permission of secured party, and
4. Provide secured party with timely monthly financial statements or other evidence that inventories are maintained at required levels

Both the note (or notes) and security agreement must follow the terms set out and agreed to in the purchase contract. See paragraph 6 under Special Stipulations in sample contract in Appendix.

All Cash Offers. Many "all cash" offers do not require a buyer to pay 100% of the purchase price at closing but they do preclude any long-term seller financing such as a note with a maturity of longer than one year. It is typical for a buyer to expect a seller to discount his asking price somewhat as the terms of sale approach an "all cash" offer. The appeal of "all cash" to a seller is obvious; he thereby avoids the risk and frustration (not to mention potential cost) of having to track down the buyer when (if) he has not received payments on time and, in extreme cases, suing the buyer. Even if seller requires a 100% "cash" sale, it is advisable to hold some money back for a few months to protect yourself against the risk of "undisclosed liabilities" and to insure that seller has met all his promises, such as providing the transition management assistance or complying with the terms of the non-compete agreement.

If a buyer assumes some of a business's debts, it is the same as paying cash, since the seller will not have to pay these debts off. You could, for example, assume a car note or equipment note or some accounts payable as a method of paying part of the purchase price as in Offers 2 and 3.

In Table 13 below are two possible offers for the purchase of Doozy. Look at Offer 1 first. The seller would get the full $100,000 value he placed on the "hard" assets in the profile and the deferred payments would be backed by promissory notes. Of course, this is not really an "all cash" offer because some of the payments are deferred. However, a buyer who is making Offer 1 is offering to pay seller the full value ($100,000) he put on the "business assets" in exchange for which he is asking the seller to let him defer the balance of the purchase price.

Although Offer 1 appears to exceed seller's asking price of $160,000, it is more favorable to the buyer than it at first appears, because: (1) the **present value** of the deferred payments for the non-compete agreement is less than the $50,000 face value of this obligation and (2) buyer will not have to worry about meeting monthly debt service obligations as he would in Offer 2. Which would you prefer: to pay $40,000 now or pay $50,000 in two years? Which would a seller prefer: to receive $40,000 now or $50,000 in two years? Maybe the seller would agree to accept $35,000 now.

In Offer 1 the seller would receive a **consideration of sale** less than the stated purchase price of $170,000, but close to his Asking Price of $160,000. To calculate the **present value (PV)** of the $50,000, discount it by a rate of interest commensurate with the risk to the holder of the note, perhaps 12%. At 12% interest (or discount rate) the present value is $39,860. The "cash" discount in this case would be $50,000 less $39,860 or $10,140, making the present value of the $170,000 offer just $159,860. See calculation below. Some sellers might accept a higher discount than 12% in order to receive more cash at closing on the sale of the business. If the seller insisted on all cash, the buyer might offer a little less, say $140,000 or $150,000, still deferring the $20,000 allocated to Management Assistance for 65 days.

Calculate: $50,000 ÷ 1.12 = $44,643 PV after one year

$44,643 ÷ 1.12 = $39,860 PV after two years

Table 13. Terms of Two Hypothetical Offers

Offer 1: Purchase for "All Cash"

	Value/Price	Terms of Payment
Down Payment (buys FF&E and Inventories-the hard assets)	$100,000	Payable at closing
60-Day Management Assistance Contract	20,000	Payable 65 days from closing
Two-Year Non-Compete Agreement	50,000	Payable in full on second anniversary of closing
Purchase Price	**$170,000**	

Offer 2: Purchase "On Terms"

Purchase Price (estimated) [54]	**$150,000**
Down Payment	50,000
Note to Seller	100,000
Interest Rate on Note	7% APR
Term of Note	Five years
Method of Payment	Equal monthly payments
Monthly Payment to Seller	$1,980

Buyer's Return on Investment and Cash Flow in Offer 2

1st Year Income Before Interest or Taxes	$36,000
Forecast 1st Year Cash Flow	42,000
Interest Payments 1st Year on Note	6,400
Forecast Income After Interest Payment	29,600
Estimated 1st Year Principal Payment	17,240
1st Year Cash Flow After Paying Principal	24,760

Which offer is better in terms of the return on your investment? Remember that your ROI is higher when the down payment/investment is lower. This will be true whether you use third party (bank) financing or seller financing. Let's use the example of Offer 2. Your investment is $50,000.

---

55 In this offer the allocation of the purchase price must be changed from the allocation in Offer 1. Perhaps the "price" assigned to the non-compete will be reduced to $30,000. Or only $80,000 allocated to the hard assets.

Before deducting interest or additional depreciation expenses, projected pre-tax income is $36,000. At 7% APR, your interest payments the first year will be a little over $6,400. This would make forecast pre-tax income about $29,600 which is a 59.2% return on a down payment of $50,000.[56]

Calculate: $29,600 divided by $50,000 = .592 or 59.2% **ROI**

The principal payments due Seller in Offer 2 (approximately $17,240 the first year) are not deducted from earnings because they go towards reducing debt.[57] However, if a buyer pays $100,000 in cash at closing plus $20,000 sixty-five days after closing as in Offer 1 (a down payment of $120,000), anticipated ROI is only 30%, or half the ROI of a buyer who pays a more typical "one-third down."[58] If any portion of the $120,000 were borrowed, the ROI would increase. With the larger down payment and an (almost) "all cash" offer, the Cash Flow 1st year, however, is greater than in Offer 2.

Calculate: $36,000 divided by $120,000 = .30 or 30% **ROI**

Suggestion: Before preparing an actual offer or letter of intent, prepare several different offers (in the simplified form shown in Table 13) with different offering prices and terms of payment. Be creative. And, then, for each hypothetical offer, calculate the probable future income, cash flow and ROI. Then, try to determine the advantages of each to the seller and to you as the buyer. And, finally, try to determine possible "trade offs" that you think a prudent seller might accept. Would he accept your price if you reduced the time of the management assistance or non-compete periods? Would you agree to a higher price if the seller would agree to extend the term of the Note from five years to six years?

---

56 Earnings from "operations" are the same before and after the purchase.
57 Note that after paying both interest and principle ($23,640), there is still $12,360 left to add to working capital under the above terms of purchase.
58 Perhaps, if the buyer offered "all cash", the seller may have accepted a price of $135,000, which would be a discount of 10%. In that case the ROI would be a little lower ($35,000÷$135,000 = .267 or 26.7%) but there would be no principal, interest or other deferred payments in the future.

What Does the Word "Terms" Mean? The "terms" of purchase can mean a lot of different things to different people. You will see the word "terms" many times in the rest of this chapter, so a clear understanding of what this word means is important. It seems instinctive, when buying a business, to assume that the word "terms" refers to the financial aspects of an offer: the price and the amount of down payment, for example. Review the "offers" in the preceding pages to see some of the more common financial terms. Actually, the word "terms" can refer to any of the hundreds of "variables" that might be contained within an offer.

It is impossible to list all the possible different terms; buyers and sellers have to be creative sometimes to put a deal together. The important thing to remember is that some aspects of an offer may be appealing to a seller and some may be "turnoffs." When you begin preparing an offer you will not know what terms will get favorable attention from the seller. But, as offers and counteroffers flow back and forth between buyer and seller, you will discover which terms the seller finds appealing. In the end it may not always be the highest price that brings the seller to the closing table. Let me give some examples:

- the buyer agrees to close on the sale within thirty (days) of seller's acceptance of his offer (because he doesn't have to wait for a bank to approve a loan request)
- the offer is clearly spelled out in only two pages-not a forty page contract filled with unfamiliar legal terms
- the terms of purchase do not require the seller to provide any management assistance after the sale
- the buyer agrees to give the seller some "outside" collateral and the buyer's wife agrees to sign the Promissory Note
- buyer will agree to pay "current replacement value" for all retail inventory instead of "seller's original cost" as he originally offered

In exchange for the buyer's acceptance of certain "terms" that the seller perceives as favorable, the seller might agree to certain terms that are more favorable to the buyer. For example:

- if the buyer will give outside collateral, the seller will reduce the purchase price in his original counteroffer

- if the buyer will assume the $20,000 balance due on one of the newer company vehicles, the seller will accept the $50,000 down payment the buyer originally offered
- if the buyer will close within thirty (30) days, the seller will provide sixty (days) of management assistance
- if the buyer will increase the down payment from thirty percent (30%) of the purchase price to forty percent (40%), the seller will agree to finance the balance at five percent (5%) interest rate instead of the eight percent (8%) requested in his first counteroffer
- if the buyer will give the seller a long term lease, perhaps ten years, on the business premises (which seller owns), seller will accept the buyer's original offer and agree not to increase the rent during the full ten years

Now, with these thoughts in mind about some of the many possible terms that can be added to an offer (to make it more appealing and to increase the odds that the seller will find an offer acceptable), let's move from the valuation process to the actual contract preparation process.

LETTER OF INTENT: Before preparing and submitting an offer or formal Purchase Agreement, sometimes it is sensible to submit what is called a **Letter of Intent**.[59] These "letters" are quite brief and set forth in very straightforward language the basic terms under which you want to buy a business. Such a letter is easier for the seller to understand and respond to than a more formal and lengthy legal document. In the case of Doozy, a letter of intent might be no more detailed than the following:

---

59 There are pros and cons to using a Letter of Intent when acquiring a small business. It is often preferable to eliminate this step, except where the buyer is requesting unusual "terms" which cannot easily be set out in a standard contract because of their length or legal complexity.

SAMPLE SIMPLIFIED LETTER OF INTENT

Dear _____,

By means of this (binding)(non-binding) letter I am conveying to you my intent to offer to purchase the following assets of Doozy Manufacturing Co. (hereafter "Business") for the price and under the terms set out below.

1. All equipment and tools used in operation of Business
2. Raw materials with an original cost of $50,000
3. All goodwill and rights to all trade names and logos
4. Unfilled work orders in hand at closing totaling $80,000
5. You will enter into a non-compete agreement and a management assistance agreement with me.
6. The price will be $150,000 before adjustments, if any.
7. The down payment payable at closing will be $50,000.
8. The balance will be paid in 60 equal and consecutive monthly installments of principal and interest.
9. The interest rate will be 7% Annual Percentage Rate.
10. Before the closing, I will inspect all equipment to see if it is in good working order and will count and value the inventories. If the inventory value is less than $50,000, the price and down payment will be reduced by the shortage.
11. The closing will be thirty days after we sign a formal purchase agreement.
12. Prior to closing, you will continue to operate in the normal manner

If these terms are acceptable to you, please signify by your signature and return to me. Within five (5) days of receipt of your signed Letter, I will present you a purchase contract on the price and terms set out above together with earnest money in the amount of $10,000.

Respectfully,   Agreed: _____
                                 John Smith, President, Doozy Mfg. Co., Inc.

_____   _____
John Doe (Purchaser)   John Smith, Individual Date_____
Date_____

Note that the letter can be a "binding" or "non-binding" offer. The purpose of the letter is to see if there is a meeting of minds between the parties regarding key points such as **price and terms** before going to the trouble of preparing the detailed contract. In the case of a binding letter, the buyer is "binding" himself only to prepare and submit a formal purchase contract within five days, if the seller accepts the price and terms exactly as set out in the letter. If the letter were non-binding, the buyer would have no obligation.

Of course, a seller is free to accept the "letter" offer subject to a few changes. The seller, for example, in paragraph two might scratch out $50,000 and substitute $40,000 or in paragraph six scratch out $150,000 and insert $160,000. In paragraph 7, he might increase the down payment to $60,000 and in paragraph nine he might increase the interest rate to 8%. Each of the changes in the letter would be initialed by the seller and the letter would be signed by the seller, before it is returned to the buyer.

Closing Costs and Service Deposits. During the negotiation process, the buyer must keep a sharp eye on his available cash reserves. If he has, for example, only $60,000 available, he should not spend the entire $60,000 on the down payment. Some must be kept for closing costs, some for working capital (if the business does not "cash flow" from the first day of ownership) and some for deposits that a buyer may have to put up in order to maintain service with service providers such as a telephone company or utility company. These costs can vary from market to market. Learn what they are in your market.

Many buyers neglect or do not think about the cost of the "service" deposits. In a standard contract (see Stipulation 11 in Sample in Appendix), these deposits remain the property of the seller. Of course, the buyer may request in his offer that all such deposits be included among the assets to be conveyed at closing at no extra cost. If a contract does not explicitly state that deposits will be conveyed to the buyer, the buyer is wise to determine the amount of such deposits and include this amount in his closing budget. Some sellers forget that there are deposits on account with these providers and, therefore, leave them in place.

If a buyer has to obtain a new lease on the business premises, the landlord may require a deposit also, typically one month's rent, sometimes both the first and last month's rent. Even though closing costs and service deposits are relatively modest, it would be wise to hold $10,000 in reserve. See other costs in the Settlement Sheets in the Appendix.

Counteroffers. Whether the buyer first submits a Letter of Intent or omits this step and submits a formal Purchase Contract to a seller, the seller is likely to respond with some changes. This "response" is called a counteroffer. Often the requested changes are quite modest. The buyer then must (1) determine how to respond to the seller in his counteroffer or (2) notify the seller that he (she) has no interest in proceeding. If the buyer accepts the seller's changes, he (1) initials them on the original Letter or Contract, and (2) returns a properly executed copy to the seller.

This exchange of counteroffers may go back and forth several times. Typically, a buyer's response is to reply to the seller by saying, in effect, I will give you what you are asking if you will give me something else, perhaps some additional inventory or some additional management assistance after the sale. Try to keep in mind what you would like the seller to do for you.

With each exchange of offers and counteroffers, the gap between the price and terms offered and the asking price and terms gets narrower and the agreements between the parties begin to reflect more fully the individuality of the business. When agreement has been reached on all points, you, as buyer, then begin to prepare the formal purchase contract. If the negotiating has been done via Letter of Intent, be sure to observe the clause regarding how many days you have to submit the Contract. Sometimes the signed Letter is turned over to your attorney or Broker who will draft the Contract.[60]

TIP: Using pre-printed contract forms provided by a broker might save a lot of money and speed up the contract preparation process. Attorneys might require several days to prepare a contract, while a broker will be able to fill in the blanks in a pre-printed contract form while you are in his office. If you choose to use a pre-printed form, it might be wise to let your attorney review it before it is submitted to the seller. If you wish to incorporate, you can also save some money by applying for a charter directly from the Secretary of State in your state. It is not required that an attorney do this for you. Closing documents, however, must be prepared by an attorney.

---

60 Brokers cannot "draft" contracts. Instead they use pre-printed contract forms that were prepared by attorneys and simply fill in the blanks.

Seller's Authority To Sign. If the owner of the assets to be purchased is a corporation (like Doozy), a corporate officer, as well as the owner individually, will sign the Letter or Contract. The Secretary of the Board of Directors of the selling corporation should sign a **corporate resolution** authorizing the President (or other officer) to enter into an agreement to sell the assets of the business. This resolution can either: (1) authorize the sale on specific terms, (2) accept an offer to purchase on the terms offered, or (3) authorize the President to enter into negotiations (sometimes exclusive) with a specific named buyer. It could be as simple as the following resolution.

RESOLUTION

*"**Be It Resolved** that the undersigned shareholders of Doozy Manufacturing Corporation (Company) authorize James P. Doozy, President, to offer for sale the stock or assets of Company on the following terms (specify terms)." And, if it is agreed as well: " The shareholders further authorize James P. Doozy to retain the firm of _____ as exclusive agent to represent Company in the marketing and sale of Company."*

If you, as buyer, want **exclusivity**, another sentence should be added to the Letter of Intent (and to any Contract that follows), substantially in the form set out below:

"During the term of our negotiations you will not enter into any negotiations with any other party nor accept any offer to purchase Business from any other party."

Even when the assets (or business) you are planning to buy are owned by a corporation, some parts of a Contract or Letter of Intent contain promises that the officers or shareholders of the corporation cannot make in their corporate capacity. For example, stipulation 5. in the Sample Simplified Letter of Intent states: "You will enter into a non-compete agreement and management assistance agreement with me." Does "you" refer to the corporation or to one or more of the officers or shareholders of the corporation? If, for example, the buyer expects the management assistance to be performed by an individual, then that individual must sign the Contract or Letter in his or her individual capacity as well as in corporate capacity. In other words, that person must sign twice. This is why, at the bottom of the sample Letter, there are two signature lines for the seller. In some cases more than two seller signatures may be required. More about signatures will be covered in the following sections.

Part II. THE PURCHASE AGREEMENT

When you have decided to try to buy a business and how to structure your offer, the next step is to prepare an offer to purchase. An attorney or experienced broker will have professionally prepared blank purchase contracts and will gladly go over them with you to assist you in structuring your offer.[61] The broker's assistance can be invaluable during this process because he knows the seller's requirements. He has probably gone over several different "structures" with his client. The broker will try to help you for another very basic reason: he will not receive a commission unless a sale is successfully consummated. See sample Contract in Appendix.

Importance of Legal Assistance. It is recommended that you hire your own attorney to review any purchase agreement (or offer to purchase) before you sign it, or sign it subject to review and approval by your attorney. After signing it, you, your broker, or your attorney can present the offer to the seller, his agent, or attorney. Submitting unsigned offers generally does not get the seller's full attention. And, if you have questions about financial and tax implications, consult your accountant before signing and submitting it as well.

Taking Title. An attorney can also advise on how to "take title" and how to file for a charter, if you wish to operate as a corporation.[62] Title is taken in the name of the entity that will buy the business. Generally, this entity is a person (individual) or a corporation. If it is to be a corporation, a corporate officer

---

61 When selecting an attorney, it is wise to remember that attorneys have specialties. Try to find one experienced in handling the sale of businesses.
62 It is not required to retain an attorney in order to apply with your Secretary of State for a charter, but every corporation needs a charter to become incorporated. As part of this process your attorney will prepare corporate by-laws and provide you with a Minutes Book.

must sign the purchase contract.[63] You can buy and own (take title to) the business in one of three ways: (1) as **a sole proprietorship** (you are the sole owner), (2) as a **partner** in a **partnership** (if you wish to have partners) or (3) in **corporate name,** if you own or wish to form a **corporation**. An existing corporation, of course, can buy and own more than one business. The "partners" could be or become shareholders in the owning corporation.

If you have decided to have partners or other shareholders, it is highly advisable to enter into a **preliminary operating agreement** or **pre-incorporation agreement** with them before you submit your offer. They may have opinions about the price and terms you offer. And it is highly advisable that they specifically authorize you in the agreement to buy the assets (or stock) of Doozy before you enter into a binding contract with the seller. Failure to have appropriate agreements between the partners or shareholders in place can result in costly and unfortunate disputes after a business is purchased. Problems between shareholders and partners could fill many books, but they generally arise because (1) no formal written agreement sets out the parties' financial responsibilities to each other or (2) how to resolve disputes when they arise. Let me cite an unfortunate case.

> **Case History: Shareholder Disputes.** Three shareholders (members) in an advertising company had signed an Operating Agreement. Their original intent was that there be four members. The Agreement was not specific enough to offer clear guidance about how to resolve disputes, but it did state that all votes required approval of 75% of the members. For better or worse, since there were only three members, nothing could be achieved without unanimity. Any member could request binding arbitration however. All three members were employed by the corporation, but the member who had been elected President had all the financial authority. Not wanting to use attorneys because of the cost or to irritate the President, no formal action was taken to resolve the disputes that arose. Three months later, the corporation (an LLC) had lost over $200,000 and the two minority members were still hesitating to involve an attorney. **Moral 1: Draft all agreements to fit the facts, i.e., the number of members. Moral 2: Don't hesitate to get help as soon as disputes arise. You could lose a lot of money.**

---

63   Sometimes offers to purchase are submitted before a corporate charter is issued. In such a case a purchase contract will include language like: "Buyer reserves right to take title (at closing) in corporate name."

As is the case with a seller, a buyer also must have proper authority to buy a business or to enter into a binding agreement to buy a business. Therefore, in addition to a pre-incorporation agreement, the shareholders or members of a corporation should adopt a **corporate resolution** that specifically sets out the authority of the person making an offer. Let's assume that you have agreed to purchase Doozy for $160,000 with a $100,000 down payment but only have $60,000 in available funds. Four friends agree to back you and put up $10,000 each. The pre-incorporation agreement states that stock will be issued to all five shareholders and that all five must put up their money by a certain date. This agreement might go on to state that the money would be used to purchase a specific business. After the corporation is formed, the shareholders should adopt a resolution authorizing you to enter into a contract with the business owner. It could be as brief as the following. The adopted resolution would be entered into the Corporate Minutes Book.

> "**Be It Resolved** *that John Doe is hereby authorized to offer to buy the assets of a business known as Doozy Manufacturing Corporation with principal place of business at (insert address) on the following terms (or at a price not to exceed $_____)* . . . . . .
>
> ATTEST, Secretary of _____ Corporation on this __day of _____(year)."

Description of Purchase Agreement. The basic blank purchase agreement (generally referred to as **Purchase Contract**) used by brokers is an uncomplicated two or three page document. It simply sets forth in binding legal language the same points of agreement listed in the letter of intent. In addition, there are almost always attachments to a contract. These are referred to as **Exhibits** and **Schedules**. They are always referenced in a contract and therefore become part of the contract. On larger or more complex transactions than the sale of Doozy, the contract might run to many more pages than the sample contract in the Appendix.

The Schedules, generally, list or describe in detail what assets it is you are agreeing to purchase, such as:

- Schedule of Furniture, Fixtures and Equipment (FF&E)
- Listing of Customer Accounts
- Schedule of Trademarks and Trade names
- Depreciation Schedule (necessary for stock sales)

The Exhibits, generally, are existing documents that set out in detail legal matters relating to the intended transaction. These may include:

- Lease on Business Premises
- Equipment Leases (on company trucks, for example)
- Employment Contracts
- Supplier Agreements
- Closing Balance Sheet on Business
- Non-Compete Agreement
- Management Assistance Agreement
- Price Sheets

There are some points in a purchase contract (and in the schedules and other documents attached to or incorporated into a contract) that only an attorney experienced in corporate law will know how to draft. These may include the seller's **warrants and representations**, escrow arrangements, non-competition agreements, and the like. The covenants and warrants in the body of the Sample Contract in the Appendix, plus the brief warrants listed in Special Stipulation 8 of the Sample Contract, are adequate for many small business sales. In addition there are "closing documents" that an attorney should draft, such as any Promissory Note that the buyer will give the seller. Despite efforts to standardize the form and content of many documents, certain documents that are valid in one state may not be valid in another state.

Notice that at the bottom of the Sample Contract (see page A-11) there are two signature lines for the seller: the first for his signature as an individual and the second for his signature as a corporate officer. If the seller is not a corporation, one signature line may be adequate to protect the buyer.

CONTRACTS AND THE LAW: Contracts are written for the purpose of protecting the parties to the contact. To me this means two things:

1. The parties to a contract each receive what they thought they had bargained for, and

2. The contract contains adequate remedies in the event that something unforeseen arises after the sale

In most cases, if a contract has been professionally drafted, and fully explained to the parties, there are no problems or misunderstandings. When problems arise it generally is because of a poorly drafted contract, not because of conscious intent to defraud or deceive. But occasionally one party or the other, more often the purchaser, is damaged financially in some way. So, it seems sensible to examine the possible causes of damage. These are: (1) the concealment of pertinent or material facts, (2) the non-disclosure of pertinent facts, and (3) the misstatement of material facts.

An example of "concealment" might be the seller's failure to tell the buyer that that there were several pending lawsuits against the selling corporation. An example of "non-disclosure" might be the omission of the fact that a corporation has several shareholders who were not aware that the majority shareholder was in negotiations for the sale of the company. An example of misstatement might be for the seller to accept an offer that clearly stated that: "all assets will be conveyed free and clear" when he knew that there were outstanding loans secured by some of the assets (cars, trucks, computers, etc.).

Another area that is open to misstatement involves a seller's customers. A seller may say that he has, for example, $100,000 in orders on the books when he knows that this is a guess or is untrue. If such a statement is a material inducement to the buyer, the buyer should check it out and include in the contract some statement from the seller binding him or making him legally liable in some way for any misrepresentation. What remedy, for example, would you have if, at closing on the purchase of Doozy, Unfilled Work Orders total only $65,000 instead of the $80,000 asked for in the letter of intent above?

A prudent buyer should be aware of several facts regarding concealment and non-disclosure. First, in most "arms length" commercial transactions, neither party has a duty to disclose to the other party all information that may have a bearing on an intended transaction. Second, a misstatement of information must result in injury or financial loss and, third, a misstatement must have been relied upon.[64] It must have been a material inducement for the buyer to go forward with the purchase.

---

64 Bergh, Louis O., *Business Law*, pages 59-61.

Only an imprudent buyer would say to himself that, if it turns out that something the seller said is wrong, "I can just sue him and collect damages." A buyer must do his own investigations and, if some representation seems important (material in legal language), require that the representation be included in the Warranties and Representations section of the contract. In other words, the buyer must "take the seller up" on what he says, if his statements have a bearing on the buyer's decision to buy or upon the price the buyer decides to offer.

Uniform Commercial Code and the Bulk Sales Act. Much fraud in the past revolved around the sale of inventory. If, for example, a company sells you its inventory for, say, $300,000 without informing you that the inventory had not been paid for, the suppliers of that inventory may have the right to come to your place of business and repossess their "goods" even though you had paid for them when you bought the business.

For reasons like that, the U.S. Congress in 1948 adopted the Uniform Commercial Code, which had as its objective not only the protection of the buyer from fraud but also the elimination of variations among the state laws governing the sale of "goods" (merchandise and other business assets). A part of this Code is the Bulk Sales Act, which was subsequently adopted by many States. Even States that did not adopt the Act *in toto* have adopted statutes that include many of its provisions.[65]

One of the purposes of the adoption of this Act was to prevent buyers from being scammed: business owners could sell their businesses, together with the goods that comprised them, to unsuspecting buyers before they had paid their suppliers. The suppliers could then repossess their "goods" and the buyers would be left with little recourse. For this reason many states require that, before a sale takes place, sellers give buyers signed affidavits listing all their creditors and the amounts owed to them.

It is then the responsibility of the buyer to notify the creditors of the impending sale and ask them to confirm the amounts the seller listed on the affidavit. In most cases notification is handled by the closing attorney, so the buyer has little knowledge of the amounts owed. The important thing is to be sure that the seller is in a position to pay off these debts before the closing or simultaneous with the closing from the buyer's (your) down payment. Check both the Accounts Payable balance and Cash balance on

---

65   Bergh, Louis O., *Business Law*, page 440.

seller's latest Balance Sheet. If your State has adopted the Bulk Sales Act provision of the Uniform Commercial Code, notification of creditors must be at least ten days prior to the closing.

If the seller is not in a position to retire these debts and convey the assets "free and clear", the buyer may consider assuming some of these debts as part payment of the purchase price. Assumption of debt is a common way to finance a business acquisition, particularly larger acquisitions, but it should not be done unless the buyer has all the facts and is protected by a "right of offset" clause in the Purchase Contract. See Stipulation 8 (**Seller Warrants**) in the Sample Contract and following discussion.

SELLERS' WARRANTIES and REPRESENTATIONS: The basic purchase contract does more than set out the terms and price that a buyer is offering. It also contains certain promises that the seller makes to the buyer regarding the condition of the business (or assets) being offered for sale. These promises are referred to as "**warranties and representations**." The seller must warrant, for example, that he (she) has good and marketable title to the assets and will remove any defects from title or Bill of Sale to make it marketable. Read carefully the paragraphs at the bottom of the first page of the sample contract and also Seller's Warrants on page A-10.

The seller also is expected to warrant something about the condition and quality of these assets and the accuracy of his (or the business's) financial statements, with language such as:

> *"All equipment is in good and working condition or will be by the time of the closing."*
>
> *"Seller warrants that accompanying financial statements for years _____ and _____ are true and accurate to the best of his knowledge."* (Include specific time periods)

Every buyer should think of other aspects of a business that the seller should warrant, since they may not all be included in a standard purchase contract or in the sample in the Appendix.

If the Contract states that certain terms and conditions must be met before a business is sold, the precise terms must either be attached to the Contract or spelled out in the Contract itself. For example, if the buyer observed that a certain piece of equipment was not working when he visited the plant, the Contract should state that there will be a re-inspection before closing. It might include the following or similar language:

> *"If any piece of equipment is not working at time of closing either (a) the closing will be delayed until Seller repairs it, or (b) Seller will reimburse Buyer the cost of having equipment restored to good working condition."*

There should be no ambiguity about the obligations each Party assumes as a condition of a sale. A failure to spell out these obligations in detail in the contract, and to spell out how and when each obligation will be satisfied, could result in serious and costly problems after the sale has been completed. Sometimes contracts include penalties for failure to complete an obligation in full or on time.

Some "attachments" to the contract are considered **closing documents** and are not available at the time the original contract is entered into between the parties. These attachments are documents that reflect what the parties have already agreed to, but which need to be put into proper legal form and, therefore, must be drafted by an attorney. An example mentioned above is the Promissory Note.

In addition to a detailed description of the four classes of business assets (listed in Chapter 3), it is normal that the purchase of a business includes two other very important assets that are not found on the Balance Sheets of most businesses:

1. **A non-compete agreement or restrictive covenant** in which the seller agrees not to compete with the buyer for a period of time (often 3-5 years) within a certain territory and in certain product lines or activities.

2. **A management assistance agreement** under which the seller agrees to provide certain specific services to the buyer after the sale for a certain period (perhaps several days or weeks at the place of business scheduled over 1-3 months, plus several hours of consultation by telephone during and after the completion of the "hands on" phase).

These two agreements are often vital to the success of a new business owner. They must be included in, or attached to, every purchase contract, if the buyer requests them to be. If the seller resists entering into such agreements, it is normal to expect the price of the business to be reduced. Note that the performance of these two assets (agreements) relies upon the owner of the business, individually. These agreements cannot be performed by the business itself. Care should, therefore, be taken to identify in the Contract who will perform the requirements of these two agreements and how much value will be allocated to them in order to protect you, the buyer, in the case of the seller's non-performance.

The terms of these additional agreements should be as specific as possible so that there is no misunderstanding after the sale has been closed regarding the seller's specific obligations or the penalty for his non-performance in whole or in part. If, for example, the seller proceeds to open a competing business after the sale, the seller may win back an exclusive product line or may take several of your key customers. Either of these events could reduce the value of the business and make it difficult for you to meet your or the business's financial obligations. For this reason, many contracts contain language stating that all or part of the deferred payments due seller will be waived if seller is in non-compliance or in violation of these agreements (or certain provisions of the agreements).

Conduct of Business Pending Closing. This section refers to how the Parties expect the seller to conduct (operate) his business between the acceptance of a contract to sell his business and the closing on the sale. Seller's "conduct of business" during this period can be critical to a buyer's success and should be covered adequately in a contract. Obviously, a buyer would not want significant changes to occur without his knowledge or approval or would not want the seller to be unavailable for consultation or delivery of documents.

The Purchase Contract in the Appendix touches on this important point only once. See the sentence at the end of paragraph 1 on page A-9. It states that the Seller covenants that his "Business will remain open during normal business hours." This covenant is not adequate to cover many things that could occur in a business between the date of signing a contract and the date of conveyance to the buyer. The standard way to cover issues concerning operation of the business is the following important covenant:

"The business will be conducted in the normal course pending closing"

However, each situation is different. The "normal course" clause above is adequate for many situations, but what is "normal" may need to be spelled out in some detail in the case of the business that you are buying. The management of inventory and the sale or purchase of expensive pieces of equipment, for example, can be issues in many acquisitions. Issues regarding employees and payroll can also be important. If a business takes on additional (and unanticipated) expense during the pre-closing period, the buyer's cash flow projections and, possibly, the price the buyer is willing to offer will have to be revised. These and similar issues can be handled by adding additional warranties or covenants (such as the following) to a contract. See **Seller Warrants** on page A-10.

> "All inventories will be replaced on an as needed basis by Seller."

> "Seller can make no material changes to the conduct of Business including the hiring or dismissing (key) employees with express written consent of Buyer."

It would not be unusual for the seller to reduce inventories or, perhaps, run them down dramatically, if not prohibited by contract. Some sellers tend to relax during this period of ownership transition; they feel their work is done and they can simply wait to pick up a check at the closing. Besides, reducing inventories will increase the Cash seller has on hand (and Cash is normally excluded from a sale), but it also in effect increases a seller's down payment since a buyer might immediately after closing have to replace merchandise. If seller reduces inventory, a business might lose some production or sales during the days or weeks following closing. This could be difficult if the buyer did not have a strong working capital cushion (in addition to his down payment).

Buyers' Warranties. Buyer warranties are not the "standard" but buyers are expected in some situations to give warranties to sellers. Such warranties are generally intended to (1) make the seller feel more secure and (2) assure seller that buyer will not "bleed" the business, that is, remove assets such as excess cash from the business while still indebted to seller. If a buyer pays himself $100,00, for example, rather than $50,000 during his first year of ownership, the business will have $50,000 less Cash Flow available to meet debt obligations.

These warranties often evolve during the negotiating process. A seller may agree to certain more favorable **terms of purchase** (such as a lower down payment) if a buyer "warrants that he will limit his personal compensation to "no more than $75,000 per year for the first three years following closing." Or, perhaps, if there is a lease in place on the business premises that the buyer wishes to assume (rather than attempting to negotiate a new lease with the landlord), the seller might require a **warrant** that the buyer will personally hold him (the seller) harmless from any future lease obligations.

Another reasonable warrant for a seller to request is one regarding insurance. Such a warrant may be worded:

> *"Buyer warrants that until the Promissory Note held by Seller is paid in full to keep all assets fully insured at their market values."*

The more willing a buyer is to offer a seller reasonable protection, the more willing a seller generally is to accept "terms" in lieu of a "cash" contract. Frankly, in my experience, most sellers do not fully understand the process of selling their businesses or the protection that may be available to them if they accept a sale on terms. They must be educated.

When purchasing stock (instead of assets), the seller is expected to warrant the net worth of the corporation. Let's say the net worth, after completing an audit, is $800,000. If the buyer buys the stock on terms, the seller might require him to warrant that "he will at all times following closing maintain a net worth of $800,000 or not less than the balance owed to seller, whichever is greater" or "maintain a net worth equal to 110% of the balance due seller." The extra 10% requirement is to protect seller from absorbing the costs of liquidation or of reselling the company in the event of a default by buyer.

Remedies for Non-Performance by Seller. What if Seller (1) does not do everything he has promised to do in the purchase agreement, or (2) if some of the promises (warranties) turn out to be overstated or false? Does a buyer have any remedies? Can the buyer return the business to the seller and get his money back? The broad answer is that "the contract does the talking." If the contract is silent on how to handle misrepresentations, the remedies may be limited to hiring an attorney to bring suit against the seller for the damages the buyer has suffered as a result of the misrepresentations. Of course, the legal process can be a costly and lengthy affair.

It is far better to spell out **remedies** in the purchase contract. See, for example, Stipulation 8 (b) in the sample contract. It reads: "There are no undisclosed liabilities, claims or pending or threatened litigation, and Seller will defend and hold Purchaser harmless from same if any shall arise from actions which took place prior to the closing." This is the so-called "**hold harmless**" clause and it should be in every contract in some form. Of course, this stipulation could be more detailed, spelling out different remedies for different infractions.

One of the most effective remedies is what is referred to as the **right of offset**. This is a right that lets the buyer "offset" certain costs against future payments due the seller. For example, if seller warrants that "there are no undisclosed liabilities" and it turns out that the seller owes the landlord money, perhaps for Common Area Maintenance (CAM) charges that had not been billed by the time his business was sold, or to the tax authorities (for non-payment of the prior year's personal property tax, for example), what could you do?

It is normally prudent to pay **undisclosed liabilities**, because failure to do so might seriously interrupt your business. There is often not time to dispute the charges with the former owner or in court. For this reason most contracts includes language that lets the buyer pay the charges and deduct or "offset" the charges paid against future payments due the seller.

Before exercising this **right of offset** the buyer must first inform the seller that he has received a bill that he did not agree to assume (or a bill that was more than the debt he agreed to assume) and give the seller time to either pay the bill or dispute it. Many contracts have wording like:

> *"If the disputed item remains unpaid ten (10) days after notification, buyer has right to pay same and deduct amount paid from next payment due seller."*

The possible existence of undisclosed liabilities (even when seller has signed all the appropriate warranties) is one important reason to always hold back some portion of the purchase price. Of course the buyer's best remedies are (1) to be thorough during the analysis and due diligence phases (2) draft the purchase agreement carefully with professional help and (3) review the results of the **lien search** which all experienced closing attorneys will perform.

Another "remedy" is to pro-rate certain predictable expenses at the closing. Most closing attorneys will do this automatically and show each party's share on the settlement sheet, but **pro-rating** bears mention here as a remedy. The monthly rent, the payroll, payroll taxes, real estate and personal property taxes and insurance premiums are predictable. Ask the attorney to split, or pro-rate, these expenses between the parties at the closing. If, for example, the seller has paid the monthly rent of $2,000 and the closing is on the 15th, the buyer will be expected to reimburse one-half or $1,000 at closing. However, if the rent had not been paid, the seller should reimburse the buyer $1,000.

EARNEST MONEY: The purpose of earnest money is to "bind" the seller to the buyer. For this reason, earnest money is often called the binder. By accepting the earnest money and letting a third party hold it on his behalf, the seller is generally agreeing not to negotiate with or even talk to other potential buyers for a certain length of time.

In virtually every case, an offer to purchase a business is in writing and accompanied by an earnest money check.[66] This check is normally held by the broker (if the seller is represented by a broker) and deposited in the broker's escrow account upon acceptance of all the terms of the offer by both buyer and seller. The broker in such cases would be the **escrow agent**. However, you might elect to have the seller's attorney or your bank hold the **earnest money**. There are many options for how and where the earnest money is held.

The amount of earnest money that is appropriate is the subject of some ongoing discussion among professionals. It seems safe to say that the standard is between 5% and 10% of the offering price. Thus, in the case of Doozy, the **earnest money binder** might be around $10,000. Conventions vary from city to city. The purpose of the earnest money is to let the seller know that you are a serious buyer. A larger binder always makes the buyer appear more serious to the seller.

At closing, the earnest money is paid to seller as part of the down payment specified in a contract. In practice the escrow agent gives the check to the closing attorney who disperses checks to the seller. The earnest money cannot be spent prior to the closing; it is simply held in escrow.

---

66 It is advisable to "let the contract do the talking." It is not advisable to ask a seller directly if he or she will accept an offer of, say, $100,000. There are too many unknowns at this stage in the negotiations. Even if a seller says, "Yes, I will accept it," the seller may not realize that your verbal offer includes (in your mind) all the inventory. The seller may intend (in his mind) to sell the business for $100,000 plus the value of the inventories.

Earnest money is not "at risk" of being lost or forfeited until all the "conditions" of the offer or Purchase Contract have been met. If any conditions cannot be met (within the times or dates stipulated in the Contract), the escrow agent must return the earnest money to the buyer, in full, when asked to do so. Be sure that the seller understands the importance of adhering to these times or dates. However, if all conditions have been met and the buyer does not close by the agreed upon closing date, the earnest money is "at risk" and could be forfeited.

Every condition must have a specific date set out by which it must be completed or removed by the responsible party. If the responsible party has not met the terms of a condition by the date specified, the other party generally has the right to withdraw from the contract or the Contract may be deemed null and void, depending upon how the Contract is drafted. The thought of reading and signing a Purchase Contract can be intimidating, but it is simply your offer to buy the assets or stock of a business. The essence of a Contract is something like this:

> "I'll offer you a price of $X and a down payment of $Y, if you will sell me your business, sign an agreement not to compete with me for five (5) years and stick around after the sale for two months to train me, provided that I can meet certain conditions (see below)."

Any offer should identify the specific assets you wish to purchase (with dollar amounts for the "countable" items such as inventories) and set out all the "conditions of sale."

CONTINGENT NATURE OF CONTRACTS: It is quite common for a contract to include a few conditions that must be met before a sale will go forward. These "conditions of sale" are generally referred to as **contingencies**. The most common involve a buyer's ability to accomplish certain important tasks before a contract is enforceable, especially the task of arranging financing to meet the terms set out in the Contract. Thus, an offer will include language like:

> "This offer is contingent upon Purchaser's ability to obtain or to satisfy the following specific conditions"

These conditions do not necessarily pertain to Doozy, or to any specific business, and are not intended to be all-inclusive, but each of them could be important. Review with your broker and attorney, or other trusted advisor, the "conditions" you feel should be included in your contract. There may be others important to your particular situation.

THIS CONTRACT IS CONTINGENT UPON PURCHASER'S ABILITY TO: (SAMPLE)

Lease on Business Premises: Secure on or before a certain date (insert date) a lease on premises, say, for five years at $10 per square foot (or at the lease rate the business now pays) from the owner or landlord.

Acquisition Financing: Obtain by <u>insert date</u> a bank loan of at least $200,000 (sometimes a specific bank is named) at an interest rate of not more than 8% annual percentage rate (APR) secured by personal assets of the buyer, with "interest only" paid for the first six months after closing.

Working Capital Loan: Borrow the sum of $100,000 at 8% APR from __name of bank__ with the inventory and equipment included in the sale as collateral for the loan.

Appraisals: Obtain qualified appraisals on the (real estate) (equipment) (inventory) etc., giving a combined value of at least $300,000.

Approvals: Receive from Seller's suppliers (customers) written approval at least (ten) (twenty) days prior to the stipulated closing date for Purchaser to assume or obtain (contracts) (dealerships) (lines of merchandise) on the same terms now in force.

Permits and Licenses: Obtain all required permits and licenses from the various governmental authorities.(It is useful sometimes to list the required permits individually.)

Earnings Confirmation: Confirm the representations on Seller's financial statements and tax returns for the past two fiscal years and do other related analyses and "due diligence."[67] Or, Purchaser's

---

67 The term "due diligence" cannot be defined specifically. It is not an accounting term. It refers to the process of doing the investigations and analyses necessary to determine that a business is in fact in the condition it was represented to be in and that all contingencies and other conditions of sale have been or can be met. See Glossary.

ability to confirm that adjusted pre-tax earnings last year, calculated on the accrual method, for example, is at least $50,000.

Compliance: Inspect business premises and determine that all equipment is in good working order and the facilities are in compliance with all applicable regulations. When buying a business that includes real estate, compliance with environmental regulations is especially important. Example: Sale is contingent upon confirmation that property is above flood levels.

Inventory: Obtain a count and valuation of all inventories (using current vendor catalogues or supplier price lists or invoices) immediately prior to closing and, if their total value is less (more) than the value offered in the contract, to reduce (increase) the purchase price and down payment by the amount of the shortage (overage).*

Accounts Receivable and Accounts Payable: Confirm account balances with customers or vendors.[68] Generally, a buyer will not assume accounts payable or other current liabilities and will not purchase the accounts receivable. If he does either, the offer should include provisions requiring the seller's personal guarantees regarding: (1) collectablity of the receivables and (2) remedies in the event that the assumed liabilities are greater than agreed. These points are necessary to mitigate the buyer's risk. See "hold harmless."

It is most unusual for the amount of inventory set out in a contract to match the amount on hand at closing. Thus, some adjustment to the purchase price is almost always necessary.

Failure to include important contingencies into a contract or to remove or satisfy a contingency can cause problems down the road. Many sellers and buyers have become impatient and decided to move ahead and close. The refrain "we can take care of that later" still rings in my ears. The following story illustrates the potential dangers in taking that approach.

---

68 Sometimes all the confirmations are not available at time of closing. Audit or other financial records as of the day of closing cannot be prepared until those records have been compiled. Contracts, therefore, stipulate that there will be adjustments made when those records are available, generally within five or six weeks of closing.

> **Case History: The Importance of Permits.** The purchaser of a security guard business failed to obtain a license from the governing state agency. In fact, he had not been told that a license was necessary. When a customer asked to see his license, the buyer was red-faced. But he promptly called the State agency and asked if they would allow him to stay in business if he promptly enrolled in the required pre-licensing class. Fortunately, the state authorities agreed, but the buyer was operating "outside the law" for months. The licensing process cost this buyer considerable time and money. **Moral: Find out what licenses are required before making an offer and include a suitable contingency clause.**

Acquisition Financing and Liens. If a contract is contingent upon third party financing, it is wise to identify specifically the assets that will be offered as collateral, because the lender, usually a bank, may require a **first lien** against them. Seller will have a **second lien** on those assets behind that lender, if he finances some portion of the sale. He may not agree to subordinate his lien rights. Doing so would particularly complicate matters (in the seller's mind) if he had to take the business back. A good counter argument is that the bank will be seller's best watchdog; the bank will do everything possible to prevent a default, including reviewing the buyer's financial statements and, maybe, limiting buyer's compensation. This potential problem may be resolved by giving the bank first lien on some assets and the seller first lien on others.

Observing Dates for Removing Contingencies. As in all contracts, dates are very important. Just as the contract specifies that the closing must occur by a certain date, so each contingency should have a specific date for its completion, satisfaction, or removal. The completion dates may be the same as the closing date agreed to in the contract. However, most buyers would want to know as soon as possible if a contingency will be met. Therefore, certain contingencies may have earlier (and possibly different) dates for their completion.

The time between contract acceptance and closing is not a time for a buyer to sit back and watch the grass grow. A thirty-day period for removing the contingencies can go by very quickly. The danger to the buyer is, if the seller becomes convinced that the buyer has not made a "good faith" effort to remove the contingencies, he will not agree to a contract extension and may, in fact, be legally entitled to enter into a contract with another buyer. You cannot simply tell the seller on the 30th day that you could not get a necessary bank loan and expect your earnest money returned.

Any offer should spell out in detail all necessary conditions of sale. This means conditions imposed upon buyer or seller. If any condition imposed upon the seller is not met by the date set out in the accepted offer, you would have the legal right then either to: (a) restructure your offer or (b) request return of your earnest money. Whether you choose (a) or (b), do so promptly and do so in writing, so that there can be no misunderstanding. If you do not notify seller, it can be assumed by your silence that the conditions have been met to your satisfaction and that the closing date does not need to be extended. However, you must be diligent in attempting to satisfy your conditions if you expect your earnest money to be returned.

Remember that your contract may include "by reference" some schedules or exhibits. If these are not attached to the contract, the contract is generally not enforceable until all parties have received and approved every document that has been made part of the contract.

ALLOCATION OF PURCHASE PRICE: As stated above, a contract or offer should specifically identify the nature, quantity and value of each asset (or class of assets) to be sold. It is understood that assets not specifically identified in the offer will be excluded from a sale, but sometimes it is helpful to also identify any assets that the parties agree to exclude.[69] This process of assigning values in the purchase contract is referred to as the **allocation of purchase price**. If it is not written out, there can be costly misunderstandings, because allocation has income tax and other implications for both parties. For you, as a buyer, the values allocated are the value that are shown on your starting Balance Sheet and are used as the basis for your future depreciation.

Let's look at a possible allocation included in an offer to purchase (the assets of) Doozy. The values given each class of assets are close to their estimated market values. From the buyer's point of view the objective to is "write off" the entire purchase price, that is, to deduct from future earnings as much of the purchase price as possible. This means assigning larger

---

[69] It is normal practice for the broker to provide the buyer with a complete description of the FF&E when the buyer is introduced to a business. See Schedule of Daycare FF&E and Description of Rental Equipment in Chapter 1.

How to Buy a Business without Being Had

values (when possible and when acceptable to the IRS) to assets that can be written down, depreciated (**tangible assets**) or amortized (**intangible assets**) and smaller values to others.

For example, you may want to add value to the FF&E to reflect the recent purchase of Doozy's new $15,000 truck. The seller may resist because he wrote off the entire $15,000 purchase price as a Section 179 expense and, as a consequence, the full value allocated to the truck will be taxed to him as ordinary income. The seller, quite logically, wants to minimize the income taxes due from the sale, so there is usually some negotiation surrounding the allocation issue. Note that the allocation in Table 14 below shows considerably more detail about values than the Letter of Intent. This is quite normal and very appropriate.

If the seller does not accept the initial offering price of $150,000 and you want to raise your offer, the price must be reallocated. In this situation, you may assign value to other assets, to the trade name Doozy, for example, or add value to the assets shown below. **The allocation, including values assigned to Goodwill, must always equal the purchase price.**

Table 14. Allocation of Purchase Price

Value of Raw Materials	$20,000
Value of FF&E, Tools and Dies (fixed assets)	45,000
Value of Miscellaneous Supplies	5,000
Value of Management Assistance	20,000
Value of Restrictive Covenant (4 years)	30,000
Value of Work-in-Process	20,000
Value of Finished Goods	10,000
Possible Offering Price:	**$150,000**

> **Case History: Missing Allocation of Purchase Price.** (Failure to make an allocation can lead to problems.) The parties did not want to hold up closing, so the closing attorney added this language to the contract: "Parties have agreed to handle the allocation of the purchase price outside of closing." The seller wanted the allocation "low" so he could keep his income taxes low. The buyer wanted higher allocations so he could "write off" more depreciation. The parties never came to a meeting of the minds. As a result the buyer could not set up his starting balance sheet and the seller could not file his federal tax return. The seller's attorney became upset with the buyer and sued him. The combined legal fees far exceeded any tax savings either party may have enjoyed from receiving a more favorable allocation. **Moral: Don't forget to allocate.**

Deductions from Pre-tax Income. In the years after purchasing a business, the buyer can probably take "tax deductions" from earnings in the amounts set out below in Table 15, or slightly more.[70] The amount of the deductions depends upon several choices every buyer must make. The most important of these choices is generally how to depreciate the fixed (or depreciable) assets acquired in a sale.

In the Doozy contract **Fixed Assets** are assigned a "contract" value of $45,000. You, as buyer, can depreciate the $45,000 in several ways. If the value is written off over five (5) years, tax deductions are $9,000 per year (so called **straight line depreciation**). You could write off 150% or even 200% of the "straight line" amount, which is **accelerated depreciation**. In Doozy's case, at 200%, your first year write-off would be $18,000. Depending upon the useful life of each asset (or class of assets), the buyer might decide to write them off in less than five years or to take a longer write-off.

If you choose to take **accelerated depreciation**, the amount of depreciation you can take will decline each succeeding year. Many buyers accept this trade-off because it is important in the early years of ownership to reduce or postpone expenses, including the expense of income taxes.

If forecast earnings for the first year are no more than, say, $36,000, there will be no income tax due. After taking $42,900 in deductions

---

[70] It is advisable to ask the advice of a CPA before agreeing to an allocation of purchase price for tax reasons because the IRS has guidelines concerning what is reasonable and defensible.

in Year 1 as shown in Table 15 below, in fact, there will be a tax loss of $6,900. This loss can be carried over to Year 2, thereby increasing Year 2 tax deductions from $21,700 to $28,600. It is important to your **cash flow** to allocate the purchase price a manner that will reduce taxable income in the years following the purchase. Remember that depreciation is a non-cash deduction; it is a write-off. The other items, such as the value assigned to management assistance, are generally paid in cash in the year in which the deduction is taken.

Table 15. Buyer's Non-Cash and Other Tax Deductions

	Year 1	Year 2	Year 3	Year 4
Depreciation ($45,000/5 years)	$9,000	$9,000	$9,000	$9,000
Management Assistance	20,000	0	0	0
Restrictive Covenant	7,500	7,500	7,500	7,500
Interest on $100,000 Note[70]	6,400	5,200	3,800	2,400
Total Deductions	**$42,900**	**$21,700**	**$20,300**	**$18,900**

The fact that most of the purchase price of a business can be written off, or expensed, over time, as appears to be the case with Doozy, supports the use of "pre-tax" income instead of "after-tax" income when estimating the **earnings value** of a business. Some appraisers disagree on this point. Use of after-tax earnings might be more appropriate when valuing businesses that: (1) are larger than Doozy and (2) sell for several times more than their book value.

If you elect to buy stock instead of the assets, the situation is different because you will use the same **depreciation schedule** that the present corporation has been using. In Doozy's case the **fixed assets** have been fully depreciated, so there would be no depreciation deduction available to you until new assets are purchased. The other deductions on Table 15 will be available.

Because some "to be purchased" assets may be owned individually (not by Doozy Manufacturing Co., Inc.), several parties must sign the Contract, even if they are the same person. This person signs in two capacities. If the Non-Compete and Management Transition Agreements are in separate documents, they must also be signed. The Contract should

---

71 The interest payments shown are not exact. They have been rounded.

clearly state which of the deferred payments (if any) the buyer will pay to the business (the corporation) and which will be paid to the owner (or other parties) personally.

After making an offer, you will probably receive a counter offer, as happened with the **letter of intent**.[72] This is normal. There are often several exchanges of offers, counter offers, and responses. Even if the price and terms of payment offered are accepted, there are often other "terms" that require further negotiation. In these cases, the business broker can be your best ally. He knows the seller and will understand the meaning of all terms used in your offer. If there is any uncertainty about the meaning of any part of the written offer, or counter offer, consult an attorney because the written word controls. Verbal agreements are not enforceable and should be avoided.

Suggestion. If it is still difficult to determine what price to offer, see if there are similar businesses on the market in your trade area. Review the Business for Sale classification in local publications. Check prices at which they are offered. If they are listed through a broker, consult the broker to learn if they are similar to Doozy in terms of annual sales, earnings history, asset value, and the like. Brokers want to be helpful because you may become a client, if you find them to be helpful.

But, for the moment, let's assume that your offer to buy Doozy has been accepted on the terms set out below and we can move to the due diligence process and the closing process.

Price: $150,000 with a down payment of $55,000

Balance: payable in two five-year notes @ 8.5% annual interest

Note 1 - $50,000 Note secured by the various inventories

Note 2 - $45,000 Note secured by the fixed assets

Monthly principle and Interest: $1,949

---

72 The (your) original contract will contain wording like: "This offer is open for acceptance until (insert specific date)." Be careful to observe and to enforce the dates in your offer because an acceptance received after the specified date will not be binding unless negotiations between the Parties to the contract have continued by mutual agreement after that date. If there are questions about this point, talk to an attorney.

Negotiating the Final Contract. This process should not be intimidating. It might be more intimidating if the seller accepted your offer without changing a word. What usually happens is that the seller signs the offer with some changes: he marks through several items in your offer, inserts new wording, initials the changes, and gives the offer back to you. This is his counteroffer. Some of the requested changes may be words; some may be numbers. In some case, the seller or his broker or attorney may insert a new paragraph covering some point that you had not addressed in your offer. Some typical changes involve price, down payment, earnest money, closing date, terms of any promissory note, and the date for acceptance of the offer (or counteroffer).

You then review the requested changes. It may be prudent to share the counteroffer with your attorney, particularly if the changes are lengthy or complicated. If you agree with the requested changes, simply add your initials beside the seller's initials. Then promptly deliver the contract with the initialed changes back to the seller. At this point the offer becomes a binding contract. It is an agreement between two parties subject, of course, to the fulfillment of the conditions set out in the final offer. If you feel that you cannot accept some of the changes, mark through them, insert what you prefer and initial.

This offer/counteroffer process may involve several exchanges of documents and, sometimes, requests for additional information. If there is a broker, the broker goes back and forth between the parties. It's his job to work out the details. For larger businesses this negotiating process may take several weeks. For smaller businesses, the process is often resolved in two or three days. In most cases (where there is a broker) you will have given the broker some idea what your negotiating positions are. This helps more the process along. During this process, it may be necessary to change the dates set out in your offer—the "acceptance" date and the "closing" date. See the last two paragraphs of the sample Purchase Contract on page A-9.

In some situations the seller will not accept your offer or make a counteroffer. This occurs very infrequently, usually when the parties are far apart in their opinions of fair value of the business. Your offer then expires if your offer or purchase contract includes these (or similar words): This instrument is open for acceptance until noon of the __ day of _____. The seller is then free to enter into negotiations with other buyers.

SUMMARY CHECKLIST for CONTRACTS: This is a review of the essential components of an offer. Does your contract (letter of intent, draft contract, offer or purchase agreement) include, at a minimum, the following information?

1. Seller's warranty that all assets will be conveyed in fee simple free from any and all defects?
2. Selling price (have you calculated the present value?)
3. Down payment at closing plus any deferred portion?
4. Amount of principle and interest to be paid to Seller? To bank or others?
5. Dates on which all payments are to be made?
6. Dates on which each payment becomes delinquent or incurs a late charge?
7. Collateral for each of the deferred obligations?
8. Terms and conditions for reducing or releasing collateral?
9. The closing date on the sale of the business?
10. List of contingencies and dates for their fulfillment or removal?
11. Right of offset clause (in case of undisclosed liabilities)?
12. Addresses to which all payments are to be sent or made?
13. Allocation of selling price, including all assets to be conveyed?
14. The earnest money? Who will hold it? When can it be returned?
15. Where and when will the Seller's management assistant be provided?
16. Under what conditions may the stated selling price be adjusted?
17. Procedures for valuing the inventory?
18. How to contact seller after the sale is complete?

It is also important to understand Parties' rights or remedies in event of:

1. Payment on any note or other deferred obligation is late
2. A loan or note is in default
3. Buyer fails to close on the sale on the date stipulated
4. Seller refuses to close (sell) on the date stipulated
5. Inventory value(s) differ from values shown in the Allocation of the Purchase Price section of the signed (final) purchase contract

6. Certain assets are not on premises or in good working order at closing
7. Seller does not provide all management assistance as promised
8. Seller violates some part of the non-competition agreement

CHAPTER 7
THE CLOSING ON THE SALE

Part I. THE DUE DILIGENCE PROCESS

After a purchase contract has been negotiated and signed by the parties, and all changes inserted in the contract in longhand have been initialed, original copies are given to each party. Then the closing process begins. It consists of two distinct parts: the **due diligence** process, which begins as soon as the contract is signed, perhaps thirty days before the closing, and **the actual closing**. That is the day when the sale occurs and ownership changes hands. With smaller businesses, this process may take only a week or two. With larger businesses, the process usually takes well over a month, especially if approval from suppliers, bankers or other third parties is needed.

The due diligence process was touched upon in the previous chapter. It essentially is the process by which the buyer: (1) confirms the representations and other promises made by the seller in the purchase contract and (2) removes or satisfies contingencies set out in a contract. Remember, a sale is almost always contingent upon the satisfaction of certain conditions by buyer and/or seller, such as "buyer's ability to obtain a lease (or lease extension) on the business premises" from the landlord or seller's ability to confirm or back up some verbal representation he made about profit or cash flow as an inducement to the buyer (to submit and offer).

The buyer of Doozy believes that the business during the last fiscal year earned $31,000 (after deducting the owner's salary) on sales of $300,000. The buyer also believes that Doozy's physical plant is adequate to handle sales of about $463,000 without the need for any new equipment. It is obviously important to the buyer to be able to confirm these assumptions. However, the Contract is silent on these matters. Why? Because the buyer was advised not to draw attention to what the business could do in the future, since the seller may at the 11th hour conclude that he "underpriced" the business and want to take it off the market. Buyer was, instead, advised to focus on two things during his due diligence process: (1) the financial results the business had reported in the past and (2) on the values of the assets to be conveyed.

The signed Purchase Contract contained only five contingencies (all fairly typical) that had to be satisfied during the due diligence period. The Contract stated:

> *"This Contract is contingent upon Buyer's ability to satisfy the following conditions:*
>
> 1. *Confirm that last year's sales were at least $300,000.*
> 2. *Obtain a new lease on the premises for five years at a gross rent of no more than $1,800 per month.*
> 3. *Obtain an independent appraisal confirming that the FF&E has a value of $45,000.*
> 4. *Confirm that Doozy had in hand at time of closing bona fide signed customer work orders of at least $60,000 and unbilled work-in-process of at least $24,000.*
> 5. *Confirm that there are on hand inventories (of resale merchandise, raw material, and finished goods) with a book value, contract value or original cost of at least $30,000."*

After analyzing Doozy's financial history, the Buyer chose to keep the Contract as simple as possible. He felt he would be adequately protected if the five conditions set out above were met or exceeded. Note that: (1) the $1,800 monthly Rent in Contingency 2 exceeds Doozy's current $1,500 monthly Rent shown on Table 7, and (2) the $24,000 Work-in-process exceeds the $20,000 value allocated in the

Purchase Price in Table 13.[73] The Seller may or may not agree to all these conditions, especially No. 4. However, the buyer felt that there might be more work-in-process in the shop than the seller had told him originally. Besides, there is no harm in asking. Condition 4 could be a useful negotiating tool.

The "contingencies" for other businesses are often lengthier. The average buyer's greatest fear is that the earnings or sales of a company have been overstated, so, often, there are several "contingencies" dealing with past earnings. If it turns out that earnings were overstated, the buyer may be hard pressed to meet his debt service requirements or to pay himself an adequate salary, so, clearly, it is important to be able to confirm that earnings are equal to or greater than represented. The following case history is fairly typical.

> **Case History: Need to Confirm Earnings.** A wholesale distributor reported pre-tax earnings of $500,000 for the past twelve months, an increase of $100,000 over the prior year. The buyer, relying upon this representation, offered $2,700,000 and inserted into the Contract a condition that he be able to confirm the $500,000[73] earnings. Seller agreed. However, **due diligence** turned up the following negative adjustments:
>
> 1. Rent of $6,000 for the last month had not been paid.
> 2. Outstanding commissions and profit sharing obligations of company totaled $150,000, and
> 3. At least $150,000 of the accounts receivable from the past year seemed to be uncollectible.

---

73 A comment on Rent: If the buyer were fortunate enough to secure a new lease at less than $1,800 per month, the savings would increase projected income. Also, Rent is what is called a "fixed expense." It will probably not change over the next five years. Most expenses are what are called "variable expenses." They will generally rise at least with the rate of inflation. When preparing your budget, always distinguish between the two.

74 In the case of businesses with substantial earnings, the "contingency" might be worded to read: "contingent upon buyer's ability to confirm pre-tax earnings within 5% or even 10% of the reported earnings."

There was no explanation for why Rent had not been paid. The profit sharing was not due until ninety days after the end of the year and was not recorded in past years until it was paid. Since pre-tax earnings equaled 10% of sales, the $150,000 in doubtful accounts receivable represented overstated earnings of about $15,000. Adding the unpaid rent, preliminary earnings were overstated by $21,000 or 4.2%, which is not very serious. The serious part is the $150,000 in accrued obligations. It turned out that the company recorded $110,000 in accrued commission obligations the year before. Thus, a negative adjustment of $40,000 appeared in order ($150,000-110,000). The total of the three adjustments is $61,000, or over 10% of the reported earnings. The buyer felt that the adjusted earnings of $439,000 ($500,000 less $61,000) were inadequate to support the price he had offered, so he requested the owner to reduce the price from $2,700,000 to $2,400,000. The seller would not budge from the original contract price. Fortunately for the buyer, the contingency in his contract giving him the right to confirm the company's earnings let him withdraw from the contract. **Moral: Be sure the contract gives the right to confirm seller's financial representations. Without it, this buyer would have been in trouble (or lost his binder).**

When Financial Statements are Missing or Incomplete. From time to time the unincorporated sole proprietorships will have incomplete financial statements. Performing "due diligence" is a little different when the statements are not as complete as Doozy's (or in the case of the business discussed above), but it is still very important; in fact, it is vital to "buying a business without being had." As a buyer you might hear a seller say that he earned, say, $50,000, but, according to the only available financial statement, the seller's business showed a small loss. Let's assume that you have found such a business and, in fact, are ready to submit an offer. How should you proceed? What kind of contingency clause or other protection should you put in your contract?

The due diligence process is often quite simple, especially when the buyer has experience in the industry. For example, buyers of convenience stores, which are "all cash" businesses, are usually concerned only with the top line, that is, the gross sales. This is true because buyers with extensive industry knowledge know exactly what the **cost of goods** is from their experience with similar stores and they know what their **operating**

expenses will be.[75] They know the rhythm of the sales, that is, the times of the day or week when sales are normally high and when they are normally low. And, they know that an average sale is exactly, for example, $8.52. They estimate that the Cost of Goods for beverage products is 20% and that beverage products can comprise 70% of gross sales. These buyers know a lot about the business they are looking at, so the sole contingency might read:

> "This Contract is contingent upon Buyer's ability to confirm that current weekly sales total at least $20,000. If Buyer does not notify Seller to the contrary by *(insert date)*, it is agreed that this contingency has been satisfied in full."

To satisfy this contingency, a buyer can count the number of customers entering the store during certain hours and watch what products the customers leave the store with. A buyer can also look at the record of purchases in a store. That's easy to do if all purchases come from one or two sources (venders). If the cost of goods is 20%, then gross sales are estimated to be five times purchases. If purchases are expected to be 40% of sales, multiply by 2.5 to get sales, and so on. This system isn't perfect, but is very useful when the owner of a business pays cash for some purchases. Simply adding up the checks posted to "purchases" in such a business will not work.

Some buyers want to count the daily receipts or review daily cash register tapes (or records) to determine sales. This is quite accurate unless the owner has paid any vendor in cash for certain purchases. If sales appear low, ask the owner if he has paid vendors in cash and if he has kept a record of such purchases.

During due diligence, one seller boasted that "this business put my four kids through college," but the business showed only a modest profit. Fortunately, the office employee (who did not want to lose her job) was very

---

75 The Cost of Goods should generally be a relatively fixed percent of Gross Sales. To calculate the percent in many small businesses it is sufficient to divide the purchases made during a period of time by the sales (or revenue). However, when it is believed that the sales figures are incomplete, it is important to get a typical Costs of Goods percent from other sources or from other similar businesses. In larger businesses, the cost of Purchases and Cost of Goods may differ substantially because of changes in Inventory levels.

cooperative. She had a complete record of purchases and knew exactly what the Cost of Goods was. After speaking with her, the buyer was satisfied that the seller's representations about profitability were accurate. To see how another buyer satisfied the contingency in his contract about sales, see Case History below.

> **Case History: Due Diligence without Financial Records.** A convenience store had no reliable records of sales or earnings. The buyer did, however, know some employees at the beer and gasoline distributors that supplied the convenience store. They told him what the value of weekly shipments had been. To these figures the buyer added the standard markup to derive an estimate of sales of these products. To determine miscellaneous sales the buyer and his brother sat in their car in the parking lot and counted the number of walk-in customers who entered the store during selected periods. The customer count was more than satisfactory. In fact, based upon this information, the buyers determined that actual weekly sales were well in excess of the $20,000 estimate provided by the seller. **Moral: When reliable financial records are not available, there are still ways to perform extensive and accurate "due diligence."**

Obviously, you should proceed cautiously when the only available financial statements appear misleading or suggest that profits are less than the owner tells you they are. However, there are almost always ways to reconstruct statements and to confirm with considerable accuracy the sales and gross profit of a small business. The basic lesson learned through trial and error by many buyers is never to buy a business without putting adequate contingency clauses in a contract to protect them in the event that it is not possible to confirm sales, cash, flow, profit or other key financial criteria.

Renegotiation. If changes in the purchase contract, in the price or in the terms of purchase, are indicated by factors that come to light during due diligence, further negotiations are needed. Since the original contract has been negotiated and accepted, I call this process **renegotiation**. The due diligence process may bring to light factors that make a business appear more profitable or less profitable to the buyer. Often due diligence brings to light positive things about a business that even the seller did not know. In such cases no renegotiation is needed.

When due diligence suggests that earnings are overstated, renegotiation is called for. Many sellers will agree to a downward adjustment in the price. Some will not. But, do not hesitate to ask. And always, put your request in writing. If the seller fully understands why you have concluded, or feel, earnings are overstated, he may be more inclined to accept some favorable adjustment. However, as you might expect, the seller's first reaction often is to become defensive. If you want to buy the business, it is important to respect seller's feelings and not lose heart.

Further negotiations, over time, may open up ways to bridge the gap between the price the seller wants and the price that you have determined is fair. Ask the seller to respond to revised offers in writing. In the seller's responses he may reveal things he would like added to the contract. These become a basis for trade offs. At this stage in the negotiating process, the total price that the seller receives from a transaction is not always the foremost thing on his mind. Listed below are a couple of responses that may lead to a successful conclusion of the renegotiation process. For example the seller might say: I will agree to reduce the contract price by $30,000 if you will:

1. Accept $20,000 less inventory (or some other value)
2. Permit me to exclude a new vehicle from the sale
3. Keep me (and my family) on the medical insurance policy during the Management Assistance period
4. Reduce the term of the promissory note (for the balance of the purchase price) from five years to four years
5. Increase the down payment by $20,000

Whatever the seller says in his responses, a written response indicates that he still wants the sale to go through. My advice is "hang in there" and continue to seek imaginative ways to bridge the gap. Some "trade offs" involve only price and terms, but others involve strategies that might reduce the income taxes a seller will owe as a result of the sale. Some involve things that seem to make the transition of ownership smoother from the seller's perspective. Changing the method for valuing inventory may be helpful. Frankly, most sellers do not know what the stumbling blocks are until after an exchange of offers. Some renegotiation may occur in a verbal exchange, but after some agreements have been reached be sure to have them appended to the contract.

Compliance with Bulk Sales Act/ Notification of Creditors. After both parties have signed the Contract, often the first task is to notify creditors. Get a copy of their addresses and send them a notice (at least ten days before closing) stating what the seller says the account balance is. The creditors will only respond if the account balance in your notice is not as shown in their records. If the contract does not indicate that you are assuming some trade debts, this step may not be necessary, particularly if you are sure that the seller has (or will have at closing) adequate funds to pay off the outstanding balances due his suppliers.

Part II. THE CLOSING PROCESS

The negotiating process and the due diligence process have both ended satisfactorily. All contingencies have now been removed or satisfied. There was no need (in the case of the Doozy purchase) to secure bank loan approval, since the seller has agreed to carry (take back) notes for the balance of the purchase price. It appears that the sale will go forward and that you are now ready to purchase the business you have found. The closing process is the last step in buying a business. It is an exiting time but a time to be careful, as well. This process begins with preparing a pre-closing checklist that lists the specific tasks that a prudent buyer must complete before taking title to his new business. A list of these tasks may include the following that I have used on my pre-closing checklist as well as some additional items:

PRE-CLOSING CHECKLIST
Tasks to Be Accomplished by Purchaser Prior to Closing
Check (✓) when done

- ☐ Transfer (establish) telephone service—Bellsouth Business
- ☐ Transfer (setup) electricity and water service
- ☐ Obtain business license and other licenses needed—County Courthouse
- ☐ Determine closing costs from your agent or closing attorney
- ☐ Open checking account and get checks printed, if an asset sale

- ☐ Obtain cashier's checks for down payment and closing costs
- ☐ Arrange for Visa or MasterCard service in business name
- ☐ Apply for approval to assume distributorships or dealerships
- ☐ Arrange for Yellow Page ad (new directory cut off is August 31)
- ☐ Obtain a federal ID number from your local IRS office
- ☐ Obtain general liability insurance binder
- ☐ Obtain other insurance (or binders) as indicated
- ☐ Arrange times and personnel to take pre-closing inventory
- ☐ Inspect premises and determine if all FF&E are on site and in good repair
- ☐ Obtain landlord's approval to assume current lease or obtain new lease
- ☐ Be sure all contingencies in your purchase contract have been completed
- ☐ Determine the time and place of the closing
- ☐ Obtain Certificate of Use & Occupancy from city hall
- ☐ Ask your Accountant to set up a starting balance sheet
- ☐ File application with the State for your corporate charter (if indicated)
- ☐ Arrange times with Seller for training and to tell employees of sale
- ☐ Call your agent for assistance if you have questions.

Suggestion. Buyers tend to focus on getting documents that the seller or closing attorney is responsible for providing. They tend to forget that they have chores to tend to as well. Do not forget to pick up a signed copy of your lease on the business premises, to pick up an insurance binder from your agent and to get all required permits and licenses. Someone at the closing table may want to see these; if a banker is involved he will certainly want evidence that these tasks have been completed. See Pre-Closing Checklist above.

TIP: Because it is sometimes difficult to know which assets to insure or at what values to insure them, some purchase contracts include language requiring the seller to keep all insurance in force at his cost for thirty (30) days following the closing.

Jack (John V. M.) Gibson

Taking and Extending Inventory. Closing normally begins the day (or evening) before the actual closing with the "taking" and "extending" of the inventory. The parties need to know if the actual value of inventory on the day of closing is more or less than the value set out in their Contract. Sometimes the parties elect to use a professional inventory service (as in the case of liquor stores) and split the very reasonable cost. Inventory services may use hand-held computers and can count, value and extend the inventory in an amazing brief time. Sometimes the parties take and value the inventory themselves. Taking Inventory is a three-step process: (1) counting the items in inventory, (2) putting prices (or costs) on the items, and then (3) extending the inventory.

Because the prices are visible in retail businesses, extending inventory usually begins with the "shelf" price. In a manufacturing business there are no "shelf" prices, but there should be price sheets showing the prices at which the products are offered for sale. In every case the "sale price" must be converted to a cost. The results of the inventory, using a retail liquor store as an example, may look something like the following:

No.	Description of Item	Unit Cost	Total
4	1.5 liter bottles of XYZ	@ $7.85 =	$31.40
7	1.5 liter bottles of ABC	@ 9.50 =	66.50
9	.75 liter bottles of XYZ	@ 4.25 =	38.25
8	.75 liter bottles of ABC	@ 5.25 =	42.00
	TOTAL Retail Price		$178.15
	Less Mark-up at 50%		<u>59.38</u>
	Seller's Cost		$118.77

When a larger business is sold, often personnel from the accounting firm representing one or both parties monitor the process by "spot checking" the inventory count. If the inventory is large, inventory sheets are prepared a few days in advance. Sometimes these sheets show current or replacement costs for each item. In other cases, the values of many inventory items are not known when the count is taken. In these cases, the inventory sheets are taken back to an office the following day and priced out from suppliers' catalogues or other price sheets. It is always helpful if the method for pricing (costing) inventory is set out in the contract.

After the items in inventory are counted, the inventory must be valued somehow to determine its cost.[76] There are several ways to do this, among them:

1. **Discount the retail price.** For merchandise in a typical retail store, take the "shelf" price of each item and discount it by the average markup. If the "shelf" prices of the wine in a liquor store total $30,000 and the average markup is 40%, the cost basis of the wine is $21,428. **Calculate:** $30,000 divided by 1.40 = $21,428.

2. **Use recent supplier price lists.**

3. **Check original purchase invoices.** Always do this, for example, in the case of automobile or equipment dealers that have large ticket items in inventory.

4. **Discount shelf price by gross profit margin.** If a drug store or furniture store has an inventory value of $500,000 (using the retail sticker prices) and has a gross profit margin of 35%, the cost basis (original cost) of the inventory is about $325,000. Often different margins are used for different classes of inventory.

   Calculate: $500,000 x .35 = $175,000 Gross Profit

   $500,000 less 175,000 = $325,000 Cost Basis

5. **Calculate the percentage of completion.** A cabinet manufacturer or manufacturer of armored truck bodies may have work-in-process, so each item or job may have to be priced individually.

The method for pricing and extending inventory is fairly standard within a given industry or market but it must be spelled out sufficiently so that the parties know they are in agreement. To do this, a contract might include language like one of the following provisions:

> "Inventory will be valued at the lower of Seller's original cost or current replacement cost" or

> "Inventory will be valued at the shelf price less 25%" or

---

76 Extending the inventory on larger businesses may take several days or more, so some of the normal closing tasks cannot be completed by the day of actual closing or the transfer of ownership. This is not a problem. However, if you feel this will occur in your case, it is wise to review the implications with an experienced attorney.

> "Inventory will be valued using prices on suppliers' latest price sheets"

Adjusting the Purchase Price. Difficulties can arise when the value of the extended inventory differs considerably from the value set out in the Purchase Contract. If there is an overage, you may not have available funds to purchase the excess. If the inventory value is less than called for, the buyer (you) may immediately after the Closing have to purchase additional inventory in order to have sufficient inventory on hand to meet normal customer requests or, in extreme cases, to stay in business. It is prudent to include in your contract provisions that explicitly cover these situations, such as:

1. "The value of inventory on hand at closing will be at least $100,000"
2. "If the value of inventories is less than the value set out above (in the Contract), The Purchase Price and the Down Payment will be reduced by the deficiency"
3. "Inventories in excess of the value set out in this Contract will be discounted by 10% or excluded from the sale, at the purchaser's option"
4. "If the inventory value exceeds $100,000, the excess value will be added to the Purchase Price and to the Promissory Note held by the Seller. The down payment will not increase."

In larger transactions your contract may include some wording like:

> "No adjustment to the Price will be made unless the value found during the Inventory count differs from the contract amount by more than $20,000" or "Value will be between $2,000,000 and $2,100,000."

Note that in the first provision, the buyer would have the right to walk away from the sale if the inventory is short. The seller would have to purchase additional inventory prior to closing at his cost to make up the shortage (or agree to convey to buyer at closing Cash equal to the deficiency). The key point is that all possible scenarios should be anticipated and remedies spelled out in the contract. Strange things concerning the values and distribution of inventory can happen.

> **Case History: Mismatched Inventory.** On the evening before the closing on the sale of a dress shop, there seemed to be far more dresses in stock than the buyer had recalled. When the inventory was extended, there was $20,000 in extra inventory. Since the Contract was silent on how to handle overages, the buyer paid the extra $20,000. It turned out that a large percentage of the dresses were in petite sizes (the seller's size) and that the seller had returned many "borrowed" items to the shop the evening before the inventory was counted. The buyer soon learned, to his dismay, that petite dresses were hard to sell. **Moral: Put clauses in the contract on (1) how to handle overages, and (2) handle mismatched inventory.**

The Purchase Price is also adjusted for reasons other than shifts in amount and cost of inventories. Review the following:

1. **Lost or misplaced items of FF&E:** The easiest way to resolve this is to deduct the values shown on the Description of Furniture, Fixtures, and Equipment attached to the Prospectus (or given to Buyer later) or in a schedule attached to the contract.

2. **Damaged equipment or merchandise:** Parties should get estimates of the cost of repairs and reduce the Purchase Price (and Down Payment) by that amount.

3. **Dated merchandise:** For example, unsold summer merchandise should be discounted if still in inventory in December. However, if a contract is silent on this point, buyers may have no recourse.

4. **Insufficient Earnings:** See Case History: Need To Confirm Earnings.

5. **Failure of Seller to Satisfy Other Contingencies**

> **TIP:** A contract does not need to provide for an upward adjustment in price in the event of excess inventory. It can simply state: "The Contract is contingent upon purchaser's ability to confirm that the inventory value on hand at time of closing totals at least $ _fill in blank_." When the buyer has counted and valued sufficient inventory to be comfortable that the contingency can be met, the counting is suspended. Thus, the seller does not know what the final value is and there is no danger of there being an unwelcome upward adjustment to the purchase price.

If possible, the count sheets are fully priced in time to give the closing attorney an exact Inventory figure. The attorney can then adjust the Purchase Price and other closing documents such as the Promissory Note, if the final figure differs from the figure in the Contract. If the count and pricing are complicated, the inventory valuation process may take several days to complete. However, closing normally proceeds as scheduled and revised closing documents are distributed to the Parties when the inventory valuation has been accepted.

Role of Closing Attorney. Today, most small business sales are "closed" by a "neutral" closing attorney. This is an attorney who specializes in business closings; he represents neither the buyer nor the seller. He represents the contract that has been reached between the parties. Closings on the sale of larger businesses require attorneys representing all parties be present to handle different parts of the closing and represent their client's interests each step of the way.

Sometimes, something can go wrong at the closing. It is at the closing that any misunderstandings between buyer and seller need to be worked out. For this reason the closing attorney will read aloud the Purchase Contract, Bill of Sale and other closing documents in the presence of the parties. It is a time to be vigilant and be sure you understand every word. Ask questions. After the closing is completed, it may be too late to "straighten" something out.

Present at the closing are the closing attorney (and/or personal attorneys), the brokers, the parties, and, sometimes, their spouses. If the buyer is giving the seller a promissory note, the buyer's spouse may be expected to sign the note. Sometimes there are two closings: one with the bank from which the buyer has borrowed some of the closing funds and then a second closing during which the Parties sign (execute) the closing documents. It helps if a list of these documents has been distributed in advance.

In the previous chapter the terms "offer" and "contract" were used interchangeably. Once the offer and the revisions to the offer have been accepted by both Buyer and Seller (referred to jointly as the "Parties") the offer becomes a Contract. A contract is an agreement that is legally binding on both of the parties who have entered into an agreement. An offer, or counteroffer, however, is binding on only the one party who has made the offer and it is only binding until the **acceptance date** set out in the offer.

Importance of Dates. A binding agreement such as a contract must include the specific dates by which different parts of the agreement must be completed. The date for closing on the sale (and conveying the business to the buyer) is the most important date. If the contract does not clearly set out a date for handing over the business, it is not a contact because there would be no way to complete the contractual obligation. The dates for removing contingencies and completing the due diligence are also important and should be observed carefully. Normally the contract states that the buyer "takes title" to the business from the start of closing day. Thus, he is responsible for expenses incurred from that time forward and is entitled to all income received.

The original offer may be worded in layman's terms, somewhat informal language, rather than in a more formal language found in a legally binding document. This is generally okay. However, informal documents often include language that is not very precise. As a result the parties may interpret parts of the agreement quite differently from each other.

After an offer has been accepted, it is often redrafted by an experienced business attorney, generally an attorney retained by the buyer, and then submitted for the other party's attorney to review. It is very important not to assume there is understanding between the parties to a contract if these "understandings" are not explicitly written down.

Although the **closing date** is an essential component of any contract, with the approval of the parties, that date is often rescheduled to permit one party or the other to complete or remove a contingency listed in a contract. For example, titles to automobiles or real estate may not be ready by the original closing date, the accountant may not have prepared a closing balance sheet, the inventory process may not be complete, or an attorney may request more time to draft some required document. Some party whose approval to the sale is necessary (a banker or franchisor, for example) may not have sent in the approval. In such circumstances it is prudent to extend the date until these documents or approvals have been prepared, received, and reviewed. However, with advice of your attorney, it is not at all unusual to proceed to complete the sale, leaving some legal details in the hands of the attorneys.

Lien Search. Remember that a seller must convey clear and unencumbered title to all assets that are to be sold. Thus, as part of the closing process, the closing attorney(s) will conduct a lien search to learn if any creditors of the selling business have filed a notice at the local courthouse (or statehouse, in the case of Tennessee) advising the public that the business owes money. It is normal that banks, finance companies, and mortgage companies that lend money to a business file a public lien against the assets that were financed. Sometimes suppliers and other business creditors also file liens. It is not unusual for a seller to be unaware that there are outstanding liens (even after the creditors have been paid in full), so you, as buyer, need to be vigilant.[77]

The Seller (or Seller's attorney) must arrange to pay off any liens against the business that might affect your ability to obtain a clear and unencumbered title to the assets that you are buying. If there is a neutral closing attorney, finding and removing liens (the lien search) becomes part of his or her normal responsibilities.

If the closing funds are inadequate to satisfy an unpaid lien: (1) the buyer can accept the asset subject to the lien and deduct the amount of the lien from the down payment and purchase price, or (2) exclude the liened item from the sale and reduce the price of the business by the value of the item. This value is often shown on the Schedule of FF&E attached to the Contract or in the **allocation of purchase price** shown on the face of the Contract. It is always wise for the closing attorney to inform Seller immediately upon finding a lien so Seller can arrange to pay it off in a timely fashion.

The Actual Closing. This is when the papers are signed and the exchange of ownership takes place. Closings can take place in the closing attorney's office, in your broker's office, or at your bank. Your attorney may prefer that closing take place in his office. All are fine. The key is for you to be sure that all closing documents have been received and reviewed several days before the scheduled closing, are fully understood by you and your attorney, and are faithful to the understandings of the Parties. **Do not proceed with closing if you or your attorney have not reviewed all closing documents in advance.** If you arrive at the closing table before an attorney has completed some required document, you might feel rushed to move forward with the closing without enough time to comfortably review the document. The attorney may feel rushed as well and so the document may contain errors and must be reviewed carefully.

---

[77] Sometimes liens are not removed even after the debts have been paid in full. If there is evidence of payment, closing attorneys will remove them.

Be sure that the results of the inventory count and the inspections of the facilities and the FF&E have been made known and that your attorney and the closing attorney are aware of any need to adjust the price set out in the Contract. These adjustments can easily be made on the closing day. The primary reason for adjustments is the change in inventory value that occurs almost daily. The final inventory value rarely matches exactly the value(s) set out in the Contract.

The closing attorney lists all monies expected to be received and dispersed at closing on a **Settlement Sheet**. (There may be separate settlement sheets for the buyer and for the seller, such as the ones in the Appendix.) This document is very important. Every buyer should review it carefully in case there are errors or surprises, such as costs that you did not anticipate. Ideally, the closing attorney should distribute a copy a few days before the scheduled closing for you and your attorney to review. Do not be hurried. And do not be hesitant to ask questions about any entry on the Settlement Sheet. The broker should be able to tell you exactly how much your closing costs will be. Ask him to pick up a copy for you when he picks up copies of the other closing documents.

From time to time there are mistakes. Sometimes even attorneys are unclear about how adjustments should be made or about other matters that buyer and seller have discussed and agreed to. The Settlement Sheet also lists any expenses that will be split, or pro-rated, between the parties, such as rent, payroll, personal property taxes, or legal fees. Normally, after a sale has closed it is difficult to get from the seller payment for items that should have been pro-rated and it may be too late to adjust the purchase price. Be very careful. Ask questions and take your time. Do not let the excitement of ownership cause you to speed up the closing process unduly.

Depending on the size of the business being sold, the actual "closing" can last several hours or more. During this period, usually neither buyer nor seller is at the place of business minding the store. Arrangements should, therefore, be made for someone to handle the daily tasks such as making deposits or writing checks. In regard to the day of closing, it should be very clear whether closing is effective at the start of business on the closing day, which is customary. If so, all sales receipts from that day are property of the buyer.

If the receipts are cash and checks, they should be deposited into the buyer's bank account. If checks are mailed to a post office box, the buyer or his agent must have a key to the post office box and arrangements must be made for the buyer to enter the business the next day. For these reasons, **it is helpful for the seller to bring with him to closing all keys necessary to operate the business.**

The buyer must bring checks to cover the closing costs and the down payment. The latter should be a cashier's check. The closing attorney should let each party know several days in advance what their share of the closing costs will be. They are often unexpectedly high, if real estate is included, so be prepared.[78] Without the purchase of real estate, these costs are surprisingly modest; the largest item is generally the closing attorney's fee, which in most markets is today equally divided between buyer and seller. If the seller has a broker, he or his firm is paid the commission from the closing funds by the attorney.

Finally, do not leave the closing table without firm agreement about some practical matters concerning the transfer of the business such as:

1. How and when the Seller will provide the agreed upon management transition assistance. Set some firm dates.
2. Whether receipts from business sales will be deposited to your (new) account or to the seller's (existing) account.
3. How much **petty cash** (or working capital) is necessary to operate the business and how much is on hand at the business.
4. Exactly when the transfer of ownership becomes effective.
5. Where the keys are, including keys to mail boxes, what they are for, and who (which employee(s)) has copies.

There may be other similar issues. Carefully think through with the Seller the mechanics of transferring both the ownership and management of the business before leaving the closing table.

After checks have been exchanged, the attorney gives you the **Bill of Sale.** This is your title to the business and a receipt for the money paid or owed to seller. The parties shake hands and the business is finally yours. Yet, some work remains to be done behind the scenes by the closing attorney. The attorney may have to pay some creditors and to record some documents. If vehicles are involved, he may still need to get new titles.

---

[78] This is because some jurisdictions require that a portion of the annual real estate taxes (city and county) be paid or escrowed at time of closing.

Follow up with your attorney (or the closing attorney) after closing to be sure that he has not been distracted and his tasks have been completed. There have, unfortunately, been closings when important tasks were somehow overlooked, such as recording a deed to real estate. See Confirmation and Bill of Sale in Appendix.

Part III. WHEN IS THE RIGHT TIME TO BUY

Anytime is a good time to buy if the price is right. Let's compare the market for small businesses with public stock markets first. People buy shares of stock in virtually every publicly traded company every day that the markets are open for trading. Why do they buy? They buy because the price, as quoted on the stock markets, appears attractive. They also buy because of the feeling that future earnings will grow and, as a result, the value of the stock, or business, will rise. This applies to small, privately held businesses as well.

Business Cycles. Whenever buying a business, it makes sense to learn where the economy is in the business cycle. What phase of the cycle are we in now? Does this suggest you are buying at the "top of the market" or at the bottom or somewhere in between? Obviously, if you feel the market is about to slow down, offering a lower price makes sense because revenue and cash flow may fall sharply. If the market is expected to come out of a recession (or economic slowdown) a higher price may be warranted.

No cycle is identical to another but some characteristics are fairly similar such as the length of a typical cycle. From 1945 to 2009 there have been eleven cycles with the "contraction" on average lasting eleven months, each followed by an "expansion" lasting on average fifty-nine months.[79] There is no way to forecast precisely when a contraction or expansion will begin or end but there are economic indicators that can be helpful in determining where in the cycle we are. The sales and earnings of some businesses follow the business cycle fairly closely while other businesses are largely unaffected. Some in fact are countercyclical, that is, they may grow while the economy is slowing down and vice versa. Which "indicators"

---

79 This data may be found on the web site of the National Bureau of Economic Research (NBER): www.nber.org/cycles.htm

would be helpful guides to timing the purchase of your business will probably require a little study.

Economic Indicators. Traditional indicators include the following five. Be sure to check them for your city, state or market area.

1. Changes in the various rates of inflation
2. Changes in the unemployment rate
3. No. of persons filing unemployment claims
4. Change (growth) in the gross domestic product
5. Monthly changes in sales tax receipts
6. Changes in various interest rates

Some local area indicators, especially those relating to real estate and construction, can help a business buyer spot trends in his market area early in a cycle. Look for:

1. Vacancy rates in commercial real estate (shopping centers and office buildings)
2. Changes in current "per square foot" rental rates
3. Changes in number (and value of) building permits issued

In addition there are many more industry specific indicators such as the number of new houses sold, new cars manufactured or changes in the prices of certain commodities (sugar or wheat if the business is a bakery, for example). My favorite economic indicator (which I could watch and measure from my office window) is the number of cars lined up each day at the drive-thru window of a major chain fast food restaurant at noon. I learned that this was a very precise measure of the propensity of the average consumer to spend or to save.

Additional information about economic indicators can be found at various sources including U.S. Department of Labor, Bureau of Labor Statistics, stats.bls.gov:80 and U.S. Department of Commerce, Census Bureau at www.census.gov

The markets over time adjust the price of each business to meet the realities of current or anticipated market conditions. Sometimes, of course, the market for smaller companies does not adjust as quickly as the public markets. And the prices at which smaller businesses change hands do not seem to fluctuate quite as widely either. It is for this reason that sometimes sellers take quite a while to lower the asking prices of their businesses. Another factor to keep in mind is that when the economy slows, sellers are much more willing to offer buyers more attractive terms, such as seller financing, as well as lower prices.

The reality in the markets for all companies, small and large, is that they trade hands when they appear to be worth more to a buyer than they are to a seller. Why would this be so? Let's look at several reasons that sellers might be willing to sell for a price less than an informed buyer might be willing to pay.

1. The seller may have an opportunity to open a new business in a different industry, perhaps with friends or with children.
2. The seller may wish to retire and move to Florida, or to travel with his wife.
3. The seller may be looking forward to having more time off to pursue other investments, or to pursue hobbies such as participating in the senior Olympics or sailing a boat around the world.
4. The seller may have simply achieved the financial goal of having sufficient means to allow him (or her) not to have to work any more.
5. The seller may have discovered that the business, in order to grow and remain competitive, requires the investment of substantial capital (persons nearing retirement age are often loathe to invest substantial new capital in their businesses).
6. The seller may be in somewhat of a rut: operating the business every day may have become boring or lonely.
7. Changes in the industry or marketplace may have persuaded the owner that he (or she) is no longer qualified to operate the business successfully.
8. The seller may be tired or facing an illness that requires him or her to cut back on the hours spent at the business.

Regardless of their age, sellers always have a motive for thinking about selling. Sometimes the motive is valid and sometimes not. Selling a small business, therefore, is really little different than saying, "I think IBM will rise more rapidly than AT&T." So the AT&T stock is sold and the proceeds are used to purchase shares of IBM. This does not mean that AT&T is unprofitable, or is in financial trouble. It means, rightly or wrongly that, in one person's opinion, IBM is expected in the future to grow more rapidly than AT&T or will be able to pay a larger dividend. The needs, expectations, and motives of buyers and sellers are different, which is exactly what makes sales happen.

Motives of sellers are often difficult to ascertain; so, **it is smart to try and buy when a Seller is ready to sell and to learn what a Seller's reasons for selling might be.** Some sellers really do not want to sell, particularly if they have nothing to look forward to in retirement except staying at home every day. They may enjoy negotiating simply to discover what the market feels their business is worth. If a seller is not sincere about selling, it is often wise to look for another business.

Owners may simply want to sell because managing the company does not seem to be as much fun or as challenging as it used to be. It may become more difficult for owners to make normal business decisions as they near retirement age. Some owners hesitate to invest in new equipment. These are both symptoms that their companies may be ready for "second generation" ownership. However, a seller may not always see these factors as reasons to sell. Some, particularly long-time owners, are very reluctant to retire. They tend to resist change. They logically worry about what they will do if they no longer have the business to run.

These symptoms may also indicate that the seller is not as content as in past years spending so much time managing the business-perhaps simply because he (she) has made enough money from the company to live comfortably. Simply put, this breed of seller no longer needs to work as hard as he (she) used to. In these cases, prospective buyers who tour a company often immediately begin asking, "Why isn't the owner doing this, or doing that?" "Why hasn't he computerized inventory?" "Why are no incentives built into employee compensation?"

These apparent lacks are more often signs that a business is worth exploring seriously, rather than signs that a business is not worthy of further study. Buyers generally ask these questions because they have substantial experience or knowledge in areas where the sellers do not. This is a good "buy" signal; but a buyer is advised to share these questions with the broker (or his financial advisor) first, because the seller might become defensive if his competence is in any way questioned by a younger and seemingly less experienced buyer.

The fact that buyers see opportunity for change suggests that they "brings to the party" resources that a business may lack to some degree. For that reason, the set of assets that comprise the business may produce a greater return in future years than it has produced in recent years for the seller. Therefore, the business is worth more to a buyer than it is to a seller, and a deal (or sale) can be crafted that is acceptable to all parties.

Conversely, if everything about a business appears to be in great shape, it may be a signal to proceed cautiously and to do additional analysis. The seller may be aware of pending changes in his market or industry, such as the entry of a large, well-financed competitor into his market, or important changes in technology that may adversely affect the business. Or the business may simply be near the end of a normal business cycle. See following story about potential problems of growth.

> **Case History: The Problem of Unbroken Growth.** I recall a situation in which a buyer purchased a business that had shown virtually unbroken growth of over 10% for many years. The buyer assumed that this growth would continue and purchased the business at a price that reflected this optimism. The Federal Reserve had just begun increasing interest rates charged to its member banks and the economy soon cooled off. The buyer was not able to meet his obligations and liquidated the business about two years after the purchase. Fortunately, there were adequate assets to cover all debts, but he did not recover his full investment. **Moral: If the business follows the cycles of the broader economy, try to anticipate when the growth will slow and make your offer accordingly.**

PRE-CLOSING CHECKLIST: As you approach the closing date, keep in mind the following questions, questions sometimes asked or remembered by buyers only at the closing table or after the closing has occurred.

1. Did you receive in advance of the scheduled closing (in time to review them carefully) copies of all contracts and other closing documents?

2. Did you read and understand the contents of all documents? If not, did you ask your broker attorney or the closing attorney to explain the points that you did not fully understand?

3. Did you observe all dates for removal (fulfillment) of the (your) contingencies?

4. Did you carefully monitor the inventory process (the count and extension)?
5. Did you remember to bring a cashier's check for the down payment to closing?
6. Did you remember to bring other required documents to closing, such as proof or insurance?
7. Have you scheduled management assistance with the Seller?
8. Have you scheduled a time for the Seller to introduce you to all critical employees, customers and suppliers?
9. Do you know where all the keys are? And who has duplicates sets?

CHAPTER 8
CONCLUSION

Many people share the dream of some day owning their own business, yet a relatively small percent accomplish this dream. Some have looked at businesses. Some have even looked at many businesses over many years yet did not get to the point of submitting an offer or closing on a sale. Why? My experience suggests that that were fearful of "being had" in some way. They did not know whom to trust and were concerned about making a costly mistake. They lacked the tools to help them make a wise choice—the choice about what kind of business to buy and the choice about what price and terms to offer.

Let's review briefly some of the more common motives that lead people to want to own their own business.

1. Meet a family's financial needs
2. Obtain or to "buy" a job
3. Provide employment for family members
4. Build a nest egg for a retirement
5. Serve as a stepping stone to greater financial success
6. Become one's own boss (I'm tired of working for someone else)
7. Achieve financial wealth and independence
8. Enjoy the freedom that comes with self-employment
9. Achieve the respect of your peers and community

These are compelling motives, so the reasons that so many people do not follow through on their dream must be equally compelling. It is prudent to understand the opportunities, risks and challenges that come with business ownership. But the main objectives are: (1) to determine with reasonable assurance that the business being studied will meet your personal financial needs and (2) to feel comfortable that the business will also be able to meet the financial obligations incurred in buying the business. There is usually a fair price at which these objectives can be met. But many buyers lack the skills to determine that price with confidence. If you develop those skills, you will be able to buy with confidence and without overpaying.

A BRIEF RECAP: It will be helpful to remember the results of the financial review of the business you have decided to purchase as well as the financial goals that you have set. These might be summarized for Doozy as shown in the table below. The **Actual Result** shown is after making adjustments to the financial statements.

Ratio or Factor (after adjustments)	Desired Goal	Actual Result	Grade or Pass/Fail
Seller's ROE (pre-tax)	35%	90%[80]	A+
Your desired ROI	40%		
Seller's Annual sales growth	15%	nil	??
Seller's Gross Profit	30%	47%	Pass
Sales per employee	$100,000	$75,000	Fail
Sales per sq. foot	??		
Cash Flow ÷ Sales	20%	12.3%	B
Income ÷ Sales	10%	10.6%	Pass
Other ?			

A business does not have to "pass" each of these goals. But it is wise to keep your goals in mind, particularly during the negotiating process. Be careful not to pay more than the fair price. At the same time, if the business is attractive, it may be foolish not to be a little flexible about price

---

[80] Refer to Table 8. Doozy's equity (net worth) appears to be $35,000. Adjusted earnings are $31,800.

and terms. Understanding the various processes or steps outlined in the preceding chapters should give one the confidence to make a wise choice and to feel secure after the choice is made. Let's recap them:

1. The search process
2. The study process
3. The financial review (analysis) process
4. The adjustment (recasting) process
5. The reconciliation (of values found) process
6. The pricing process (determining an offering price and terms)
7. The contract preparation process
8. The negotiating process
9. The contingency removal/fulfillment process (due diligence)
10. The closing process
11. The post-closing/management assistance process

UNLOCKING VALUE: In addition to these ten traditional steps to buying a business, there are some other useful steps in preparing a buyer to make a wise choice and in negotiating a good contract, that is, in deciding if a business will meet his specific needs and goals. The first step is a process that I call "unlocking value." Can a buyer find more value in a business than the seller can? We have previously discussed a few ways to do this. Below is a recap with a few additional suggestions.

1. A business may have hidden assets, assets such as underutilized plant capacity, or work-in-process.
2. There may be potential outlets for some products or services that the current owner for some reason has not identified or developed.
3. There may be more efficient and up-to-date ways to manufacture or market company products such as by more fully utilizing the power of computers.
4. There may be related products or services the business might economically market to its present customers.

5. There may be surplus assets, such as excess inventories of some items that can be sold and converted to cash, thereby reducing the effective purchase price of the business.

6. A business may unlock value by improving operations in some fashion, perhaps by increasing output per man-hour or by adding performance bonuses to compensation.

7. Employees and customers may have valuable ideas about improving many aspects of the business. Talk to them. Many first generation owners have not talked to their customers or employees in a long time.

8. Owners may have been overpaying for equipment or for resale merchandise or making unnecessary purchases. Review Schedule 1 on page 11. Would you have paid $1,200 for your desk? Review Case History on page 14. How much did this landscape contractor overpay for his merchandise?

THOUGHTS FROM SEASONED BUYERS: The second useful step is to talk with seasoned buyers before making your decision. Let me share some guidelines that business buyers say they found helpful or wish they had heeded. Some were learned from painful experience.

1. Beware of buying a business if you are not able to perform or complete the full due diligence process after your purchase contract has been accepted.

2. If you can verify seller's financial statements, and if the statements have been audited, the business may be worth a premium. If the statements cannot be verified, the business may be worth a little less than your analysis suggests. Proceed cautiously.

3. Don't automatically pay a premium if the business has had years of unbroken growth. It may be at the top of its natural business cycle. "My advisors told me," said one disappointed buyer, "to look for a business that has had double digit growth each year for at least five years."

4. Before the sale, be sure to review the accountant's **opinion letter** for any comments about the way financial statements have been compiled. One buyer says, "I didn't know that accountants were supposed to attach an opinion letter to the financial statements,

How to Buy a Business without Being Had

but I sure wish I had read it earlier." If there is no opinion letter, it may be wise to ask why.

5. Remember that a business's value depends upon the return it will give after the sale. What a business earns in the future is far more important than what it has earned in the past. Because it made money in past years does not mean it will make money in the future.

6. Beware if key documents, such as corporate resolutions, have not been prepared and signed in advance of the closing or if signatures are missing on closing documents.

7. Small businesses are different from large ones. The work rhythm is different. In larger businesses there is often time to study problems at length before making or implementing a decision. In small businesses, decisions need to be made promptly.

8. Focus on the business. Do not be distracted, because time is of the essence (as stated in most standard contracts). Customers, suppliers and employees can quickly sense if the new owner is "in charge" and paying attention to business.

9. It is helpful if the seller will: (1) inform the employees that there has been (or will be) a transfer of ownership and introduce you to the employees in an open meeting, and (2) introduce you to key suppliers and customers. Introductions are often more effective if made in person. "I wish I had put these stipulations in my contract," says another buyer.

10. Calculate carefully your working capital needs. After the sale is closed it may be too late to borrow more money.

11. Find a knowledgeable lawyer to prepare your closing documents but try to avoid the need for more lawyers or going to the courthouse after the sale. Most legal problems arise because the original documents are not fully understood or drafted in sufficient detail.

AFTER THE SALE: The third step is to keep your eyes open after the sale has taken place. Keep track of your forecast budget and monitor the cash flow carefully. Keep track of questions you wish to ask the seller during your management assistance time and schedule the first management assistance session before leaving the closing table. It may be useful if the contract gives you permission to call the seller at home after work hours when you have time to talk without the distraction of taking care of business. Ask him to give you both daytime and "after hours" telephone numbers and travel schedules, in case some questions need prompt answers. Here's one reason why:

> **Case History: Bank Account Problem.** The purchaser of a daycare center wondered why she had not received reimbursements from the State for certain "scholarship" children. It turned out that the state had sent all reimbursement checks to the previous owner's bank account and that, immediately following the closing, the former owner had left town on vacation. This resulted in such a lack of cash flow during the first month of ownership that it almost bankrupted the business.[80] **Moral: Before closing, let customers know how to remit future payments, or require seller to tell customers where to remit payments or transfer company mailbox (and key, if there is one) to you.**

The first weeks or months after the sale is completed is not the time to be distracted. A new owner needs to take charge and to act decisively; yet not change the "old way of doing things" without careful thought. The first Case History (in Chapter 1) illustrates this point. This next Case illustrates how important it is for the buyer to be ready to take over management of the business upon taking ownership.

---

81 Some Management Assistance Agreements (or the paragraphs in the Purchase Contract) spell out exactly when and for how long a buyer may talk with the seller. And they also spell out penalties if the seller violates his part of the agreement. Sometimes the penalty is simply forfeiture by the seller of the money allocated to this agreement.

How to Buy a Business without Being Had

> **Case History: Scheduling Management Assistance.** The owner of a dress shop was fortunate to have found a buyer; she was nine months pregnant when the closing occurred. The buyer opened the shop on Monday and discovered there were no employees at work. Desperately she looked for phone numbers but could find none. She tried to contact the seller, but, alas, the seller had gone to the hospital to deliver her baby. And the buyer had important appointments scheduled that took her away from the shop. It was several days before she found the phone numbers and could work out a schedule with her new employees. **Moral: Be sure you know what will happen your first day of business and plan for it in advance.**

Forecasting (Again). Forecast both your annual and monthly expenses carefully. These forecasts become your budgets—a twelve-month budget and a monthly budget. Your expenses will be different from the Seller's. Include your anticipated **debt service** in the forecast expenses. Revise your monthly operating budget every month for a few months after the sale. Do not rely solely upon a budget prepared before or immediately after the acquisition because there are always surprises. And reserve in the budget enough cash for the lumpy expenses such as annual business taxes and insurance premiums. Finally, remember that in a small business **the owner gets paid last.**

One of the reasons for going forward with the purchase of Doozy is your hunch that under your leadership both sales and profits could increase by 10% per year during the next few years.[82] Since our analysis (refer back to Table 9) suggests that Doozy had an adjusted pre-tax income last year of $31,000, this means you project that Doozy will earn $34,100 (before income taxes) the year after you buy the business. Now, test this projection by preparing a twelve-month budget using your anticipated expenses as shown in Table 16.

The forecasts in the pre-acquisition pro forma Income and Expense Statement are a good starting place for preparing your monthly budget. A more useful budget may include more expense accounts than are included

---

[82] Ten percent growth may seem high. In reality this "growth" number is the sum of the rate of inflation plus real growth. If inflation is 5%, real growth is only 5%. And part of the real growth is from management changes rather than from an expanding economy.

in Table 16. For example, each type of insurance and tax expense might become a separate line item, since these items are paid in different months. Try preparing an income statement using different revenue and cost of goods assumptions as well. Using your estimates, it appears that Doozy may earn $34,354, slightly more than the projected 10% increase. The $34,354 is calculated before making interest or principle payments.

Suggestion. Some costs may be greater for a new owner than for a previous owner. Payroll taxes and insurance premiums come to mind. Check both carefully before preparing your budget. Older businesses over time earn a lower SUTA (state unemployment insurance) tax rate than you would qualify for, if they have a favorable unemployment claims history. New businesses start at the highest rate. In regard to insurance costs, contact several carriers. See if buying all policies with a single carrier will result in lower aggregate premiums. Do not automatically continue the policies or levels of coverage the seller had in force, since it may have been years since he "shopped" different carriers. However, if premiums or other costs will increase, make the owner aware of this; it may help in your negotiating.

Table 16. Purchaser's Twelve-Month Income and Expense Budget (Projection)

	Amount	% Change
Revenue from Projected Sales	$330,000	+ 10%
Cost of Goods Sold @ 24%	79,200	+ 10%
Gross Profit	**$250,800**	+ 10%
Owner Salary	50,000	+ 4%
Employee Wages Excluding Owner's Wife	71,060	+ 10%
Part-Time Office Worker	6,000	New
Payroll Taxes @ 10% of Payroll Costs	12,705	+ 6%
Rent (new five-year lease)	20,000	+ 11%
Bookkeeping Service	1,800	New
Insurance—All Policies	11,000	+ 10%
Utilities	15,840	+ 10%

Telephones	4,410	+ 5%
Office Supplies	2,640	+ 10%
Taxes and Licenses	2,860	+ 10%
Gasoline	3,300	+ 10%
Advertising Including Yellow Page Ad	2,730	+ 5%
Part-Time Shop Employees	4,400	+ 10%
All Other Expenses Including Reserve	2,000	+ 100%
Sub-Total	**$210,746**	
Depreciation	5,000	0%
Total Expenses	**$216,446**	
Projected Income (Pre-Tax)	**$34,354**	
Income as % of Projected Sales	10.4%	

Some people do pay too much for a business (or buy on overly restrictive terms) and quickly run into difficulties. They often say they are drowning in debt service. This is really just another way of saying that a business did not meet a buyer's cash flow expectations or that the buyer did not forecast the expenses carefully enough before purchasing it. To prevent a cash flow squeeze in the first few months of ownership, some prudent buyers put a clause in the purchase contract that says that payments due the seller will not begin until sixty or ninety days after the closing. The best way not to be "had" when buying your business is to do your homework. Forecast carefully.

Try to forecast monthly revenue and cash flow as well as expenses. Revise the forecasts as results of operations become clearer. All forecasts need periodic revision. One key to a business like Doozy is to learn how much working capital you will need before the next job is completed, shipped, and paid for. This could be a different amount every month.

In most retail businesses, sales occur daily and are paid by customers in cash. In a custom manufacturing business there may only be one or two sales a week.[83] Thus, the new owner will need to have enough working capital to pay bills and wages in the meantime. Be careful not to spend

---

[83] In Doozy's case, customers must give Doozy a deposit when an order is placed. This deposit should be transferred to the Buyer in whole or in part when the business is sold, if a customer's order has not been completed. Sometimes this deposit is split between the parties according to the percentage of the work that has been completed at the time of the sale.

all your available cash on the down payment. **Just because Doozy has positive earnings does not mean that Doozy will have a positive cash flow every week or month of the year.**

The timing, the price, a cooperative seller, reliable financial records and careful financial analysis—these are important parts of the answer to how to "buy a business without being had." But the most important is to find a business that feels comfortable to you in terms of your unique set of skills, resources, experience and expectations, and one that you feel will be able to grow under your management and direction.

FIVE YEARS AFTER THE SALE: You might ask yourself, "If you could buy Doozy for $150,000 with a $50,000 down payment and achieve 10% annual growth in sales, what would my financial situation look like five years later?"[84] Well, three good things would have happened as you will see on Table 17 below.

1. You would have paid off the $100,000 promissory note held by the seller, and you would own Doozy free and clear of debt.
2. If things went according to plan, your business would have **retained earnings** of $95,177 (see Cumulative After Tax Income in Table 17), and
3. You would have **cash on hand** of $99,582 (Subtract the estimated Income Taxes of $16,798 payable over the first five years from the Cumulative Cash of $116,380).

Pre-Tax Income for Year 1, your first year of ownership, is projected to be $34,100. See Part I of Table 17 below. Refer back to Table 11. With 10% growth, Pre-Tax Income is projected to be $49,926 by Year 5. The Deductions shown in Part II are taken from Table 15. They include $9,000 in Depreciation expenses each year under your ownership ($45,000 for the FF&E ÷5 years = $9,000) plus interest due seller on the $100,000 purchase money note (or two notes) that the seller will carry if he accepts your offer. Both the projected EBITDA and projected Cash Flow in Table

---

84 If there is no growth beyond the 1st year projection shown in Table 16, there would still be adequate Cash Flow ($39,354) to cover the principal and interest due the seller (P&I on $100,000 @8% paid over 60 months is $24,332/year). This is less than 2/3 of the forecast Cash Flow.

17 are the same because your projected Depreciation charges are included in the Deductions in Part II.

Table 17. Purchaser's Projected Five-year Income and Cash Flow

Part I	Year 1	Year 2	Year 3	Year 4	Year 5
Pre-Tax Income	$34,100	$37,510	$41,262	$45,387	$49,926
Depreciation	+5,000	+5,000	+5,000	+5,000	+5,000
Cash Flow	39,100	42,510	46,262	50,387	54,926
Debt Service (P&I)	-23,761	-23,761	-23,761	-23,761	-23,761
Cash Balance	16,339	19,749	22,501	26,626	31,165
Cumulative Cash (Pre-Tax)	$16,339	$36,088	$58,589	$85,215	$116,380
Part II					
EBDITA (lines 1 and 2 above)	$39,100	$42,510	$46,261	$50,387	$54,926
Deductions (see Table 15)	42,900	21,700	20,300	18,900	17,400
Taxable Income	(3,800)	20,810	25,962	31,487	37,526
Income Taxes-estimated	0	-2,552	-3,894	-4,723	-5,629
After-Tax Income	(3,800)	18,258	22,068	26,754	31,897
Cumulative After-Tax Income	($3,800)	$14,458	$36,526	$63,080	$95,177

The **Cash Balance** left after Debt Service and Income Taxes (the portion not needed for working capital or new equipment) could have earned interest. See line 5 of Part I. This potential interest income is not included, but if it were, the Income and Cash Flow would be greater than shown.[85] The **Cash Flow** shown above in Part I assumes that there were no major capital expenditures, or other unforeseen expenses, during the first five years of ownership. If this is so, after five years the business (and you) would have Cumulative Cash, after deducting estimated federal income taxes, of $99,582.

Calculate: $116,380 less income taxes of $16,798 = $99,582

---

[85] At an estimated 2% annual interest on the collected balance, projected interest income after five years would be between $4,000 and $5,000.

This is almost a 100% return (**ROI**) on your original $50,000 investment (excluding closing costs). Since the full cost of Doozy has been paid off and you own the company free and clear of debt, we must add the value of Doozy to the Cash to find the true **ROI**. The best part is that Doozy will probably have grown in value above your purchase price. If these assumptions regarding projected earnings turn out to be true, and the 5:1 P:E is still applicable, Doozy after five years may have a market value of over $250,000.

Calculate: 1. EBITDA after Year Five: $54,926 x 5 = $274,630

2. Pre-Tax Income Year Five: $49,926 x 5 = $249,630

All in all, not a bad return on a $50,000 down payment or on a $60,000 investment for that matter, if the seller required the larger down payment. Your investment has enabled you to create a business asset and Cash that after five years of ownership are together worth $350,000 or more. This is a potential ROI of 600% and this is why people want to own a business.

Calculate: Forecast Cumulative Cash $ 99,582

Forecast Value of Doozy 250,000

TOTAL Return (rounded) **$ 350,000**

During the past five years the budgets had room for increases in Owner's Salary. The first year salary was budgeted at $50,000. If the salary grew each year by 8%, it would now be $68,025. Perhaps, also, some of that Cumulative Cash could have been paid to the owner as additional salary or bonus.

While these numbers may seem modest to some, the processes, strategies, and case histories are applicable to business acquisitions of all sizes. A $100,000 investment may have turned into a business worth $700,000 five years later (with cumulative cash). Perhaps a $1 million investment would turn into a $7 million business.

Five years after the sale, most businesses are doing fine. The purchasers of those businesses have been able to retire their debt (pay off the loans they took out to help finance their purchase) and pay themselves a steady and growing salary. Although many of the Case Histories in this book deal with problems, they do not represent the norm. Purchasers who did their homework, sought professional assistance and had properly drafted purchase contracts, avoided most of the problems outlined in these Case Histories, at least the problems associated with the purchase of their businesses.

Contract problems and problems stemming from misrepresentation normally occur early in a purchaser's period of ownership. Most contracts provide for after-the-sale adjustments that protect the purchasers from financial loss or from "being had" in some other way. However, sometimes, even five years later, problems can occur. This is the subject of the final Case History below.

> **Case History: Shareholder Liability.** The buyer of a business had two minority shareholders. These two shareholders had loaned some money to the buyer and received shares of stock in exchange. Three years later the business was sold. The new owner soon ran out of working capital and took the business through a bankruptcy. The court reduced the monthly payments on the Note due the original owner. When he heard this, the original owner sued the minority shareholders, demanding the balance of the Note be immediately paid in full. The judge agreed. It turned out that the shareholders had signed the original purchase contract as individuals rather than in "corporate capacity." Actually, it was not required that they sign in any capacity since they were not officers of the corporation. But, because they had signed, the court held them personally liable. **Moral: Always be careful what you sign and do not sign if a signature is not required. It could be costly.**

SUMMARY: Many buyers whose investments did not turn out as well as they would have liked say that they wished they had taken more time before buying their business—time to study the business and its industry more in depth, time to negotiate more imaginatively, time to draft a contact more carefully and time to perform more adequate due diligence.

Taking time is an important key to making a successful investment. Taking a little extra time to review carefully the financial statements may reveal hidden assets, hidden income, or hidden inconsistencies in the financial reporting. Undertanding a business and its industry and markets will always put a buyer in a position to negotiate better terms of purchase.

If you like a business, do not be discouraged by the initial asking price or by your disappointment when you first look at a set of financial statements. Things are not always as they first appear. It is equally important to trust your judgment when an attractive opportunity is available. If your contract is well drafted and includes the necessary contingency clauses, you should be able to buy a business without being disappointed.

Not all acquisitions will grow as rapidly as projected above for Doozy, an inflation adjusted growth rate of 5% a year. Some, of course, will grow much more rapidly depending upon the markets they serve. Some few businesses will show no growth at all. Yet all of these can turn out to be successful investments if the owner/operator buys on the right terms, at a fair price, and keeps a sharp eye on cash flow.

How much to pay for goodwill remains a tough question for many buyers. Buyers want to see a lot of tangible assets. And their bankers want to see a lot of collateral. But, remember that a business that makes more money with fewer assets is the better business. Finding creative ways to finance an acquisition without using a bank may be the answer. And remember also that in today's so-called "information economy" the most important assets in a business may be knowledge assets: the contracts, data bases, contacts, customer files, software, specifications, manuals and the collective memory of where a business has been and what it has learned. Be sure to identify and define these assets as carefully as you identify and count the inventory.

You have now completed the Ten Steps to Successfully Buying a Business set out in the **Introduction**. And you have taken a look at how your business might have performed during the five years after you bought it. There are, in conclusion, a few basic guidelines that seem to summarize the lessons drawn from the real life experiences covered in this book.

1. **Do not overpay.** Try to determine a fair price (a fair value) to pay for your business. There is a small but important exception to this guideline: do not be driven by "leaving no money on the table." If your projections indicate that the business will have adequate cash flow, the price is probably fair. Remember that it might take

a lot of time (and lost salary) to find another equally attractive business.

2. **Don't buy a business that doesn't feel comfortable to you** (even if you feel that the price is a great value). It is hard to define "comfortable." Think about whether you are comfortable with the products, the customers, the suppliers, the facilities, the employees, the location and the size and complexity of the business or, in other words, the more important non-financial characteristics of the business.

3. **Be sure that your purchase contract will protect you from unforeseen events.** Perhaps you discover a material misrepresentation by the seller. Or perhaps there is an economic slowdown or rapid rise in interest rates. Does the contract give you protection to the extent practical?

4. **Be sure that the seller has some financial interest in your success.** There are many creative ways to accomplish this. Some, but certainly not all, have been discussed in the preceding chapters of this book: seller financing, a solid management assistance agreement with the seller, and appropriate consequences in the event of violations of any of the seller's warranties and representations.

5. **Be sure that you are adequately capitalized.** Defining precisely how much capital will be adequate can be difficult or even impossible. The key is to think through various potential scenarios (events that are likely to occur at some time in the future) and to project how you could handle them.

6. **Finally, stay involved in your business.** Most businesses do not run by themselves; they need steady guidance. Usually no area of involvement is more critical to your success than "watching the cash." Be sure that safeguards are in place to prevent overcharging by suppliers, malfeasance by employees, late payments by your customers and the other basic aspects of good financial management.

These guidelines, plus the Steps, Tables, TIPS, Suggestions and Case Histories, should help you to buy a business with confidence and avoid disappointment and unnecessary financial crises in the years ahead.

Glossary of Terms

Over many years in the business brokerage industry, the author has observed that small business owners are not, in general, very concerned with accounting matters. Their objective is simply to run their businesses profitably. Consequently, business owners and the people who advise them (including business brokers) do not always use financial or accounting terms very precisely.

The author recalls one conversation with an owner who stated that his business had income of around $300,000. After some time, it became clear that the owner was using the term "income" to mean the revenue coming into the business, that is, his "sales." He did not mean "bottom line income" or pre-tax earnings, as the author had at first assumed. There was a big difference between those two meanings.

It is important always to learn the definition of all terms used during the process of studying, valuing, and negotiating the purchase of a business. It is equally important to learn the definitions that other people are using. Consulting an accounting textbook is recommended. It is hoped that the layman's definitions in this Glossary (and used in the world of small business) will be helpful to you. Above all, do not hesitate to ask the meaning of any terms you hear; it can help you avoid many potential problems.

Accounting (Keeping Books). Most businesses "keep books" in some fashion or other. Smaller, unincorporated businesses sometimes "keep books" quite informally. Corporations, however, generally keep books according to standard accounting principles referred to as GAAP. These "books" consist, at a minimum, of three documents: a Statement of Income, a Balance Sheet and a Cash Flow Statement. The Balance Sheet shows the current and fixed assets at the top and the current and long-term liabilities at the bottom. The Cash Flow Statement shows changes in the "cash position" of a company from year to year. Books are kept on either the "cash" or "accrual" method but in some small businesses a combination of both is (incorrectly) used. Sometimes tax returns are prepared on the cash basis while internal company books use accrual accounting. Thus the "income" on tax returns may (legitimately) not match income on the company books.

Book Value. The Book Value of a business (or of an individual asset) is found on a company's Balance Sheet. It is the difference between the book value of its assets and the book value of its liabilities. The Book Value of the assets is the original cost of the assets less any accumulated depreciation. Book values may differ significantly from their market values. In fact, the market values are generally considerably higher. In other words, the Book Value of a business should not be confused with its Market Value. Book Value is a poor measure of a business's worth.

Cash Basis. The term "cash basis" refers to one of the two basic methods of accounting. Books are kept on the **cash** method or on the **accrual** method. If books are kept on the cash method (as they are in most small businesses), sales are reported when the cash payment is received; and expenses are reported when they are paid. Thus, businesses could have many expenses (bills) that have not been paid and are, therefore, not recorded. In such a case, the book value may overstate the real value of the business. Likewise, some sales may not always be recorded or recorded in the month they were made.

Cash Flow. The term "cash flow" generally refers to the sum of the reported earnings plus all "non-cash expenses" such as depreciation and amortization less two things: 1) payments for the purchase of depreciable equipment and 2) payments that reduce a company's debt. We can look at daily, weekly, monthly, or annual cash flows. Net cash flow would be cash flow less principle payments due on a company's debt and income taxes.

Consideration of Sale. This term is often used by lawyers, brokers and accountants. It refers to the price stated in an offer or contract. It is usually the sum of all the payments that a buyer offers to pay the seller. In other words, the Consideration of Sale is the sale price of a business. It may differ from the Present Value. See below.

Cost of Goods Sold. On the financial statements of many smaller businesses, the Gross Profit is calculated (shown as) Sales minus Purchases. This practice can lead to erroneous gross profits and, more importantly, incorrect gross profit margins. To correctly calculate gross profit, we must deduct the Cost of Goods Sold from Sales. If a business (during some time period) had purchases of $150,000 and the inventory increased by $50,000, the gross profit could be understated by $50,000. Likewise, if inventory decreased by some amount, the gross profit could be understated. The correct way to calculate the cost of goods (products/services) sold is: Add the Beginning Inventory to Purchases and then subtract the Ending inventory. The idea is to learn what it actually "cost" to produce the reported sales.

Thus the Cost of Goods is sometimes called Cost of Sales or Cost of Production. This is the cost of making or assembling the goods sold and may logically include the cost of factory labor and equipment depreciation in addition to the purchase of resale merchandise and other supplies and materials. When comparing Gross Profit margins be sure to learn what "costs" are included in Cost of Goods.

Debt Service. Debt service is what it costs literally to "service" the debt(s) of a business. It includes both principal and interest payments and includes debts owed to the seller, as well as debts owed to banks, finance companies and other parties.

Due Diligence. The term "due diligence" cannot be defined specifically. It is not an accounting term. It refers to the entire spectrum of analyses and investigations necessary to determine that a business is, in fact, in the condition it was represented to be in. Due diligence, more specifically, refers to investigations undertaken by a buyer or his (her) agents during the period between the acceptance of the Purchase Contract and the closing on the sale. The object of this process is to assure the buyer that all the contingencies and other conditions of sale can be or have been met. Sellers also occasionally conduct "due diligence" on the buyers, particularly if the buyer asks the seller to finance part of the purchase price of a business.

Earnings. The term "earnings," as it is used in this book, is defined as the earnings of a business after paying a salary to the business owner that is consistent with present market salaries for persons in similar positions. Earnings, such as Doozy's, are also pre-tax earnings, that is, earnings calculated before paying or accruing federal or state income taxes, but after deducting all business expenses, including depreciation expenses. The terms earnings, income and profit are often used interchangeably. The term Net Profit (or net income) is earnings after paying (or accruing) applicable income taxes. When looking at "earnings" of an unincorporated business, be sure to learn if the owner has deducted any salary for himself (herself).

EBIT. EBIT stands for: Earnings Before Interest and (income) Taxes. Some analysts use EBITDA: Earnings before interest, taxes, depreciation and amortization. The object of both is the same: to standardize the "earnings" of different businesses so that they may be more accurately compared. Some new businesses may be highly leveraged and pay lots of interest but pay little or no income taxes. Older businesses may have no depreciation and therefore appear quite profitable and pay a lot of income taxes. In other respects the businesses may be identical (and be worth the same).

Financial Statements. Businesses normally prepare monthly and annual financial statements. A financial statement always includes two parts: a Statement of Income and Expenses and a Balance Sheet. It should include a third, a Cash Flow Statement, but often does not in the case of small business. But ask if one can be made available. The term Income Statement means the same as Profit & Loss Statement or P&L. Statements should also include an opinion letter from the CPA or Preparer but rarely do. Be leery of relying heavily on statements if there is no opinion letter or if the letter has exceptions. Although many businesses do not compile statements on a regular or timely basis, this is generally not cause for alarm.

General Ledger. Most businesses have a general ledger. It is a daily record of all transactions: receipts, disbursements, credits and debits. It also shows daily cash balances and overdrafts. If a business's records are computerized it is easy to generate a general ledger. Of course, this record contains confidential information, so it would not be freely distributed to buyers until the negotiating or due diligence process was well along.

Goodwill. The term "goodwill" used in its accounting sense refers the difference in value between the purchase price of a business and the value assigned to the assets included in the sale. Under this definition, it is well to remember, goodwill can have either a negative or positive value. In a broader sense, goodwill refers to the general reputation of a business. However, it is advisable to try to specifically value the goodwill and to identify all the individual intangible assets that make it up. Sometimes we look at goodwill as that collection of assets that do not appear on company's balance sheet. It can include logos, the trade name of the business, customer lists, work orders, contracts, catalogues, proprietary software, and many other assets essential to operating a business.

Gross Profit. This is an important term. It is calculated by subtracting the Cost of Goods from Sales (Revenue). For retailers and wholesalers the Cost of Goods is the cost of the merchandise the business is selling. For manufacturers Cost of Goods is the cost of making the manufactured products. Some manufacturers only show the cost of materials; others show the cost of materials, labor and plant overhead (all necessary costs of making the products). If calculated correctly, Cost of Goods is adjusted for fluctuations in the value of inventories on hand. However, many small businesses just use the cost of purchases as their Cost of Goods. Year-over-year and month-over-month gross profit is expected to be a relatively constant percent of Revenue.

Income. The term income (earnings or profit) is used in several ways. It refers to how much a business earns. In some sole proprietorships (unincorporated businesses) Gross Income may refer to sales (the top line) and Net Income (the bottom line) refers to earnings. There is no pre-tax and after-tax income in sole proprietorships since the income derived from these businesses is combined with the proprietor's other income.

Liens. Liens are legal restrictions placed on certain assets by creditors. For example, when we buy a car on terms, the bank or other creditor will retain a lien on the car for as long as money is owed on it. Generally, a lien is recorded at the local courthouse or with the state. Recording makes it a public record. When buying a business, the purchaser will do a "lien search" to determine if it is "free and clear" of any indebtedness. If money is owned, the debt (lien) must be paid off before clear title can be conveyed. This "search" is done during due diligence. Lawyers check at the courthouse or statehouse to see if there are recorded liens on any assets. Unless the buyer agrees to assume an outstanding debt (as part payment of the purchase price), the business owner (seller) will have to pay off the debt before the business is sold. In actual practice, liens are removed and debts paid from closing funds by the closing attorney a day or so after the sale.

Liquidity. The term "liquidity" refers to the ease (or speed) with which an asset, generally a financial asset, can be converted to cash or some equivalent. If it might take even a week or more to convert an asset into cash, it is considered "illiquid." By this definition, most businesses are very illiquid.

Market Value. The price at which an asset (or business) would exchange hands, after adequate exposure to the market, between a willing buyer and a willing seller, each informed of the relevant facts and neither under duress.

Net Worth. The term "net worth" has a specific accounting definition: it is the (sum of the book value of a business's assets) less the (sum of the book value of a business's liabilities). Net worth is also called Book Value, because it is found on the company books. Remember that all liabilities and assets are not recorded promptly or fully on the balance sheet of many companies. For example, there may be goods-in-transit that have been pre-paid but not put on the balance sheet until they are received at the place of business. There may be unrecorded payroll obligations and bonuses.

If financial statements have been audited by a C.P.A. (which is rare in the world of small business), we can assume that the net worth is accurate. Unaudited statements, on the other hand, frequently show an inaccurate net worth. The net worth figure is likely to be more accurate in companies that keep books on the accrual method. Generally net worth includes no value for any class of goodwill. An exception would be a business that bought another business and acquired goodwill in the process. The fair market value of a business includes the presumed value of the items of goodwill.

Opinion Letter. Audited financial staements always have an Opinion Letter from the accountant (auditor) at the start of the statement. Many unaudited statements are not accompanied by opinion letters, which is unfortunate. This "letter" will set out the accountant's concerns about a business or it may state that there are no concerns about the manner in which the staements were complied. In either event, the letter is important and should be read.

Present Value. Deferred payments, such as payments that the buyer of a business promises to pay to the seller of a business at some future date, are generally worth today (at the present time) less than their face value. Thus, the Face Value of a Purchase Contract (sometimes called the Consideration of Sale) may be more than the Present Value. A good way to look at this is to answer some questions: What would you be willing to pay today for a $10,000 Promissory Note payable at the rate of $1,000 a year over a period of ten years without interest? What would you pay if the Note carried interest of 6%? Or 10%? What would you pay if the maker of the Note had declared bankruptcy at some time in the past? Your answers to these questions are the Present Values of these obligations.

Value. There are many meanings to the word "value" but, in the final analysis, value is always in the eye of the beholder. The "appraised" value of a business or of a piece of equipment is an appraiser's opinion of value. When referring to inventories, we can speak of "replacement" value, that is, what it would cost to buy (replace) today. The "market" value of something is the price for which it can be sold in its present condition. Then there is "present" value, that is, the current value of a future income stream. What an informed buyer would pay today for, say, $1,000 a year payable for ten consecutive years is its present value. See above. Book value is the value at which an item is carried on a company's balance sheet.

Work-in-Progress. This term refers to an important and often hidden asset: the value of the work output of a business which has begun but has not been completed, billed to the customer or (often) put on the books. Shop employees at Doozy may have been working on a $30,000 custom order for weeks. All materials may have been purchased and paid for and the labor completed, except for a final coat of finish. In that case, the work-in-progress (WIP) could be worth the contract price less the cost of the finish coat and a 10% profit margin, or about $25,000. In such a case the Book Value (or Net Worth) of a business would be unstated by $25,000.

Working Capital. The strict definition is Net Current Assets less Net Current Liabilities. It is an important measure of a company's fiscal health. In layman's terms, working capital refers to the money (capital) a business needs to operate. It is not the start up capital necessary to open a business or money needed to buy a business. Said differently, working capital is the amount of money needed until the cash flow from operations is adequate to fund the ongoing operations of a business.

The amount of working capital needed at different times of the year differs in different types of businesses. Many retailers, for example, may realize 50-60% of their annual sales during the Christmas season. They may operate at a deficit cash flow for ten months of the year. Working capital is needed during these months to cover that deficit. Retail businesses whose customers pay by check or cash do not need as much working capital as businesses that bill their customers each month and carry accounts receivable. The exception to this rule is businesses that are highly seasonal and must lay in (and pay for) large amounts of inventory well before sales pick up, such as businesses with large Christmas sales.

Index

A

Acceptance date, 172
Accounting, 5, 62, 168, 199
Accounts expense, 15, 74, 189
Accounts Receivable, 6, 39, 46, 79, 148
Accrual accounting, 62
Accrual method (basis), 148, 199–200, 203
Acquisition financing, xvii, 147, 149
Add backs 68, 74
Adjusting (the Purchase Price) 170
Adjustments (to earnings), 12, 70–71, 216
Agreement, binding, 135, 173
Allocation of purchase price, 114, 150–52, 174
Annual percentage rate (APR), 37, 109, 125–26, 129, 147
Appraisal(s), 213
Asking Price 3, 35, 36, 37, 43, 86, 109, 124
Assets, 31–32, 39, 41–43, 46–49, 51–54, 77–83, 113–19, 122–23, 139, 141–43, 149–53, 199, 201–4, A-2–A-3, A-5–A-6
    Classes of, 46–47
    Current, 39, 204
    Excess of, 49
    Hidden, 4, 48, 80, 102, 185, 195, 203
    Overstated, 67
    Sale, 31, 114, 166
    Tangible (fixed, hard), 39, 41, 43, 47, 77, 86, 103, 151, 196, A-2
    Unrecorded, 83
Attorney. *See* closing, 172

B

Balance Sheet, xvi, 5, 39, 48, 52, 66–68, 77–80, 82–83, 88–89, 92–94, 96, 100, 199, 203, 215–16
Balloon note (payment), 121
Bill of Sale, 139, 172, 176–77, A-14
Blue sky, 43
Budget, 101, 161, 189–90, 194
Bulk Sales Act, 138–39, 166
Business (type of), 25, 35, 54, 61, 106, A-2

    Advertising company, 134
    Cabinet manufacturer, 33, 74, 86, 169
    Ceramic products, 48
    Convenience store, 22
    Day care, 13
    Dental lab, 52, 94
    Dress shop, 171, 189
    Forklift distributor, 91
    Furniture store, 23
    HVAC equipment sales, 23
    HVAC service, 41
    Industrial equipment sales, 13
    Landscape contractor, 18, 186
    Liquor store, 22, 91, 95, 168–69
    Manufacturing, 20, 22, 31–33, 41, 48, 73–74, 80, 87, 101, 129, 132, 135, 153, 168, 191
    Personal services, 20, 26
    Photo processor, 18
    Professional services, 20–21
    Restaurant and bar, 91
    Retail, 10, 20, 41, 43, 46–47, 52, 60, 74, 81, 90, 95, 99, 105, 118, 168–69
    Security guard service, 26
    Service company, 41
    Veterinary practice 23
    Wholesale, 20, 47, 161, A-2
Business brokers, 9–11, 15, 154, 214
Business cycle v, 56, 57, 107, 177, 181, 186, 218
Business valuation, 31, 39, 215
Buyers Agreement, 11

C

Capital (see working), xvii–xviii, 46–47, 107–8, 118, 126, 130, 147, 176, 187, 191, 193, 204, A-2
Capitalization (cap) rate, 44–45
Cash flow, xvii, 4, 6, 28, 67, 88, 91–92, 104–5, 108–10, 125–26, 130, 187–88, 191–93, 199–201, 216
Cash method, 200
Charter (corporate), 131, 133–34, 167
Checklist(s) 53, 166, 167, 214, 218
Closing (on sale of business), xviii, 50, 67, 79, 83, 119–21, 123–26, 129–30, 139–40, 144–45, 147–49, 159, 166–67, 169–77, 187–88
Closing attorney, 138, 144–45, 152, 166–67, 172–77, 181, 202, 217, A-10, A-13
Closing costs, xviii, 130, 166–67, 175–76, 194, A-10, A-12
Closing documents, 131, 136, 140, 172, 174–75, 181, 187, A-10
Collateral, 37, 121–23, 147, 149, 156, 196

Common Area Maintenance (CAM), 144
Comparable sale, 86
Compensation issues, 75
Compliance, 122, 141, 148, 166
Condition(s) (of sale), 140
Conduct of business 141, 142
Confidentiality, 9, 11, 29, A-1
Consideration of Sale, 200, 203
Contingency(ies) clauses, 149, 162, 217
Corporate resolution(s), 132, 135, 187
Cost (original), 13–14, 39, 50–51, 67, 78, 94, 96, 119, 129, 160, 169, 199
Cost of goods sold (COGs), 44, 63, 95–96, 190, 200
Counteroffers, 131, 172
Covenant (not to compete), A-8, A-10
Customer base, 24
Customers, xiv, 4, 6, 11, 24–25, 27–28, 46, 48, 118, 147–49, 163–64, 185–88, 191, 203–4, A-3–A-4

D

Daycare Business 12, 16
Dealer(ship), 10, 21–22, 39, 67, 116, 147, 167
Debt service, 18, 104, 108–10, 124, 161, 189, 191, 193, 200
Deduction(s), 37, 69, 152–53, 192–93
Default (clause), 122
Deposits (customers/service), 66, 79, 130, A-11
Depreciation
    Accelerated, 152
    Straight line, 152
Depreciation (schedule), 135, 153
Discount(s), 105, 169
Discounted cash flow, 103–4
Down payment, xviii, 18, 36–38, 54, 75, 100, 109, 120, 125–26, 129–30, 135, 145–46, 170–71, 192, 194
Due diligence (process), xvii–xviii, 147, 161–65, 173, 200–202, 217

E

Earnest money, 76, 129, 145–46, 150, 156, A-8–A-9, A-12
Earning, 32–41, 44–46, 51–60, 63, 65–76, 78, 84–94, 96, 99, 103–4, 152–54, 161–62, 164–65, 199–202, 215–16
    Capacity, 99, 216
    Multiple, 44, 52, 55
    As percent of sales, 59, 85
    Value, xvi, 14, 31, 34–36, 40–46, 78–79, 82, 94, 104–5, 119, 125, 151, 170, 199–200, 202–4

Earnings
  Restated, 84–86
  Retained, 89, 192
EBIT(DA), 63–64, 106, 192, 194, 201
Economic indicator(s) 177–178
Embezzlement, 90, 92
Employee(s) xiv, 4, 5, 7, 9, 10, 11, 15, 20, 24, 25, 33, 34, 35, 38, 68, 69, 72, 73, 74, 75, 76, 79, 90, 91, 92, 96, 100, 101, 108, 111, 115, 142, 163, 164, 167, 176, 180, 182, 184, 186, 187, 189, 203, 1, 3, 10
Escrow (agreement)(agent), 136, 145–46
Excess Earnings Method, 103
Excess inventory, 44, 49–51, 66, 119, 171, 186
Exhibits, 135–36, 150
Exit strategy, 25, 27
Expenses (non-operating/operating), 13, 66–67, 91, 93, 96

F

Fair Market Value 49, 52, 59, 65, 77, 80, 82, 86, 94, 203
Fair price xiv, 18, 45, 65, 113, 184, 196, 214, 216
Financial statement(s) 15, 33, 42, 67, 68, 72, 90, 93, 162, 201
Fixed assets (FF&E), 13–14, 33, 41, 43, 47, 83, 96, 125, 135, 150–53, 160, 167, 171, 174–75, 192
Forecast(ing), 101–2, 104, 110, 125–26, 152, 187, 189, 191–92, 194
Foreclose, 122

G

General ledger, 60, 76, 201
Goodwill (value), 39–44, 47, 53, 55, 81, 86, 103, 114, 116, 129, 151, 201–3, 213, 215, A-2–A-5
Gross profit (margins), 44, 63–64, 73, 91, 94–96, 107, 164, 169, 190, 200, 202, 216, A-6

H

Hidden assets (value), 48, 80, 185, 195
Hold harmless (clause), 144, 148

I

Income, 12–16, 34, 36–39, 41, 53, 63–69, 72–78, 88–90, 96, 102–5, 125–26, 150–53, 189–95, 199–203, A-2–A-6
  Approach to value, 72, 86
  As percent of sales, 59, 85
  Pro forma, 109, 189
  Statement, 67, 73–74, 76, 84, 88–89, 94, 96, 190, 201, 215–16, A-6
  Weighted, 86

Incorporate(d), 31, 33, 114, 133, 136
Insurance, 13, 15, 33, 66, 68–69, 73, 76, 79–80, 83, 92, 96, 115, 143, 167, 189–90
Intangible assets 39. *See under* assets
Inventory, 34–35, 43–44, 47–51, 66–67, 89, 92–96, 100, 107–9, 118–19, 129, 138, 145–48, 167–73, 175, 200
    Count (taking of), 168, 170, 175, A-10
    Normal levels, 51
    Obsolete, 50, 78
    Service, 168
    Turnover, 43–44, 108

K

Key customer, xiv, 141, A-4
Key employee 101
Keys (to success), xiv

L

Late payments, 122
Law(s), lawsuit, 66, 115, A-7
Lawyer(s), 11, 187
Legal (assistance), 133
Letter of intent, 126, 128, 131–32, 135, 137, 151, 154, 156
Liabilities, 31, 63, 67–68, 73, 77–79, 83, 96, 114, 118, 120, 144, 148, 199, 202–4, A-10
Lien (first search), xviii, 144, 173–74, 202
Line(s) of credit, 46, 107, A-4
Liquidation, 78, 143, A-5
Liquidity, 38, 45, 202

M

Management assistance, 24, 120–21, 123–26, 131, 136, 140, 151, 153, 157, 165, 182, 187–89, A-8–A-9
Minutes (book), 133, 135
Misrepresent(ation) 83, 90, 110, 111, 137, 143
Missing allocation 152
Missing Inventory, 100
Monthly financial statements, xv, 56, 62, 72, 123, 216
Monthly sales 15, 17, 56, 60, 61, 62, 102

N

Negative goodwill, 43–44, 215
Negotiating, xvii, 117, 120, 131, 143, 161, 165–66, 180, 185, 190, 199, 201
Non-compete agreements, 114, 116, 136
Non-compliance, 141

Non-disclosure (Agreement) 137, 1
Non-financial criteria, 23, 215
Non-performance (by seller), 143

O

Obsolete inventory, 50, 78. *See also under* inventory
Opinion letter (accountant's), 84, 186–87, 201, 203
Opinion of value 49, 63, 203

P

Payroll service, 77
Penalties 122, 140, 188
Percent of sales (value), 108
Petty cash, xviii, 176
Pilferage (embezzlement), 92
Plant capacity, 99, 185
Pre-closing checklist, 166–67
Pre-incorporation agreement, 134–35
Pre-tax earnings (income), 38–39, 52–53, 55, 59, 72, 74, 89, 148, 161–62, 199, 201
Present value 104, 105, 124, 156, 200, 203
Price to earnings ratio, 45, 52
Profit margins, 58–60, 64, 84, 91, 107, 200, 204
Promissory note, 120–21, 124, 136, 140, 143, 165, 170, 172, 192, 203, A-7, A-13
Pro-rate(ing), 144–45
Prospectus (profile of business), 12–13, 171

R

Ratios (price to earnings), 45, 52
Real estate, 20–21, 33, 46, 51–52, 87, 119, 145, 147–48, 173, 176–77
Real growth, 189
Recasting (financial statements), 67
Reconciliation (reconciling) 103, 185
Red flag(s) 14, 214
Remedy(ies), xvi, 137, 143–45, 148, 156, 170, 217
Renegotiation 164, 165
Replacement (value, cost), 94, 103, 108, 119, 169
Reported sales, adjusting, 60
Restated earnings, 84–86. *See also under* earnings
Restrictive covenant, 140, 151, 153
Retained earnings, 89, 192. *See also under* earnings
Return on assets (ROA), 35–36, 41, 43, 108
Return on investment (ROI), 35–38, 54, 87, 125–26, 194
Right of offset, 139, 144, 156

Risk (factors), 38

S

Sale price(s) 81, 119, 168, 200, 2, 3, 12
Scam, 138
Schedules (part of contracts), 84, 135–36, 150, 188
Seasonal 51, 62, 121, 204, 218
Security agreement, 122–23, A-7
Settlement Sheet, 145, 175, A-13
Shareholder(s) 114, 134, 137, 195
SIC codes, 22
Sole proprietor(ship), 116, 134
Spreadsheet, 12–13, 15, 68, 73–75, 96, A-6
Standardizing statement, 63
Stock sale, 78, 113–14, 135
Suggestion, 13, 52, 72, 74, 82, 87, 126, 154, 167, 190
Summary 41, 60, 61, 62, 70, 4
Summary (of monthly sales), 60–61
Supplier(s), 10, 115–16, 136, 148, 169, A-4

T

Ten Steps xvii, 196
Terms of payment 81, 125, 126, 154
Terms of purchase xiv, xvii, 100, 113, 126, 127, 143, 164, 196
Terms of sale 120, 123
TIP, xviii, 28, 51, 71, 75, 77, 82, 90, 95–96, 131, 167, 171
Title (taking), 114, 133, 166
Turnover (turns), 43–44, 50, 108

U

Undisclosed liabilities, 114, 120, 123, 144, 156, A-10
Unemployment insurance, 190
Unlocking value, 185
Unrecorded, 48, 66–68, 83, 91, 94, 203
Unscrupulous 7, 111

V

Value glossary
    Asset, 4–6, 31–34, 36–44, 46–49, 51–55, 77–84, 86, 102–4, 113–19, 121–25, 137–43, 149–54, 173–74, 199–204, A-2–A-6
    Book, xvi, 14, 31, 40, 42–43, 67, 78, 90, 94, 119, 153, 160, 199–200, 202–4
    Fair market, 31, 48–49, 52, 59, 65, 77, 80, 82, 86, 94, 203
    Goodwill, 41–43, 53, 55, 86, 103, A-2–A-3, A-5
    Present (of income stream), 103, 203, A-3–A-4

Valuing (business, contract, inventory), 46, 87, 106, 156, 165, A-5

W

Warrants (ies), 136, 138–39, 142–43, 217, A-1, A-9–A-10, A-14
Working capital, xvii–xviii, 46–47, 107–8, 118, 126, 130, 147, 176, 187, 191, 193, 204, A-2
Work-in-process (progress), 47, 80, 203

Bibliography and Suggested Reading

Books:

Bergh, Louis. *Business Law.* 6th ed. New York: Ronald Press, 1964.

Berthelette, Eric, and Kresen, Frank, editors. *The Entrepreneur's Planning Handbook*, revised ed. Denver: Entrepreneurial Foundation, 1997.

Domash, Harry. *Fire Your Stock Analyst.* Prentice Hall 2006.

Gumpert, David E. *How To Really Create a Successful Marketing Plan.* 3rd ed. Boston: Inc. Publishing, 1996.

Lereah, David A., The Rules For Growing Rich: Making Money In the Information Economy. Random House 2000

Morris, Joseph, and James N. Brendel. *Mergers and Acquisitions: Business Strategies for Accountants.* Hoboken: John Wiley & Sons, 1995.

Pratt, Shannon P., Robert F. Reilly, and Robet P. Schweihs. *Valuing a Business: the Analysis and Appraisal of Closely Held Companies.* 3rd ed. Chicago: Irwin Professional Publishing, 1995.

Price, Courtney, Mack R. Davis, and Richard H. Buskirk. *Sample Business Plans: Premier Fast Track.* Denver: Premier Entrepreneur Programs, Inc., 1994.

West, Tom. *The 2003 Business Reference Guide.* 13th edition Concord, MA: Business Brokerage Press, 2003.

Articles:

Gibson, John. "The Need for Forensic Accounting in Valuing Small Businesses," 2004. Allied Buisness Group.

Gibson, John. "Notes on Value of Goodwill in Small Businesses," 1999. Allied Buisness Group.

Jones, Gary E., and Dirk E. Van Dyke. "Using the Black/Green Approach to the Build-Up Summation Method."

Miles, Raymond C. "Placing the Subject Business within the Range of Market Values," 2005. Buisness Brokerage Press.

Discussion Questions, Checklists and Study Guides

Introduction

1. Why do some businesses fail?
2. Why are some buyers disappointed in the financial results of businesses they bought?
   Identify as many possible explanations as you can.
3. A business should have enough "cash flow" to cover four essential things. What are they? Discuss why each is critical to your success.
4. There are 10 distinct steps to go through to successfully negotiate a fair price and purchase a business. Can you name them?

Chapter 1 Why Buy a Business?

1. Are there advantages in buying an established business rather then starting a new business? List them.
2. What are the differences between first and second generation businesses?
3. How can we find businesses that might be for sale?
4. What is the role of a business broker? Are there advantages to the buyer in using a broker?
5. What documents should a seller provides to a potential buyer? When should he provide them?
6. What should you look for in your first review of a set of financial statements?
7. Name some of the obvious (or potential) "red flags" related to the operation of a business? To the financial statements?

Chapter 2 What Kind of Business To Buy?

1. What are the major "types" of businesses? Discuss the characteristics of each.
2. List some important non-financial criteria to take into account when placing a value on a business?
3. What are some of the factors that have led to the slowdown in growth in certain industries? Or to their eventual disappearance?
4. Why should it matter to you, as a buyer, what kind of business to buy?

Chapter 3 Business Valuations

1. List and discuss the three major approaches to valuing a business.
2. What secondary sources of data might be helpful in doing a business valuation?
3. Identify and discuss some common financial measures for (a) describing a business and (b) comparing one business to another.
4. Discuss whether Business 1, 2 or 3 (on page 26) is more valuable and why you think so.
5. Discuss how to determine if a set of financial statements has been prepared on the "cash" basis, "accrual" basis or a combination.
6. List and discuss reasons why reported sales or expenses may not be fully accurate.
7. Is there any indication that all expenses have not been posted? Has Rent been paid for the current month? Depreciation? Interest?
8. Are there unexplained deviations between the amount of expenses posted for some accounts in different reporting periods?
9. What differences can be found in the financial results of different kinds of businesses or businesses in different industries? Think of the Balance Sheet as well as the Income Statement)
10. Under what conditions would you expect a business to have no goodwill? Or negative goodwill?
11. Is the business growing? What is the rate of growth when adjusted for inflation?
12. What earnings multiple is appropriate for each (type) of business? Discuss.

Chapter 4 Adjustments to Financial Statements

1. Discuss and list frequently encountered non-operating expenses.
2. How can we tell when earnings (profits) have been overstated? List.
3. How can we tell when earnings may be understated? List indications.
4. What is the advantage of looking at monthly financial statements in addition to the annual statements?
5. When does it make sense to "weight" the earnings?
6. List and discuss some of the kinds of account entries that suggest it is necessary to make adjustments to the income statement?
7. Are the Cost of Goods and the Gross Profit calculated accurately?
8. When should adjustments be made to the Balance Sheet of a company?
9. Recast the financial results for the Daycare spreadsheet shown on page 10? What is the actual pre-tax income, cash flow and EBITDA for each year?
10. What, in your opinion, would be a fair price for the Daycare?

Chapter 5 Earnings Capacity and Other Valuation Factors

1. Explain the concept and the importance of "earnings capacity."
2. Explain what the term "cash flow" means. Explain "cash flow from operations."
3. Explain the process of reconciling values and why it may be important.
4. How can you spot items in the current operation of a business that should be changed?
5. Can you spot items that can easily be changed with new management?
6. What impact would these changes have on future cash flows? Profits?
7. What valuation factors/ratios could be red flags to a potential buyer?
8. What does the expression "let your contract do the talking" mean?

Chapter 6 How To Structure a Purchase Agreement

1. What are the critical elements in an enforceable purchase contract?
2. What are some of the elements of a contract that each purchaser has control of?
3. What remedies does a buyer have when a seller defaults on some provision (the Seller's Warrants for example) in a purchase contract?
4. What remedies does a seller have when the purchaser defaults? Explain how these work.
5. Why is the "allocation of the purchase price" important and what are some of the considerations that a buyer should focus on?
6. How can the allocation favor the seller and how can it favor the buyer?
7. What contingency clauses should normally be in a contract?
8. What warranties and representations should be in a contract? Which protect the buyer and which protect the seller?
9. Describe the financial structure of a typical contract that includes "seller financing."
10. Discuss the circumstances under which you might buy the "stock" of a company instead of buying "assets."

Chapter 7 The Closing on the Sale

1. Explain the "due diligence" process. Why is it important to a buyer?
2. List and discuss what "approvals" may be necessary before the closing.
3. What are a buyer's options if the due diligence reveals that one or more contingencies have not been met?
4. List and then discuss the basic components of the closing process.
5. Discuss the more commonly encountered methods for taking and valuing the inventory of a business?
6. What does a "closing attorney" actually do? What should he do?
7. What role should a buyer's attorney play in the contract preparation, due diligence and closing processes?

8. Does it matter when to buy a business? When in the business cycle? When in the seasonal cycle of a business?

Chapter 8 Conclusion

1. List in order the various "processes" that should take place before the closing on the purchase of a business occurs?
2. Discuss the components of each "process."
3. List the commonly cited reasons for buying a business.
4. Discuss how it might be possible for a purchaser to "unlock" additional or "hidden" value in a business.
5. Discuss why positive "cash flow" is so critical to the success of a business purchase.
6. What are some of the things that should happen after the sale/purchase of a business to help ensure each buyer's success?
7. How would you know if your purchase of a business has been a success?
8. Why do some businesses fail and some succeed?

Checklists:

1. List and discuss the various documents and data that you would expect a business owner to provide to his broker or to prospective buyers when offering his business for sale.
2. List the "red flags" you might find in a set of financial statements and discuss several appropriate ways to handle them.
3. List the various personalized sections (stipulations, covenants or agreements) that you would require be added to a standard Purchase Contract. Discuss why they should be added.
4. List the usual attachments (Exhibits and Schedules) to a Purchase Contract (as well as some unusual attachments).
5. List and discuss the tasks which you feel must be completed (or questions that must be answered) before:
   a. scheduling the closing on the sale/purchase of a business, and
   b. leaving the closing table

APPENDIX
CONFIDENTIALITY & NON-CIRCUMVENTION AGREEMENT

The undersigned prospective purchaser ("PURCHASER") hereby agrees not to disclose to or discuss with any third party, other than PURCHASER's employees, investors and other professional financial advisors who shall also be covered by this agreement, confidential information provided by seller ("SELLER") or his agent, Allied Business Brokers Mid-south ("BROKER") with respect to a company identified through a summary profile titled: LIQUOR AND WINE STORE ("BUSINESS"), and dated February 3, 2009, and to keep confidential the company's business affairs including the fact that BUSINESS may be available for purchase.

PURCHASER warrants that he has contacted BROKER and is entering into this agreement for the purpose of considering an acquisition of a business.

PURCHASER agrees not to use confidential information provided by BROKER for competitive purposes, and to keep in strict confidence all information relating to BUSINESS that could be used to the detriment of BUSINESS or its owners.

PURCHASER agrees to not circumvent or contact directly the owners, employees, suppliers, competitors or customers of BUSINESS without permission of BROKER.

PURCHASER agrees to not make any offer to invest in or purchase the company except through BROKER, and will be liable to BROKER for any fees that would be owed should PURCHASER circumvent BROKER.

PURCHASER acknowledges that serious monetary damage to BUSINESS and its owners could result from improper or unauthorized disclosure of Confidential Information, including the fact that the owners of BUSINESS are considering a sale of referenced business.

Upon request, PURCHASER will either return to BROKER all written confidential information provided and/or covered under this Agreement, including original documents and all copies or reproductions, or certify that said confidential information has been destroyed.

Should SELLER or his agent find it necessary to engage the services of an attorney to enforce the terms and conditions of this Agreement, prevailing party shall be entitled to collect reasonable attorneys' fees in connection with any successful enforcement activity.

AGREED & ACCEPTED _____ DATE: _____
                          Authorized Signature
PURCHASER NAME:_____
COMPANY: _____
ADDRESS: _____
TELEPHONE: _____

NOTES ON VALUE OF GOODWILL IN SMALL BUSINESSES

Introduction: The sale price of most successful small, privately-held businesses includes a "value" in excess of the value of its tangible assets. In other words, the price for which successful businesses will sell (their market value) is expected to be greater than the value of the individual assets used in the operation of each business. This excess value is often referred to in the courts and by others as "goodwill." Sometimes it is referred to as a "going concern" value. This latter term makes a distinction between businesses that are in operation and businesses that are going out of business.

How much goodwill to assign to a business is always a matter of discussion. The simplest yardstick I have developed is that the goodwill value is expected to be about equal to one-year's adjusted pre-tax income. Of course, such a yardstick fits no business exactly. The actual or appraised value of the goodwill varies all over the place even for similar businesses in the same industry. In fact today, there are probably "yardsticks" for each major type of business: retail, wholesale, manufacturing and service. They are good starting points but are not very reliable measures. Service businesses tend to have the fewest tangible assets and the greatest goodwill value if measured as a percent of the prices at which these businesses typically sell.

Based on information from various business brokerage firms, it is generally agreed that about one-half of all small businesses cannot be sold as going concerns.[1] They, therefore, cannot be expected to have any "going concern" or goodwill value and will probably be sold for a price close to the value of the individual assets. The most commonly observed reason for this situation is the lack of demonstrated and sustainable income. Here we are using the term "income" to mean any pre-tax profit in excess of a normal salary for the proprietor or operator (if the operator is not the proprietor).

If we are being technical, the term "income" is really what is left over after:

- payment of a compensation package (including salary, payroll taxes and other normal benefits such as health insurance) equal to the "going rate" in each marketplace to hire someone with the skills necessary to replace the operator, plus
- paying a return on the value of the assets used by a business (the return generally is thought of as interest at a rate at which a small business owner could borrow money)

---

[1] What qualifies a business to be called a going concern can be debated. For purposes of this discussion a good definition might be: a business that is sufficiently stable financially that a buyer would not have to inject additional working capital into it to keep it running.

Thus, a business can appear on paper to have some income and, therefore, appear at first glance to deserve some goodwill value in the marketplace. However, after subtracting a reasonable compensation package and subtracting a return on the value of the assets, this apparent income might disappear. Let's use as an example a business that during the most recent year:

- paid a salary package of $40,000 to the owner
- showed pre-tax profit of $25,000 and
- had assets valued at $150,000

If a competitive package in the market was $60,000 and we use a 10% cost of money (interest), what looked at first like a profit of $25,000 becomes a loss of $10,000 and any potential goodwill value quickly vanishes. Why? The answer is that few buyers would consider buying a business for more than the value of its assets ($150,000 in this case) that did not earn at least enough to cover interest on the purchase price and a reasonable compensation. This does not mean that such a business is not saleable; it only suggests that the sale price of such a business might not include any goodwill value.

There are some other keys to determining the existence of goodwill value, and the value of that goodwill in a given situation, in addition to the existence of income. Some of these other keys are:

Transferability The goodwill must be transferable to a new owner. This means that the accounts, and other intangible assets, must survive a transition of ownership. If a new owner can keep the revenue and income stream (enjoyed by the former owner) intact after the purchase of a business, the goodwill is indeed transferred. Often, we should assume that some accounts can be transferred and that others cannot be. In either case, the goodwill value can be expected to diminish over time, sometimes quite rapidly. In other cases, under new ownership, revenues and income will grow and a business will flourish without the previous owner, in which case the value of goodwill might increase.

Organization If the technical knowledge and business concept that produced the historic incomes in a business disappear when the owner, founder or operator leave, the goodwill value will evaporate very quickly. In fact, it might leave with the former owner. If, on the other hand, there is an organization in place that consists of trained, competent and loyal employees, a business may never miss the departure of the former owner and the "goodwill" tends to remain in place. In fact, a business may blossom under a new owner (the so-called "honeymoon effect") because a new owner needs to listen to and respect the knowledge and ideas of employees and customers far more than the former owner, in many cases, needed to or cared to.

Contracts Some business operators are fortunate enough or farsighted enough to have in place relatively long-term contracts with suppliers, customers, employees, landlords or with other entities critical to the survival and growth of a business. If these contracts are automatically rescinded, or have to be renegotiated when an owner leaves (or sells), there is uncertainly surrounding the continuation of the revenue stream and income stream of a business and, therefore, of it's goodwill. Some examples might be a line of credit with a bank, an exclusive distribution agreement with a supplier, or a long-term lease with a landlord. These factors are all small but important examples of goodwill, each of which can be transferred, sold or valued independently.

Let's consider for the moment what would happen if a business were near the end of its lease and the landlord wanted to increase the annual rent by 20% or if a key supplier wanted to give the distribution rights to a competitor. Both landlord and supplier may have been loyal to the former owner for years and, knowing he was considering retirement, held off on making any major changes. Let's assume that the annual rent that the owner/seller has enjoyed is $60,000 a year. If a buyer (or the current owner) had to pay $75,000 during the coming five years, annual income would be $15,000 less. If 20% of revenue was from products purchased from the key supplier and no alternate supplier could be found, this loss could quite literally wipe out a business's bottom line (income). Businesses survive this sort of double whammy, but such a double whammy would reduce income and consequently reduce the value of the business and its goodwill.

Customer Contacts If customers rarely had personal contact with the prior owner, as is the case with many retail establishments, his or her departure would matter little. Also, there are some business-to-business establishments where there has been little or no personal contact between owner and customer. However, if the only contact between customer and the business is through the owner, it may be difficult and very time consuming for a new owner to obtain new orders.

An example that comes to mind is a typical "sales rep" organization. The transfer of the goodwill of such a business is made easier if the former owner willingly signs a non-competition agreement with a new owner. The former owner can also enter into a "management contract" with a new owner, under which the previous owner agrees, among other things, to introduce the buyer to all key customers. Such agreements become yet another intangible asset which forms part of the Goodwill.

Another example of the value of customer contact is a business that has done business for many years under the owner's name. Even if the business continues to operate under the same name after it is sold, it is not the same business if the owner whose name is on the marquee is not there to greet customers. Many restaurants fall into this category.

Summary: The determination of the existence of goodwill and the magnitude of its value, we can see, depends upon many discrete variables. Each must be taken into account by the appraiser.

However, overriding all other factors, it is the degree of probability that the income stream enjoyed by one owner can be transferred to another owner that determines the value of the Goodwill. Markets dislike uncertainty and, if uncertainty exists regarding the efficient transfer of the intangible assets discussed above, the prudent buyer or investor will discount the goodwill value which otherwise might seem to exist. Many small businesses are fragile and cannot adjust very rapidly to the changing demand of the market place or changes in the environment in which they operate.

If it is determined that no goodwill exists, then we are left with selecting the proper asset value criterion to use in valuing a business. There are, in general terms, three separate criteria: <u>value in use, value in place, and liquidation value, the price that the assets will bring under a situation in which a business will cease operation and the assets must be sold off one by one, or in lots.</u>

The asset value "in use" is far higher in most cases that the value which the assets would bring in a forced or "going out of business" sale. Also the value "in use" is higher than the value of the assets "in place." The reasoning is that it costs someone time and money to assemble the aggregation of assets into a viable, smoothly operating business. In a "going business" the equipment, the counters and shelving all have been installed in a workable configuration. These assets clearly have a use and can be used efficiently and profitably. And the skill with which they have been assembled and installed can, to a very real degree, determine the profitably of a small business. Assets that are simply "in place" may or may not contribute to the production of income.

Although it is not at first apparent to a skeptical buyer, these "configurations" evolve over many years of trial and error. A lot of effort and experience (translate: time and money) go into determining the optimal mix of assets as well as their configuration. The cost is often money well spent by a seller and money that a buyer will not have to spend. During this trial and error process, owners learn which assets are essential to the efficient and profitable operation of their plants (or businesses of any kind) and which are disposable or surplus. And this is why good businesses (some with very few visible assets) can justify a goodwill value well in excess of the value of their tangible assets and why other businesses that are "rich" in assets have no goodwill.

Copyright 1999, John V. M. Gibson, President, Allied Business Brokers, Inc. Distribution or reproduction without express written permission of the author is strictly prohibited.

Bigger Cabinet Corporation, Inc. Spreadsheet 2001-2007

	2007	2006	2005	2004	2003	2002	2001
Gross Sales	$4,365,729	$3,931,819	$3,180,802	$2,852,704	$2,677,929	$1,265,757	$2,222,255
Cost of Sales	2,816,790	2,592,498	2,100,668	1,897,314	1,767,932	956,704	1,648,880
Gross Profit	1,548,939	1,339,321	1,080,1334	955,390	909,997	309,053	573,375
% Gross Profit	35.48	33.38	33.23	32.74	33.25	24.01	25.47
Operating Expenses							
Advertising	69,386	79,630	67,431	32,372	22,787	11,719	21,127
Auto	4,812	5,509	7,713	6,831	7,383	2,518	4,707
Bad Debts	6,204	58,312	(35,348)	2,508	25,874	0	(2,115)
Credit Card Fees	8,939	12,214	15,667	14,654	12,948	0	0
Bank Charges	49	495	1,413	1,098	30	10	90
Canteen	507	1,477	1,409	(636)	(480)	(59)	(158)
Depreciation	31,677	18,701	15,262	14,039	12,715	2,766	4,609
Donations	900	575	0	0	120	350	250
Dues	820	775	925	805	805	30	30
Meals	846	502	207	227	21	18	73
Equipment Rental	1,022	1,172	834	0	0	0	46
Insurance	121,373	130,009	142,869	147,559	122,573	78,242	122,146
Trash Collection	1,152	989	2,381	1,512	935	647	1,093
Miscellaneous	75	135	1,094	174	623	0	487
Repaire	10,881	10,174	7,732	12,283	4,816	2,023	6,259
Office Supplies	14,637	15,540	12,676	5,190	8,584	3,065	5,045
Temporary Office	811	1,139	624	448	0	0	0
Payroll Taxes	76,138	77,382	62,895	55,102	47,943	26,744	46,253
Pension/ Profit Sharing	160,800	87,906	20,182	0	41,950	0	0
Professional Fees	11,104	18,777	14,051	37,993	11,631	6,450	9,295
Postage All	6,280	5,971	5,461	30,531	37,038	20,270	31,534
Rent	60,000	60,000	60,000	60,000	60,000	30,000	50,000
Salaries							
- Owner	272,846	96,000	96,000	48,000	0	0	0
- Children	83,577	83,577	83,577	83,577	83,577	41,788	0
- Other	530,294	486,423	457,674	395,809	357,188	191,455	0
Taxes and Licenses	8,873	9,678	15,840	16,020	15,350	128	12,408
Telephone	37,258	34,267	28,786	23,498	25,207	11,969	19,784
Travel	1,394	1,187	1,057	722	179	0	0
Utilities	19,679	25,687	18,860	18,830	22,925	10,384	20,147
Total Expenses	1,542,333	1,350,205	1,107,990	1,009,194	922,722	448,327	742,633
Operating Income	6,606	(10,884)	(27,856)	(53,796)	12,725	(139,274)	(169,258)
Miscellaneous Income	(20,948)	(12,776)	(1,935)	(3,994)	(5,490)	(3,389)	(3,593)
Disposal of Asset	6,177	(1,175)	6,375	12,213	5,297	0	0
Income Taxes	6,264	2,945	269	0	3,307	3,400	3,400
Other Income	9,523	11,006	(4,709)	(8,219)	(3,114)	(10)	193
Pre-Tax Income	$ 16,130	$ 122	($32,565)	($62,015)	$ 15,839	($139,284)	($169,065)

Notes: (1) The figures shown for Salaries—Owner Children are taken from W-2s. On Income Statement, Salary—Children is combined with Salaries—Other.

(2) Results shown for 2002 are for six months only as result of change of Fiscal Year.

Sample Promissory Notes
Promissory Note (with Installments)

$100,000

Dated: November 27, 2002

For value received, Johnny B. Buyer (Hereafter "Borrower"), 112 East 112th Street, New York, New York 12231, promises to pay to Bob B. Bigger (Hereafter "Lender") the principal sum of $100,000 together with nine percent (9%) annual interest on the unpaid balance.

Borrower agrees that this note will be paid in forty-eight (48) equal and consecutive monthly installments of principal and interest of _____ with the first payment due on the 15th day of January 2003 and on the 15th day of each month thereafter until paid in full.

If any installment is not received within ten (10) days of the due date, Borrower agrees to pay Lender a late fee of exactly $100.00. Late fees not received by the due date of the next installment shall be added to the principal balance and accrue interest.

Borrower further agrees that in the event three consecutive installments are not received by the due debt, Lender, at his option, demand the entire unpaid balance of principal and accrued interest will become immediately due and payable.

If Lender brings suit against Borrower to recover an unpaid balance due and prevails in a lawsuit, Borrower will pay legal fees and court costs which the court finds reasonable.

Agreed:_____   _____
         Johnny B. Buyer   Witness

Promissory Note (Secured)

$100,000

Dated: August 15, 2004

For value received, Borrower, Thomas B. Buyer, of 201 Second Avenue, Syracuse, New York 22124, promises to pay to Lender, George A. Smith, of 505 East Elm Street, Syracuse, New York 22134 the sum of one hundred thousand dollars and no/cents ($100,000.00) together with interest at the rate of eight percent (8%) on any unpaid balance.

Payments are payable in sixty (60) consecutive monthly installment in the amount of $_____ beginning the 1st day of October 2004 and on the 1st day of each month thereafter until paid in full.

This note is secured by a Security Agreement dated August 15, 2004 setting forth conditions agreed to by Borrower. Borrower acknowledges that default or breach of any of these conditions permits Lender, at his option, to demand full and immediate payment of any balance due under this note.

Note may be prepaid at any time in whole or in part without penalty.

_____
Johnny B. Buyer   Date   Witness

PURCHASE CONTRACT

STATE OF: Tennessee
COUNTY OF: Shelby

This **Purchase Contract** entered into this the ___ day of _____, 2008, by and between _____ (hereinafter Seller) with an address at _____ _____, and _____ _____ (hereinafter Purchaser) with an address at _____ _____. Purchaser and Seller are hereinafter jointly termed the Parties. Purchaser has paid to Allied Business Brokers (hereinafter Broker) the sum of _____, as earnest money and part payment of the Purchase Price. On the dates herein stated, Purchaser agrees to buy and Seller agrees to sell all goodwill, trade- marks, trade name(s), logos, contract rights, customer lists, and other tangible and intangible assets, including but not limited to those listed below, of the business known as _____ _____ (hereinafter Business) located at _____ _____ with the exceptions, if any, of the excluded assets listed in Special Stipulation 1 on the next page:

All furniture, fixtures, and equipment as further described in attached Schedule A	$ _____
Resale inventory and supplies (valued at Seller's cost) in the amount of	$ _____
Leasehold improvements	$ _____
Management Assistance (see Stipulation 3 following)	$ _____
Covenant(s) Not to Compete (see Stipulation 4 following)	$ _____
_____	
_____	
TOTAL	$ _____

The Purchaser agrees to pay to the Seller at closing the following:
Earnest Money, Above Acknowledged	$ _____
Payment by Cashier's or Certified Check	$ _____

And additional payments, or assumption of debt, as follows:
1. _____ $ _____
2. _____ $ _____

making the **Total Purchase Price** for Business prior to adjustments, if any, called for herein in Stipulation 8

                                                                         $ _____

The Seller covenants and agrees to bind its heirs, executors, administrators, successors, or assigns and to convey the said Business and/or property to said Purchaser or applicable heirs, executors, administrators, successors, or assigns, in fee with proper deed, capital stock, bill of sale, or title (whichever is applicable), with all marital and homestead rights waived (if applicable); free from any and all defects and encumbrances except such as are herein agreed to be assumed by the Purchaser. Seller agrees to pay for any action required to remove any defects from title or bill of sale or other instrument in order to make it good and marketable. Seller further warrants, represents, and agrees that Seller has good and marketable title to all of the real and personal property and other assets of the Business being sold hereby. Seller also agrees that from the date of acceptance of this Purchase Contract through the day of closing of the sale, that the Business will remain open during normal business hours.

Upon the tender of such deed, capital stock, bill of sale, or title, above mentioned, the Purchaser agrees to comply fully with the terms of this Purchase Contract. All taxes, assessments, rents, and insurance premiums are to be prorated to date of closing, by the Parties, outside of Closing.

Time is of the essence. Parties agree to work diligently to satisfy all conditions and contingencies of the intended sale set forth in this Purchase Contract. This Purchase Contract constitutes the sole and entire agreement between the Parties hereto and no modification or amendment shall be binding unless in writing and attached hereto and signed by all parties to this agreement. No representation, promise, or inducement not included in this Purchase Contract shall be binding upon any party hereto.

Purchaser agrees that its/his/her/their failure to comply with the terms hereof within the stipulated time gives Seller the right to retain the amount paid in escrow as liquidated damages; and Seller agrees to equally divide this earnest money with Broker for services rendered in regard to this Purchaser without any reduction of fees that may be due Broker on a sale of this business to another Purchaser. The Seller acknowledges that Broker cannot guarantee payment of check or checks accepted from the Purchaser as earnest money.

This instrument shall be regarded as a bona fide Purchase Contract by Purchaser or Seller who first signs to the other and is open for acceptance by the other until noon on the _____ day of _____, 2008, by which time written acceptance of such offer must have been actually received by Broker who shall promptly notify the other party, in writing, of such acceptance. If accepted as set forth herein, this Purchase Contract becomes **LEGALLY BINDING** upon both Parties and upon their heirs, executors, administrators, successors, and assigns.

The closing of this sale shall be on or before _____, 2008. The following **SPECIAL STIPULATIONS** are an integral part of this Purchase Contract and shall, if conflicting with printed matter, control.

SPECIAL STIPULATIONS TO PURCHASE CONTRACT

1. **ASSETS EXCLUDED FROM SALE** (if any): _____
   _____

2. **MANAGEMENT ASSISTANCE**: Seller will, for the consideration stated, if any, provide management assistance and training after closing consisting of _____
   _____
   _____

3. **COVENANT NOT TO COMPETE**: For the consideration stated, if any, Seller agrees not to compete for _____ years from closing as owner, part owner, investor, manager, consultant, or permanent employee (except as an employee of the Purchaser), without Purchaser's prior permission, in the following types of business within the area defined below:

   Type(s) of business: _____

   Restricted area: _____

   Other restriction(s): _____

4. **PAYMENT OF CLOSING COSTS**: Parties agree to retain a closing attorney to prepare the closing documents and handle the closing, and agree equally to share the attorney's fee and other closing costs and fees, provided they do not exceed $_____ each.

5. **CONDITIONS PRECEDENT TO CLOSE**: Seller agrees to meet the following conditions at its expense: _____
   _____
   _____
   _____

6. **SECURITY FOR DEFERRED PAYMENTS**: _____
   _____
   _____
   _____

7. **INVENTORY COUNT AND ADJUSTMENTS TO THE PURCHASE PRICE**:
   _____
   _____
   _____
   _____

8. **SELLER WARRANTS**: Seller hereby represents, warrants, and agrees:

   a. All financial statements of Seller furnished relative to this Agreement fairly reflect the financial position and results of operations of Seller for the periods indicated. (Parties may list these statements here:)

   b. There are no undisclosed liabilities, claims, or pending or threatened litigation, and Seller will defend and hold Purchaser harmless from same if any shall arise from actions which took place prior to the closing. If there are undisclosed liabilities, Buyer may, after giving Seller ten (10) days notification to dispute or satisfy such liabilities, pay same and deduct amount paid from next payment or payments due Seller.

   c. All equipment to be conveyed to Buyer will be in normal working condition at time of closing.

   d. All inventories to be conveyed to Buyer will be in good and marketable (and current) condition at time of closing.

9. **CONTINGENT NATURE OF CONTRACT**: Parties agree that this contract is contingent upon the satisfaction of the following conditions prior to the closing date set out above or amended by the Parties. However, Parties agree to be diligent in securing their prompt satisfaction.

   a. _____
   _____
   _____

   b. _____
   _____
   _____

   c. _____
   _____
   _____

10. **PAYROLL**: All payroll and payroll tax liability accruing to the close of the sale shall remain the responsibility of the Seller. Immediately from and after closing of this sale, all subsequent payroll expense shall be the sole responsibility of the Purchaser.

11. **DEPOSITS**: Any and all amounts currently on deposit for the benefit of the Business for utility service, phone, rent, etc., are the property of the Seller and are not included as part of the sale. Purchaser shall deposit such amounts as necessary to continue the operation of the business. Customer deposits held by the Business shall be divided as follows: _____
_____

12. **INCORPORATION BY PURCHASER**: It is agreed that the Purchaser may elect to incorporate. In such event, the new corporation shall become the Purchaser, and the Purchaser shall cause the corporation to ratify all of the terms and conditions of this Purchase Contract. Further, Purchaser shall continue to be personally liable for the performance of this contract, covenants, and agreements and the payments of any unpaid balance owed to Seller hereunder.

WITNESS the hands and seals of Purchaser and Seller this day, month, and year below written. Each Party acknowledges that each has read this Purchase Contract in its entirety and has had the opportunity to seek legal counsel.

_____	_____	_____
PURCHASER	**Witness**	**Date**
_____	_____	_____
SELLER (individual signature)	**Witness**	**Date**
_____	_____	_____
SELLER (corporate signature)	**Witness**	**Date**

SAMPLE SETTLEMENT SHEETS
PURCHASER'S ACCOUNT

SELLER: ABC Enterprises, Inc., (d.b.a. Amoco of Casino Strip) and its Shareholders
6804 Casino Strip Blvd.
Robinsonville, MO 31664

PURCHASER: Horacio Mendoza
5339 Horseshoe Trail
Jonesboro, AR 39115

CHARGES:
	Sale Price	$194,000.00
	Legal Fees and Other Closing Costs	$ 1,000.00
	Proration of 2005 Property Taxes	$ 3,058.32
	Adjustment to Contract Price	$ 6,000.00
	Balance Due Bank	$ 3,993.00
	Filing Fees	$ 20.00
	TOTAL CHARGES	$208,071.32

CREDITS:
	Earnest Money Deposit	$ 20,000.00
	TOTAL CREDITS	$ 20,000.00

BALANCE OF PURCHASE PRICE DUE FROM
PURCHASER AT CLOSING: $188,071.32

The undersigned has examined the above statement and hereby acknowledges that the same correctly reflects the disbursements made for his account and benefit, and the undersigned hereby states that this transaction has been consummated in accordance with his understanding and agreement with the Seller of this property.

March_____, 2005   Horacio Mendoza, Purchaser   _____

SETTLEMENT SHEET
SELLER'S ACCOUNT

SELLER: Julius M. Barnstead
                1944 South Angela
                Memphis, TN 38104

PURCHASER: Greenspace Landscapes, LLC
                9847 Farmington Road
                Welllington, TN 38002

BROKER: Sam Cantor & Company

CREDITS: Sales Price: $110,000.00
                                          TOTAL CREDITS: $110,000.00

LESS:

Commission to Broker	$11,000.00
One-half closing attorney fee	$ 450.00
Promissory note to Seller	$40,000.00
UCC LienSearch	$ 150.00 (est.)
Payoff Outstanding Liabilities:	
Chase Auto Finance	$ 6,189.12
Fifth Third Bank	$10,620.50
Courier fees	$ 30.00

                                          TOTAL CHARGES: $ 68,439.62

                NET PROCEEDS TO SELLER AT CLOSING: $ 41,560.38

I have examined above statement and hereby acknowledge that the same correctly reflects the disbursements made for my account and benefit, and I hereby state that this transaction has been consummated in accordance with my understanding and agreement with the Purchaser of this property. I further understand that the business is not shown on the City or County tax rolls for personal property taxes. In the event an assessment for such taxes is made after closing, I agree to pay all such taxes assessed for the period up to closing. Items marked as "estimate" are estimates only and are subject to change after closing.

Date: _____   Seller: _____

CONFIRMATION AND BILL OF SALE

FOR AND IN CONSIDERATION of the sum of one hundred fifty thousand dollars ($150,000) in hand and of which receipt is hereby acknowledged, John A. Ranger (Hereinafter "Seller") of 82 East 82nd Street, New York, New York 11223 does hereby grant, convey sell, transfer and deliver to George B. Buyer (Hereinafter "Buyer") of 112 112th Street, New York, New York 12233 as business know as Doozy Cabinet Manufacturing Company, Inc. with an address of 123 32nd Street, Newark, New Jersey 12345 (Hereinafter "Business") under the terms of the attached Purchase Agreement dated August 14, 2007.

SELLER warrants that he is the lawful owner of Business and has the legal right to sell same and will defend title of Business against any and all legal claims and demands.

AGREED this ___ day of _____ 2007:

SELLER: _____ BUYER: _____

WITNESS:

    Signature _____

    Print Name _____

ALLIED BUSINESS BROKERS, INC.
PROFILE NO: JG-039-068 *(Rev. 9/24/98)*

555 Perkins Ext., Suite 418
Memphis, TN 38117
(901) 767-2354
FAX: (901) 761-9244

Blender of Dry Mixes for Dairy & Seafood Processors

This three and one-half year old company blends mixes which are used by both the dairy products industry and by fish and poultry processors. The present accounts are located in six states from Florida to Oklahoma. During the company's first two years of operations the company blended mixes primarily for the dairy products industry. As margins declined, the owners curtailed shipments of dairy products in favor of formulating and selling product to meat processors. The last shipments of dairy mix were in October 1997. The largest volume blended since that time has been for catfish processors. As of June 1998, monthly sales are back to 1996 levels of about $100,000 per month. Sales for June 1998 exceeded $130,000.

ORGANIZATION: The company is a Tennessee corporation with 9 stockholders who collectively pledged $231,250 at time of incorporation. As of June 30, 1998, pledges of $218,250 had been paid. The President of the company is the largest shareholder with 30% of the outstanding shares.

FACILITIES: After 2 ½ years of operation in Arlington, TN, the company moved in June 1997 to Ocala, FL where it leases 3,000 square feet from one of the stockholders. This move was made because of proximity to several dairy accounts. Today the largest concentration of accounts is in the Mississippi delta. After moving to Florida, much of the equipment was upgraded and replaced. Virtually all equipped in stainless steel and will meet EPA's strict standards. The Balance Sheet shows an original equipment cost of $232,000.

MANAGEMENT: The daily operations are managed by the President's son in Ocala. The President, who still lives in Tennessee, is responsible for sales and has been assisted by several commissioned sales persons who receive average commissions of 5-6% of each sale. Technical support is provided by a Ph.D. Chemist with many years experienced in both meat and dairy products. In addition there are 2 ½ hourly personnel receiving an average of $7.50/hour and the President's daughter who was paid $20,000 for accounting and bookkeeping assistance.

REASON FOR SALE: Three factors are responsible for the decision to sell: the plant manager is going back to college in the fall; the President has recently had serious back surgery; and the landlord needs the space occupied by the company.

FORMULATIONS: The formulations are custom blended. They serve to reduce dehydration and discoloration of frozen products as well as extend their shelf life. The sale will include the rights to the use of all formulations. The trade names and formulations are owned by the founders of the Company individually.

OTHER ASSETS IN SALE: A summary of assets to be sold and their approximate values are shown below:

Accounts Receivable - guaranteed	$ 120,000
Raw materials and bags (at cost) - guaranteed	20,000
Finished Goods @ 80% of selling price	10,000
All furniture, fixtures and equipment	120,000
Rights to use of formulations and trade name	50,000
Management assistance & Non-compete	25,000
Miscellaneous supplies, tools, etc.	5,000
	$ 350,000

RECENT DEVELOPMENTS: In January 1998, Company negotiated very favorable pricing with its largest raw material supplier. In May 1998, Company raised prices to its customers by about 2.5%. These two factors should improve the gross profit margin by 4-5% points.

ASKING PRICE: $350,000   If $250,000 is paid at closing, Purchaser may pledge accounts receivable and inventories to a first lien lender. Seller will carry note for balance at 9%.

DISCLAIMER: *This report includes information obtained from sources believed to be reliable but no independent verification has been made and we do not guarantee accuracy or completeness. Opinions expressed are subject to change without notice. This report should not be construed as a request to engage in any transaction. The price and terms shown above are subject to change without notice.*

Source of Data for Tables: The Catfish Institute 1997

MARKET ANALYSIS: The industry (blenders of dry mixes) is driven primarily by the increase in the volume of shipments of frozen foods in recent years. Processors and retailers alike want the product to retain a fresh look and texture as long as possible. It is important also that the product not lose weight through dehydration while frozen. These factors are particularly true in the meat and seafood processing industries.

In the case of seafood, until recent years, most product was shipped and sold fresh. Therefore, sales were tightly clustered around seaports and coastal cities. Traditionally, fish like trout, bass and salmon were served fresh; frozen fish had little appeal. This has changed radically and now the average family as well as many schools and other institutions serve frozen boned filets and fishsticks. Fish today is easier to prepare and eat and sales have soared; demand has outstripped traditional sources of supply. Therefore, domestic production of pond raised fish (acquaculture) has become a large and growing industry. For recent U.S. production (1995) see Table 1.

Table 1
1995 U.S. AQUALCULTURE PRODUCTION

	Pounds Produced	Pounds Sold
Salmon	34,000,000	80,000,000
Trout	55,000,000	61,000,000
Crawfish	55,000,000	33,000,000
Catfish	447,000,000	351,000,000

Table 2
U.S. CATFISH PRODUCTION
Pounds of Live Weight Catfish Processed

1997	524,959	1990	360,435
1996	472,000	1989	341,900
1995	446,686	1988	295,109
1994	438,269	1987	280,495
1993	458,013	1986	213,756
1992	457,367	1985	191,616
1991	390,870		

In volume, the growth in catfish production has been the greatest. However, the increase in the percent of pond-raised salmon and trout is impressive. Table 2 shows the steady increase in catfish production by pounds of live weight processed since 1985. According to the Catfish Institute, average consumption nationwide of pond-grown catfish in 1997 had grown to 1.0 pounds per capita from .4 pounds per capita in 1985.

Because of this growth and the concentration of catfish consumption in the Mid-South, the Company decided in 1997 to concentrate on developing formulations for use by catfish processors. The owners now estimate that the Company has 50% of the catfish drymix market after only one full year of production. Note on Table 3 that the consumption (by weight) has more than doubled in several states between 1986 and 1996 most notably in Texas, California, Tennessee, Arkansas, Michigan and Florida. Most notable is the fact that several of the most populous states (Ohio, Pennsylvania, New York) are not shown. Also note that California, our largest state, consumed only .54 pounds per capita. These data suggest that there is ample market for continued growth in catfish consumption.

Table 3
CATFISH CONSUMPTION BY GEOGRAPHY

	Estimated 1996 Population	Pounds (000's) Consumed 1986	Pounds (000's) Consumed 1996	1996 Rank	Pounds Consumed Per Capita	1996 Rank
Texas	18,000,000	28,000	47,500	1	2.64	4
Illinois	11,500,000	14,000	23,500	2	2.04	6
California	30,500,000	6,500	16,200	3	.53	15
Louisiana	4,300,000	11,300	16,200	4	3.76	2
Tennessee	5,000,000	4,200	16,100	5	3.22	3
Arkansas	2,450,000	5,100	14,000	6	5.71	1
Florida	14,000,000	2,200	13,500	7	.96	12
Mississippi	2,700,000	7,000	11,000	8	.41	16
Alabama	4,100,000	6,000	10,000	9	2.44	5
Michigan	9,400,000	1,500	8,100	10	.86	13
Missouri	5,200,000	5,000	7,500	11	1.44	7
Georgia	6,800,000	5,000	6,750	12	1.00	11
Indiana	5,600,000	2,400	6,200	13	1.11	9
Kentucky	3,750,000	1,200	5,000	14	1.33	8
N. Carolina	6,800,000	1,400	4,350	15	.64	14
Oklahoma	3,250,000	2,500	3,500	16	1.08	10

Because of declines in catches in recent years, it seems fair to assume that pond production of other species (Trout and Salmon) will also continue to grow and that consumption of frozen fish will become more popular in many markets where fresh fish are not readily available.

Source of Data for Tables: The Catfish Institute 1997

Printed in Great Britain
by Amazon.co.uk, Ltd.,
Marston Gate.